Convergence

Spiritual Journeys
of a Charismatic Calvinist

by

Sam Storms

President of
Enjoying God Ministries
P. O. Box 481814
Kansas City, MO 64148
www.SamStorms.com
www.EnjoyingGodMinistries.com
sam@enjoyinggodministries.com

Convergence: Spiritual Journeys of a Charismatic Calvinist

Copyright © 2005 by Enjoying God Ministries

For additional copies, visit www.SamStorms.com or www.EnjoyingGodMinistries.com

Published by Enjoying God Ministries
    P. O. Box 481814
    Kansas City, Missouri 64148
    e-mail: info@enjoyinggodministries.com

ISBN 0-9771739-0-9

Unless otherwise indicated, all Scripture quotations are taken from: The Holy Bible: English Standard Version, copyright © 2001 by Crossway Bibles, a division of Good News Publishers. Used by permission. All rights reserved.

Cover design: Ron Adair (www.RonAdair.com)

First printing, 2005
Printed in the United States of America by Bethany Press International

Affectionately dedicated to
my Grandsons

Joseph Konrad Liang
and
John Benjamin Liang

"May God forever incline your hearts
to walk in
the integrity of His Word
and
the fullness of His Spirit"

Table of Contents

Introduction

What hath Orlando to do with Anaheim?

In January, 1991, I accepted a friend's invitation to attend a conference in Anaheim, California, hosted by the Association of Vineyard
Churches. There were some 7,000 people in attendance at the five-day event,
many of whom had come from countries other than the U.S. The week was
filled not only with biblical preaching but also exuberant and extended times
of worship, prophetic utterances, prayers for healing, and other emphases
and practices that had come to be associated with John Wimber and the
Vineyard movement of which he was the leader until his death in 1997.

At the end of the conference, I boarded a plane and returned to my
home in Oklahoma. With only a day or two of rest, I again took flight, this
time in the opposite direction (some would say both geographically *and* theologically!). I traveled to Orlando, Florida, where I was to speak for the second consecutive year at a conference sponsored by R. C. Sproul's Ligonier
Ministries. Again, there was Christ-exalting worship (but without guitars or
dancing), lots of Bible teaching, and plenty of prayer, but few if any for physical healing.

Many of my friends and colleagues over the years have questioned
my wisdom, if not my sanity, in seeking to live and minister in both worlds.
Some of those from "Orlando" have insisted, often zealously, that people who
speak in tongues rarely engage in serious theological reflection. They've tried
to convince me that people who pray expectantly for miraculous healings are
inclined to minimize the importance of Greek exegesis. Quite a few have suggested that my being a Calvinist is inconsistent with belief in the spiritual gift
of prophecy.

Those from "Anaheim" have also voiced their concerns. Some fear
that my unflinching affirmation of the sovereignty of God will either kill my
evangelistic zeal or undermine any sense of urgency in prayer, or perhaps
both. They are often suspicious of my emphasis on the mind and the critical
importance of history and tradition. Although few have said it openly, I can
sense their uneasiness with my persistent and meticulous habit of subjecting
all claims of supernatural phenomena to the test of Scripture. Beneath it is the
worry that excessive devotion to biblical precision will either breed dogmat-

ic arrogance or quench the Spirit or, again, both.

I didn't buy into such false dichotomies then, and I don't now. Yet there are many who continue to insist that the theological differences and consequent ecclesiastical and personal divisions between cessationists and charismatics are perfectly illustrated by the geographical distance between Orlando and Anaheim. These same individuals would conclude that the possibility of bringing them closer together in anything other than a superficial way is remote at best.

There's no escaping the fact that a serious, and occasionally vitriolic, breach exists between Word-based evangelical cessationists and their more experientially oriented charismatic cousins. Most are familiar with the efforts to build a bridge between Roman Catholics and evangelical Protestants. Attempts to promote unity among a variety of protestant denominations, as well as within those denominations, continue unabated. But little if anything has been said, even less done, about the mistrust, caricature, and often denunciatory recriminations that pass between these two evangelical groups. Can anything be done?

Several attempts have been made, and I discuss them briefly in chapter five. So what distinguishes mine from the others? What makes *Convergence* different? The answer is found in the three-fold focus of this book.

First, I don't write as an outsider to either perspective. In the first four chapters I describe in considerable detail my own spiritual pilgrimage, one that has taken me from the lofty intellectual heights of evangelical academia to the "sawdust trail" of charismatic revivalism. I have lived and ministered and mingled in both camps and to this day would find my closest and most trusted friends spread equally between them.

There was a time when I thought my spiritual journey was unique. I hope that was due more to ignorance than hubris, but in any case I've come to discover that others share a similar pilgrimage. They've told me of their abiding love for Scripture and the foundational role it plays in both life and ministry. But they also describe stunning supernatural encounters that brought revelation (perhaps through a dream or vision), healing, and even deliverance from demonic oppression.

In sharing the details of my life and exposing them to the searchlight of Scripture, I hope you will see the possibility, dare I say *necessity*, of embracing the strengths of both "Anaheim" and "Orlando" (as well as rejecting their shortcomings). I'm sure you would agree that it's easier to type with both hands, to run a marathon with two legs, and to read this book with both eyes. Christian life and ministry are also more effective when both mind and heart, both Word and Spirit, both principle and power work in tandem for the sake of the kingdom.

A second distinctive element in this book is the effort I've made to identify both the strengths and weaknesses in both the cessationist or Word-based world of mainstream evangelicalism and the charismatic or Spirit-empowered world of those who affirm the contemporary validity of all spiritual gifts. In doing so I hope to shed light on why both churches and individual Christians tend to gravitate toward one or the other. Thus my aim in Part Two is to broaden our understanding of both camps by engaging in what I hope is an honest and forthright (and at times painful) exercise of self-examination.

Thirdly, I've chosen to focus in Part Three on the issue of hearing God's voice, not simply in Scripture but also in the gift of prophecy, dreams, visions, and so-called spiritual impressions. I have two reasons for this emphasis.

First, as you will quickly see, my personal journey in the last twenty years has been significantly influenced by supernatural encounters involving the gift of prophecy. This makes it important for me to provide something of a biblical and theological case for the validity of the extra-biblical revelatory ministry of the Spirit and to respond to objections so often brought against it.

But second, and more important still, this is the issue that serves to divide the two camps more so than any other, speaking in tongues notwithstanding. There was a time, primarily in the sixties and seventies, when the charismatic phenomenon was referred to simply (and somewhat derisively) as "The Modern Tongues Movement."[1] Today the spiritual gift of prophecy has supplanted that of tongues as the focal point of debate. What concerns and even frightens many evangelicals isn't the thought of an unintelligible prayer language or even the claims made concerning physical healing. Their greatest suspicions are reserved for those who insist they've heard God speak, whether audibly or internally, by dream or vision, but in all cases beyond (but never contrary to) the infallible written Word of God.

I'll have considerably more to say in the next chapter on why *Convergence* was written. For now, my prayer is that you will recognize, as I have, the critical and urgent necessity for all Christians, of every theological and denominational stripe, to wrestle with the divorce that has occurred between Word and Spirit, and to commit our energy to seek the heart of God for a glad and glorious reconciliation.

One more comment is in order before we begin. Ironically, few in either party to this division believe that a divorce has occurred in their *own* experience! Word-based cessationists refuse to concede that they have diminished the role of the Spirit or failed to acknowledge and embrace the fullness of God's power for life and ministry. They would take offense at the suggestion that they have denied anything God has affirmed concerning the nature and function of spiritual gifts or the role of the affections in Christian experience.

Charismatics typically react with no less surprise to the argument that they have, to some extent, failed to build faithfully on the foundation of the final and all-sufficient canon of Holy Scripture. They loudly proclaim their allegiance to the totality of God's written word and its unquestioned authority over their lives and bristle at the slightest hint that the Bible is anything other than central and controlling when it comes to what they believe and how they live.

I'm no longer surprised when I hear comments like, "O.K., yes, there is a divorce of sorts, but not in our family! It's that church across town that has put asunder what God hath joined together. But not us!" I can only ask that as you read *Convergence* you be open to the possibility that the separation of Word and Spirit and the suppression of one in favor of the other is more real and determinative in the way you live as a Christian than you formerly acknowledged. After all, what use is a proposed solution if no one recognizes that a problem exists?

---

[1] One immediately thinks of the book with that very title written by Robert Gromacki and published by Baker Book House in 1967.

PART ONE

My Spiritual Journey

Chapter One

A Prophetic Pilgrimage

If you had seen me in the early days of 1988, or perhaps spent time with me as I fulfilled the routine tasks as pastor of a small, independent, Bible church, you would never have guessed what was at hand. I certainly didn't!

By all appearances, I was a fairly typical graduate of Dallas Theological Seminary, although perhaps a bit more Calvinistic than most. I was committed to the inerrancy of Scripture, expository preaching, evangelism, and world missions. I still am. My convictions concerning the sovereignty of God were expressed in a book on the doctrine of divine election,[1] a view from which I have not deviated in the least. Nevertheless, over the course of the next six months I experienced a fairly significant transformation in my theological understanding that bore both immediate and long-term, as well as controversial, results.

A number of friends heard that my theology had changed significantly since 1988, but few suspected that, in 1993, I would become a pastor and teacher in a Vineyard church. Neither did I. At first, most were hesitant to ask why. But as the months passed, I received an increasing number of phone calls and letters from life-long friends who wanted to know how this former Southern Baptist, now Bible church Calvinist from Dallas Theological Seminary, could end up at the Kansas City Vineyard.[2]

So I decided in 1994 to write a brief account of "My Journey" (releasing it under that title) hoping that it would put to rest rumors that I had become a heretic, or worse still, that I was on the verge of insanity (believe it or not, I actually heard reports that both interpretations were circulating). What you are now reading (in the first four chapters) is an updated and vastly expanded version of that initial chronicle.

But before I go any further, I think a word of justification is in order.

Why I Wrote this Story

Like some of you, I was glued to the movie screen several years ago as Jodi Foster sat atop her car in the film *Contact*, surrounded by giant satellite dishes pointed skyward, as she waited patiently, listening for a voice, a beep, a vibration, a whisper, any sound that would verify her deeply held belief that we are not alone in this vast universe. Like many of you, I walk through a typical bookstore and marvel at the dozens, perhaps hundreds, of books published only in the past couple of years that focus on angels and alleged personal encounters with them, together with volumes on everything from communication with the dead to the latest discoveries on physical healing.

Although it's now seen only in re-runs, just a few years ago the Sunday night CBS television show "Touched by an Angel" became the second most popular program in that network's prime-time schedule, trailing only "60 Minutes" in the ratings. Today we have an almost countless array of programming devoted to spiritual, paranormal and often overtly supernatural subjects. Everyone, it seems, apart from a few hardened skeptics, are at least open to the possibility that "God" or an "angel" or a "deceased friend" or some unidentified "extra-terrestrial celestial" either has or will speak to us or make contact in some supernatural fashion.

My purpose in this narrative is certainly not to add to the hysteria surrounding much of this religious obsession. On the other hand, I do believe, as I trust you do as well, that there is a God who speaks and that He has inscripturated His "word" for us in the pages of the Bible. I also believe, again as do you, that there are countless "spiritual emissaries", for lack of a better description, commonly called "angels", who do God's bidding and often communicate His will.

I must still answer the question, though, "Why write about supernatural events that are so personal and uniquely tied to one particular individual? Doesn't that lend itself to exhibitionism and elitism?" The point is well taken. So permit me to explain why I've written this story.

In the first place, although what you will read happened to me and my family, we believe God intends for it to be a source of encouragement to the entire body of Christ. Our heartfelt conviction is that the work of the

Holy Spirit in prophetic ministry and the attendant supernatural activity with which it is so often associated is designed for the whole body of Christ. A frequent comment from those who heard about my journey was: "It isn't right for you to deny to the rest of the church the testimony of God's supernatural activity. When we heard about what you had experienced it increased our faith. We said to each other, 'Well, if it could happen to him, it can happen to us, too.'" The point is, what you are about to read is *God's* story, not ours. It belongs to him, and thus to all his people.

This especially hit home to me when three of my former classmates at Dallas Seminary, all of whom now teach at a prominent theological seminary, asked to meet with me to hear my story. This wasn't the first instance of such a request. I've met with dozens of pastors and scholars who, for any number of reasons, have begun to question their theology of the Spirit. Most, if not all, of them testify to being in something of a spiritual rut. A few are disillusioned to the point of contemplating leaving ministry altogether. Some have fallen into serious depression. Sadly, several have endured personal tragedies which their theological education had ill prepared them to handle. But they all, without exception, express their frustration with a ministry that lacks power and appears so dissimilar to what they read about in the New Testament.

Most of them have pleaded with me to write this book. As I shared with them what I've discovered in Scripture and in personal experience, their eyes lit up with renewed hope and longing and expectation for what God might do for them as well. This book is for the whole body of Christ. But having myself been a pastor and professor for thirty years, you will forgive me if I write with a special eye on those who minister daily to the church and the academy, longing for a fresh and empowering touch from a living, loving, speaking God.

A second reason I feel it's important to publish this story is because we have precedent for it in Scripture. On several occasions the biblical authors would rehearse the story of Israel's experience in Egypt or tell of the miracles God performed in the wilderness or recount the mighty acts of deliverance from her enemies. Their intent in this was to draw attention to God and his faithfulness to the promises of the covenant. When the people hear of the mighty deeds God has done in the past, their confidence in his ability to do them yet again both in the present and the future is greatly enhanced. This can only help to energize our seeking of God for all he has promised.

God instructed Habakkuk to "write the vision [and] make . . . plain on tablets" (Habakkuk 2:2) what he had been shown. Although my history is certainly neither inspired nor infallible, as was that which Habakkuk experienced, there is, nevertheless, a principle in what he did that we would do well to imitate. It is this: when God acts in grace and power to make himself known, to heal, to deliver, and to awaken the soul to the glory of his presence, his people must hear of it and read of it that they may lie prostrate before him and ascribe to him all praise and honor and glory.

It's no small matter when the people of God forget his mighty deeds. Israel certainly had a short memory. In Nehemiah 9 we read of a corporate confession of sin in which special attention is drawn to their failure to remember the "signs and wonders" (v. 10) which God performed against Pharaoh in delivering Israel from bondage in Egypt. They refused to obey and "were not mindful of the wonders that you [God] performed among them" (v. 17). Whether it be great miracles of deliverance or small manifestations of mercy and kindness, we must be diligent to recall and retell the wondrous things God has done for us.

But in doing so we must never yield to the contemporary infatuation with glitz and bang and sensational sights. The supernatural is never an end in itself. Signs and wonders are designed to "signify" something beyond themselves and evoke "wonder" in those who witness them. What they point to is God and the revelation of his goodness and faithfulness in the redemption of his people. The awe and wonder are not in mere deeds of power but in the God who transcends the boundaries of our experience and shatters the limitations we so often place upon him.

Thus, although it would be a serious mistake to equate the stunning signs and wonders of Scripture, many of which bore redemptive-historical significance, with the supernatural experiences of anyone today, the latter are not for that reason to be neglected or treated with scorn. The God whose omnipotent breath parted the Red Sea and mighty hand raised Jesus from the dead is the same God who today speaks gently in the hearts of his children and tenderly touches them with healing mercy.

Third, this is not simply a story about a single individual, but one that hopes to focus on the sovereignty and providential power of God. This is a story about the God in whom all things consist (Colossians 1:17). This is a story about the God who works all things according to his will (Ephesians

1:11). This is a story about the God who upholds all things by the word of his power (Hebrews 1:3) and is committed to the summing up of all things in Christ (Ephesians 1:10). Finally, this is a story about hope, about how God can transform lives and deliver from oppression and satisfy the soul in a way that nothing else in life can. My desire is to draw attention to the majesty and glory of the God in whom we live and breathe and have our being (Acts 17:28) and to instill hope in the hearts of those who may have given up on him or concluded that he is either uninvolved or indifferent toward their needs.

Lastly, I believe a book that chronicles and confirms the reality of prophetic ministry today is especially important in view of the attacks being launched on this particular arena of the Spirit's work. It's becoming a commonplace for self-appointed disciplinarians in the body of Christ to ridicule and mock prophetic ministry and come dangerously close to slandering those who are involved in it. Although this story is not intended as a thorough-going response to such attacks, I do pray that it will re-focus the faith of God's people on the reality of the supernatural and revelatory work of the Spirit which the Bible so clearly urges us to pursue. Only you the reader can be the judge if I am successful in doing so.

A Brief Chronology

As I noted above, until March of 1988 my life and ministry were both uneventful in terms of what one might call overt supernatural activity. In fact, my life until then had been boringly predictable and, well, easy. I've always identified with Hubbell Gardiner, the character played by Robert Redford in the film, *The Way We Were*. In one of the opening scenes, Gardiner's essay is read aloud in class by his college English professor. The film only gives us the first two lines, but they stuck with me these many years. The title to his essay was, "The All-American Smile." It began with these words: "In a way, he was like the country he lived in; everything came too easily to him. But at least he knew it."

I'm incredibly grateful for the life God has given me. But in many ways, "everything came too easily to me." Friends, academic achievement, athletics, jobs, relationships. They all came too easily. But, like Hubbell Gardiner, at least I knew it. All that was to change in 1988. Not that life suddenly became significantly harder or more painful, but it certainly became more exciting! And frightening, in many ways. Entire new vistas of spiritual reality opened up and I began a journey that continues today.

My spiritual roots are in the Southern Baptist Convention. My grandfather was a personal friend of W. A. Criswell, long-time pastor of First Baptist Church in Dallas, Texas, and my mother once served as secretary to R. G. Lee, pastor of Bellevue Baptist Church in Memphis, Tennessee. I was converted at the age of nine during a revival service at First Baptist Church of Shawnee, Oklahoma, the town where I was born and raised.

If our family missed a Sunday service, morning or night, it was exceptional to say the least. At the age of ten, during the closing hymn of an evening service at First Baptist Church of Midland, Texas, I sensed the call of God into full time Christian ministry. I heard no voice, saw no vision, witnessed no miracle. But the awareness of God's presence was no less real and the clarity of his call no less riveting.

I survived the decade of the sixties and entered the University of Oklahoma in the fall of 1969. Ann and I were married in May of 1972 and were both graduated a year later, she with a degree in Journalism and mine in History. In September of that year I entered Dallas Theological Seminary, from which I received my Th.M. in Historical Theology in 1977. For the last three years of my seminary experience (1974-77) I served as interim pastor of a small Presbyterian Church where I cut my teeth, so to speak, on expository preaching and pastoral counseling.

Upon graduation I joined the staff of Believers Chapel in Dallas, a non-denominational Bible church of about 1,000 people, and stayed there until August of 1985. I was honored and blessed to serve with and, better still, learn from S. Lewis Johnson, longtime professor of New Testament and Systematic Theology at Dallas Seminary, and later of Trinity Evangelical Divinity School in Deerfield, Illinois. During this time I also received my Ph.D. in Intellectual History from the University of Texas at Dallas. My intention had always been to teach in a seminary or graduate institution of some sort. But the Lord had something else in mind. In August of 1985 we moved to Ardmore, Oklahoma, where I became senior pastor of Christ Community Church, a small non-denominational Bible church.

My expectations for ministry in Ardmore, at least initially, weren't much different from what I had while pastoring in Dallas. The eight years I spent there were rich and joyful. As you will soon discover, the last five years

(1988-1993) proved to be a momentous, dare I say, breathtaking season. I'll return to that in a moment.

In August of 1993, Ann, Melanie, Joanna and I loaded our belongings in a moving van and made our way north from Ardmore, Oklahoma, to Kansas City, Missouri. It was a move I never thought I'd make. Several offers to leave Ardmore had come my way, but I rarely gave any of them a second thought. It never crossed my mind that I would leave this church where I had served as Senior Pastor for eight years and the people we loved so deeply to join the staff of Metro Vineyard Fellowship, home of the well-known, so-called "Kansas City Prophets".

Our seven years in Kansas City were wonderful, but they too came to an end in 2000. Much to my surprise, I was offered a position teaching theology at what many believe is America's premier Christian liberal arts school, Wheaton College in Wheaton, Illinois. While there I taught an array of theology courses in both the undergraduate and grad programs. But our time in Wheaton proved to be shorter than we expected. After four years in the classroom, God led us to return to Kansas City and establish Enjoying God Ministries, providing me with the opportunity to write, pursue itinerant ministry, and develop a website (www.SamStorms.com) that I trust will be beneficial to the body of Christ.

Such is the chronological framework of the last thirty years of my life. But it does not begin to explain the stunning encounters I've had with God and the radical transformation that has occurred. Such is the substance of this story that I've chosen to call, *Convergence.*

I must also confess my reluctance to share the details of this story, not only for the reasons already stated, but because I've always found the idea of anything approaching an autobiography distasteful and pompous. My prayer is that nothing I say will draw attention to myself but instead will cause you to look more closely at the Scriptures and to the God whose leading I have tried to follow these past few years.

If anything I say sounds self-serving, please forgive me. I'm writing this because I care deeply for the people who have loved us and prayed for us and supported us and been patient enough to sit under my ministry these many years. Truly my heart's desire is that you understand what has happened and why. I hope and pray that the Lord Jesus Christ is exalted in the chronicling of this journey.

A Word about the Title

Why *Convergence*? Why *Spiritual Journeys of a Charismatic Calvinist*? Even before answering those questions, I need to define some important terms that will appear repeatedly throughout the book.

First, the word "cessationism" may be new to some of you. It has nothing to do with the decision of the South in the nineteenth century to secede from the North! That is "secessionism," not "cessationism". Cessationists don't deny that "miracles" may still occur by the sovereign will of God (well, some do). But they do deny that God imparts "miraculous gifts" to individuals within the body of Christ. The alleged "cessation" of such gifts as prophecy, speaking in tongues, the interpretation of tongues, healing, miracles, word of wisdom, word of knowledge, and the discerning of spirits, is a view embraced widely in the evangelical community, although, for obvious reasons, I sense that its popularity is beginning to wane.

Second, the word "charismatic" is typically used of someone who not only believes in the perpetuity of all spiritual gifts but also actively prays for, expects, and employs them in ministry. I emphasize this point because there are many in the evangelical world who, on the one hand, would concede that the New Testament nowhere explicitly teaches the cessation of certain spiritual gifts but, on the other hand, make little or no effort to pursue or cultivate the exercise of such gifts either in their personal experience or that of the church corporately.

Such folk, for obvious reasons, would not care to be called either "cessationists" or "charismatics". There is a sense, then, in which they are *theologically charismatic but experientially cessationist*! They affirm the theoretical potential for such gifts to exist but devote little energy to pursue or employ them as essential elements in the Christian life. The gifts may well be valid, they say, but their lives reflect virtually no expectation that such manifestations will actually occur. And when they do, allegedly, occur they are greeted with more than a little skepticism.

This raises the delicate question of why someone who does not believe the Bible teaches cessationism would not, in turn, actively pursue spiritual gifts and happily welcome their use in the context of the local church. I've heard a wide range of answers. Some contend that whereas the New Testament doesn't explicitly affirm cessationism, neither is it sufficiently clear in its affirmation of a charismatic orientation to life and ministry to warrant the kind of effort necessary to implement such phenomena in either their personal agenda or corporate church experience. Or if the potential exists for such miraculous gifts to be operative in our day they have yet to witness their occurrence in anything approaching a biblically credible and empirically verifiable way.

A few have told me that they simply don't have the time or skill to properly integrate the charismatic dimension into church life and have resigned themselves to focusing their energy on whatever unique calling or vision God has granted them. One such pastor said to me: "Honestly, I don't know how to do it without either splitting my church or detracting from other aspects of kingdom life that I regard as more important." There may yet be other reasons why a person is theologically charismatic but experientially cessationist that would require drawing conclusions concerning motives of the heart that I have neither the freedom nor discernment to address.

Returning now to the issue of terminology, some have begun to employ the label "continuationist," insofar as it emphasizes that all gifts of the Holy Spirit "continue" throughout the course of church history and into the present day and, should they appear, are designed by God to operate according to the same principles as they did in the first century of church life. The label "charismatic", sadly, is not only used pejoratively and often as a condescending slur, it is theologically ambiguous and bears cultural implications as well. One need only note that it is used to describe people as different theologically as Wayne Grudem and Gordon Fee, at one end of the spectrum, and Benny Hinn and Oral Roberts at the other. Has the term outlived its usefulness? Perhaps, but I suspect that it is probably here to stay, whether we like it or not.

So, where does that leave us? For the sake of convenience and simplicity I will employ the term "cessationist" to refer *both* to those who deny the validity of miraculous gifts today *and* those who may not embrace that denial but live and minister as if it were true. In point of fact, my concern in this book is less with their view of spiritual gifts and more their stress on the centrality of the Word and how that affects the way they envision life in the kingdom of God.

Likewise, I will use the terms "charismatic" and "continuationist" interchangeably throughout this book. Again, my concern is not so much with the arguments they employ to prove the perpetuity of all gifts as it is with their emphasis on the affections and the role of supernatural phenomena in the life of the believer.

If at any point you find yourself uncomfortable being labeled with either of these tags, convinced that you fall into *either* camp or *neither* camp, feel free to discard them. I hope you'll still be able to appreciate the distinctions I've drawn and the orientation toward Christianity and the church that they produce.

So, why the title? Why the sub-title? First, a word about the latter. Having already defined "charismatic", an explanation is in order about my choice of the label "Calvinist". When I'm asked, and I'm asked often, "Sam, are you a Calvinist?", I immediately respond with a request of my own, "Tell me what you mean by 'Calvinist'. Then I'll tell you if I am one." Often the person then defines "Calvinism" as a non-evangelistic, fatalistic system of theology, devoid of life and joy, in which God is portrayed as an inflexible bully who takes sadistic glee in sending people to hell whether they deserve it or not. "If *that* is what you mean by 'Calvinist', then I most assuredly am *not* one!"

It's because of such caricatures of Calvinism that some advised me against using the term in my sub-title. "It will only confuse people," they insisted, "and probably make your charismatic and Arminian friends so angry they won't even bother to read the book." But it's important you know that I'm using the term "Calvinist" not so much for its emphasis on the sovereignty of God in salvation as for its elevation of the centrality of Scripture and the life of the mind.

Without diminishing the emphasis that other Protestants have placed on Scripture, the Reformed tradition is especially well-known for its focus on the primacy of both the Word and the intellectual dimension of Christian faith. If Calvinists are known for anything, aside from their emphasis on divine sovereignty, it is the rich doctrinal tradition they have built and cherished and defended these past five centuries. The same cannot be said for the Charismatic movement (with a few notable exceptions).

If Calvinism has elevated the Word and mind, charismatics have given pride of place to Spirit and heart. In fact, they have often done so in conscious and explicit reaction to what they believed was an excessively cerebral approach to Christianity, one they feared would quench the work of the Spirit. Their fears have not been entirely unwarranted. But no less concerned are those in the Reformed tradition who are quick to point to the emotional excess and doctrinal laxity that often attend those who speak in tongues and pray expectantly for physical healing. Both sides have legitimate complaints. Both sides have justified fears.

Hence our need for *convergence*. But the convergence of what? I'm certainly not attempting to make a case for the convergence of cessationism and continuationism. These are two mutually exclusive views on the perpetuity of spiritual gifts. Perhaps someone else can make a case for a theological *tertium quid*, but I'm not the one to attempt it (convinced, as I am, that it can't be done). I most assuredly pray and strive for a *relational* unity among both groups and a recognition of the vast theological ground they hold in common. But that is not my primary concern.

Nor do I intend to argue for the compatibility of belief in the sovereignty of God in salvation and the utilization of all spiritual gifts for ministry. Believing, as I do, that the apostle Paul was both a Calvinist and regularly healed the sick and prophesied renders this a moot point. Even the committed cessationist who acknowledges that Paul embraced a Calvinistic soteriology will have to concede that, at least in the first century, the two perspectives were entirely harmonious.

In calling myself a "Charismatic Calvinist" I run the risk of incurring either ridicule or disbelief. The ridicule will probably come from my Calvinist friends who are offended by what they perceive as the theologically shallow and hermeneutically naïve orientation of many charismatics. My charismatic friends will be amazed that a person, for example, who claims to have "heard God's voice" could affirm something so seemingly archaic and spiritually stifling as predestination.

In early July of 2005, *Christianity Today* magazine featured Jack Hayford in its cover story, entitled "The Pentecostal Gold Standard." Hayford minced no words in expressing his opinion of Calvinism: "Reformed theology," said Hayford, "has … ended up creating a monster of theology that dampens the place of our passion and partnership with God."[3] Not a few of my Reformed friends brought this to my attention and again expressed their incredulity that I could embrace Hayford's doctrine of the Spirit while holding fast to Calvin's doctrine of salvation. Of course, my response is that I don't: both my charismatic view of the Spirit and my Calvinistic view of salvation derive, I believe, from the apostle Paul!

I also expect that my cessationist Arminian friends will want me to point out that they, no less than Calvinists, are devoted to the centrality of Scripture. But the fact remains that I *am* a Calvinist, not an Arminian, and the doctrine of sovereign grace in the salvation of sinners plays an incredibly crucial role in my understanding of Scripture and our experience of God.

So, notwithstanding the incredulity of many on both sides of the theological divide, I unashamedly affirm the traditional five points of Calvinism, popularly known as "TULIP", and I regularly speak in tongues. I stand in the theological tradition of John Calvin and Jonathan Edwards (aside from their commitment to cessationism) and embrace the ministry praxis of John Wimber and Jack Hayford. And no, I don't believe they are mutually exclusive. It's not unusual for me, in consecutive weeks, to speak at a theology conference hosted by Presbyterians (who affirm the Westminster Confession of Faith) or Reformed Baptists, on the one hand, and at a healing seminar hosted by a Vineyard church or the Assemblies of God, on the other (although there's a strong likelihood that such groups will now find that my "convergent" theology disqualifies me from both venues!).

That said, I've decided to use *both* the term "Calvinist", because of that tradition's identification with the Word, *and* the term "Charismatic", because of its focus on the Spirit. If "Word" and "Spirit" are themselves problematic as labels, I simply ask you to put aside your objections momentarily until I have had opportunity to unpack and analyze what their use entails. I won't engage early on what I develop at length later in the book, so suffice it to say that I am committed, because I believe God is committed, to the unified reality and world-changing power of both Word and Spirit.

Here is how *Webster's New Collegiate Dictionary* defines "converge": "to tend or move toward one point or one another: come together: meet; to come together and unite in a common interest or focus."[4] The division that currently exists (although, as noted earlier, neither side will admit to having minimized the other) is unbiblical and destructive, both of what God envisioned for individual believers and the corporate body of Christ. My prayer is that my own journey toward wedding the two, as set forth in the pages that follow, will prove beneficial in helping us heal the breach. Whether or not I accomplish that remains to be seen. But of this we may all be sure: God is displeased by this divorce. He longs for reconciliation. So do I.

Conclusion

One final word before we begin. Some will read this book anticipating a fresh proposal on how to move beyond our traditional denominational identities or perhaps a programmatic strategy for creating a new ecclesiological infrastructure that avoids the pitfalls of the past. I only ask that you put those expectations to the side. My purpose is not to convince Presbyterians that they need to become Pentecostals, or to persuade those in the Vineyard to embrace the ways and means of Southern Baptists.

My aim, rather, is to encourage all believers of every tradition, denomination, or whatever "movement" with which you may identify to look honestly at your own weaknesses and the "other guy's" strengths, and be willing to make whatever subtle or overt changes the Word of God requires.

I hope all of us will ask of ourselves, "In what ways have I marginalized or suppressed the work of the Holy Spirit, and in what ways have I minimized or ignored the centrality of Holy Scripture?" "What can I learn from my charismatic brother or my evangelical sister across town?" "How might I personally benefit from a more courageous trust in the power of the Spirit?" "Have I given myself to the study of God's Word and submission to its directives as thoroughly and consistently as it deserves?"

These and undoubtedly countless other questions posed in the pages that follow are designed to awaken in every heart serious self-examination. My desire may be utopian, but I can't help but long for the convergence in mind and heart, in belief and behavior, in corporate and individual experience, of both Word and Spirit. If such were to occur, if even in small measure, perhaps we, like the early church, might be charged with having "turned the world upside down" (Acts 17:6).

---

[1] *Chosen for Life: An Introductory Guide to the Doctrine of Divine Election* (Grand Rapids: Baker Book House, 1987).

[2] The church in Kansas City was first made known to the evangelical world at large through an article in the January 14, 1991, issue of *Christianity Today* magazine (pp. 18-22). The title was, "Seers in the Heartland: Hot on the trail of the Kansas City prophets," authored by Michael G. Maudlin.

[3] The article, written by Tim Stafford, can be accessed on-line at www.christianitytoday.com.

[4] *Webster's New Collegiate Dictionary* (Springfield, Massachusetts: G. and C. Merriam Company, 1979), 246.

Chapter Two

❊

Stirrings of the Spirit

My first twelve years of Christian ministry in Dallas, Texas, were almost exclusively devoted to in-depth and meticulous study of Scripture, for which Dallas Seminary had effectively prepared me, and the expositional proclamation of that Word to the people, first, of Dallas Independent Presbyterian Church, and second, to the congregation at Believers Chapel.

Nothing in what follows should be interpreted as regret for the emphasis of those years. The problem wasn't with what I was doing, but with what I had consciously excluded. If there were problems, and there were, it was the absence of a robust and biblical perspective on the ministry of the Holy Spirit. The problem wasn't that I focused obsessively on the Word, but that I lived in fear and ignorance of the power of the Spirit. And I do not believe for a moment that the former was the cause of the latter.

As noted, Pneumatology, or the doctrine of the Holy Spirit, was not high on my list of theological priorities during this tenure of ministry. If I thought about the Spirit, or taught on the subject, it was in relation to personal sanctification and the Christian's struggle with sin. I rarely, if ever, gave much consideration to the issue of spiritual gifts other than to insist, often with considerable disdain for those who disagreed with me, that miraculous, or what we erroneously called "sign" gifts, were no longer operative in the church. I went to great lengths to convince my congregation that people who thought about miraculous *charismata* probably did so as an excuse for *not* thinking about more substantive theological issues such as the Trinity or soteriology (the doctrine of salvation) or eschatology.

The prevailing image in my mind of the typical charismatic was someone with a deficient educational background who was emotionally unstable, intellectually lazy, and envisioned the Christian life as a Spirit-empowered leap from one mountain top experience to another. I simply couldn't bring myself to believe that anyone who was committed to the rigors of biblical exegesis and the depths of theological analysis would sprinkle their prayers with what appeared to me as meaningless gibberish. People of substance, people of character, so I contended, were not given to public displays of emotion: they did not weep, they did not move when they worshipped (other than to turn the pages of a hymnbook), and by no means, for heaven's sake, did they dance in church!

I and some of my colleagues were also prejudiced against what we referred to as "charismania" because of our belief that virtually all who embraced it were soteriological Arminians. We were Calvinists, and darn proud of it. Nothing seemed more outrageous than the notion of a Charismatic Calvinist (the Apostle Paul notwithstanding!). If ever there were a contradiction in terms, there it was.

People who exalted the sovereignty of God and labored for his glory to the exclusion of all human boasting simply couldn't believe that speaking in tongues was a legitimate spiritual exercise for this day and age. Glossolalia was for those who had little regard for the life of the mind. Such verbal incoherency was the playground of people with mush between the ears. Those who relished the reading of Calvin's *Institutes* and delighted in parsing Greek verbs were not impressed with claims of angelic encounters or miraculous healings. And above all else, no one in their right mind could affirm the finality and all-sufficiency of Scripture while contending that God still spoke through revelatory prophetic words, dreams, or visions.

When we did get around to discussing the doctrine of Pneumatology, the Spirit's primary, if not sole purpose, was two-fold: to awaken the mind, by means of Scripture, to the glory of Christ, and to empower the believer to resist the temptations of the flesh. Anything beyond that was not only unnecessary, it was distracting, and even potentially dangerous.

On to Oklahoma

When I left Believers Chapel in August of 1985 to assume the position of Senior Pastor of Christ Community Church in Ardmore, Oklahoma, that is the theology I took with me. For the first three years of ministry there, the people heard a similar message. It was not uncommon for me to ridicule, from the pulpit, no less, the beliefs and behavior of charismatics and to warn my congregation about too close an association with those who attended charismatic churches.

But it was more than just a theology. It was an attitude. A disposition, a socio-economic prejudice. I may not have said it aloud, but my suspicions were that the charismatic "experience" probably had its greatest appeal among low-income, gullible, psychologically weak, and culturally unsophisticated folk. If there were "successful" charismatics, they were probably shrewd advocates of the health and wealth gospel who had figured out a way of fleecing others of their ilk. Let's be sure we call this attitude or belief or assumption what it is: arrogant and evil.

This isn't to say that ministry during this period of time in Oklahoma was unprofitable. Far from it. Although somewhat routine, my experience with the people of Christ Community Church was profoundly enriching both spiritually and relationally. The Lord united us with a family of believers who have proven to be one of the greatest blessings we've ever known. To this day many of our closest friends in Christ are still active in the Ardmore church.

During these first three years I preached verse by verse through the Scriptures and did my best to honor God and serve his people. But I was growing increasingly frustrated by the problems people faced and my apparent inability and lack of wisdom to help them.

By God's design my counseling ministry was beginning to expand at a pace that caught me by surprise. The vast array of problems and addictions and devastation that people had endured in life was almost overwhelming. Although I value my seminary education, nothing from the classroom had prepared me for the harsh realities of human sin and the daily onslaught of demonic attack on the people God had called me to pastor.

Each day I went to the office wondering if there was possibly anything new in the human condition that I might confront. Invariably, and tragically, the answer was Yes. Their pain was more than I could handle. I felt helpless to help. For all my education and experience, it began to dawn on me that I really didn't understand the human soul, how it thinks and feels and reacts and adapts to abuse and sin and temptation. I needed help if I was going to be of help to others.

I decided to attend a week-long seminar in Dallas conducted by Dr. Larry Crabb and his associate at that time, Dr. Dan Allender. I'm not sure what happened that week, other than to say that I left the seminar a changed man (or at least committed to change). My best guess is that God used certain things Larry said and especially the examples of people to whom he ministered to open my heart to the depths of human pain. My life had always been pretty easy. I was raised in a Christian home. We weren't perfect by any stretch of the imagination, but I can honestly say that I came from one of the few truly *functional* families in America (that is, assuming you believe what the experts tell us about how *dysfunctional* family life has become).

But something happened that week in March of 1988. I have tried to tell the story in my book, *To Love Mercy* (Navpress; now out of print). To be brief, the Holy Spirit awakened my heart to see, perhaps for the first time, how badly people were hurting. I thank God daily for Larry Crabb, his friendship, and the impact his ministry has had on my life and my approach to being a pastor. Beyond the learning of new ideas and an introduction to a biblically sound philosophy of counseling, I left Dallas with a new passion for people and a burning desire in my heart to help them.

The point of my telling you this is that I believe what God did in March of 1988, in terms of my relationships with people, was preparatory to what would be a radical renewal in my relationship with God himself. I hear others tell their story and it seems as if in most cases the vertical relationship is first affected and only then the horizontal. With me it was the other way around. I don't know why. But God first humbled me by exposing the selfish and relationally distant nature of my ministry to people and only then did he choose to transform my relationship with him. It's hard to explain, but there's something about weeping with those who weep that makes the heart less resistant to the stirrings of the Holy Spirit. Like everyone else, I expect to struggle with pride for the rest of my life. But I am thoroughly convinced that in March of 1988 God graciously poked a big enough hole in my arrogance and ego to prepare a path for his entry into my life in a way I had never thought possible.

The Ceasing of Cessationism

Like most graduates of Dallas Theological Seminary (at least, in the 1970's), I was a cessationist (see Chapter One for a definition of this and other related terms). The charismatic perspective, on the other hand, was not a view generally tolerated at Dallas Seminary or in the circles of evangelicalism in which I had customarily moved.

For the first fifteen years of pastoral ministry I never questioned or doubted the doctrine of cessationism. In fact, regrettably, numerous cassette tapes of my teaching are still in circulation in which I affirm cessationism and warn the body of Christ concerning the dangers of the charismatic movement. On numerous occasions I went out of my way in a sermon or Sunday School class to alert others to what I perceived to be the theological errors of those who believed in the on-going validity of spiritual gifts.

Everything began to change when I read a book by Donald A. Carson entitled *Showing the Spirit: A Theological Exposition of 1 Corinthians 12-14* (Baker, 1987), but please don't hold Carson accountable for whatever errors you may detect in my thinking! Nothing in particular stirred me to read it, other than my appreciation for (but not always agreement with) everything he writes. But this book rocked my theological world. Carson's careful treatment of 1 Corinthians 12-14 exposed the errors in a number of arguments I had used through the years to defend cessationism. I will always be grateful to him for enabling me to read and interpret the Scriptures in the way that I believe God intended them.

It's important to make clear that I didn't reject cessationism because of some spiritual experience or miracle I witnessed. To that point in life I had never seen a miraculous healing or been the recipient of a prophetic word, nor had I ever dared raise my hands in worship, whether in private or public. I rejected cessationism because, in the solitude and safety of my study at Christ Community Church, I became convinced the Bible didn't teach it. I embraced the biblical validity of all spiritual gifts for the church today before I ever personally experienced them (with one exception, as noted below).

Carson's book also alerted me to the danger of embracing theological arguments based largely on one's respect for the person from whom you first learn them. The traditional arguments for cessationism, to which I respond in detail, by the way, in my contribution to the book *Are Miraculous Gifts for Today? Four Views* (Zondervan), were taught with great vigor and clarity by several of my professors at Dallas Seminary. The fault didn't so much lie with them as with me. I believe they are sincere men of God who are convinced that Scripture teaches cessationism. Sadly, though, I never took the time or invested the energy to carefully investigate on my own whether the arguments they presented were in fact biblical. I simply embraced them because of the immense respect I had for these men and the surface plausibility of their position. Carson's book drove me back to the text of Scripture and disclosed the fallacy in those arguments that I had so unthinkingly embraced for so many years.

Perhaps the most painful part of this particular theological shift was the discovery of one of the primary reasons I had so long resisted the full range of the Spirit's gifts. Beyond the biblical arguments to which I would appeal, I was, quite frankly, embarrassed by the appearance and behavior of many who were associated with spiritual gifts in the public eye. I didn't like the way they dressed. I didn't like the way they spoke. I was offended by their lack of sophistication and their overbearing flamboyance. I was disturbed by their flippant disregard for theological precision and their excessive displays of emotional exuberance.

By this time, however, I was so utterly persuaded by the biblical evidence for the perpetuity of the gifts of the Spirit that I was determined not to permit the fanaticism and failures of a few (or even of many) to affect how I read the Scriptures or how I ministered in the church. The fear of guilt by association has a far greater, more subtle, and more insidious influence on what we believe than most are willing to admit.

My convictions on this subject of the gifts of the Spirit were becoming known not only to the church in Ardmore but to my friends all around the country. Even in my book, *Healing and Holiness: A Biblical Response to the Faith-Healing Phenomenon* (Presbyterian & Reformed, 1990; now, thankfully, out of print), most of which I would prefer *never* to have written, I explicitly rejected cessationism. But it wasn't until March of 1993 that I took a bold step out of the theological closet, so let me jump forward several years before I return to the flow of our narrative.

A Return to Dallas Seminary

Dan Wallace, a long-time friend and currently a professor of New Testament at Dallas Theological Seminary, invited me to deliver a paper at the southwest regional meeting of the Evangelical Theological Society, to be held, of all places, on the campus of DTS! He wanted me to address this theological shift in my ministry. I consented. There I had the opportunity to explain why cessationism was, in my opinion, unbiblical. (The paper I presented at that meeting became the foundation for the article that later appeared in the book *Are Miraculous Gifts for Today? Four Views*.)

Several students at DTS as well as a dozen or so faculty members attended the session. They were all gracious and receptive, though not necessarily convinced! I was especially honored that Lewis Johnson (who died in February, 2004) attended the meeting. I honored, loved and respected Dr. Johnson as much as any man I've known. The debt I owe him is incalculable. The words I wrote of him in the book *Continuity and Discontinuity* (Crossway, 1988), a volume published in his honor, are no less true today than then.

My rejection of cessationism had already become evident in my preaching and in the life of our church in Ardmore as early as 1989. I not only advocated the gifts, I also encouraged the humble pursuit and practice of them (cf. 1 Corinthians 14:1). But I couldn't ask or expect my congregation to embrace something without first providing them with a cogent biblical foundation for it. So I preached verse by verse through Acts on Sunday mornings and taught a twenty-eight week series on the person and work of the Holy Spirit on Sunday nights. Slowly but surely we began to utilize the gifts in our home groups and eventually, where appropriate, in the public meetings of the church. There were skepticism and hesitancy on the part of some, but the church was remarkably open to what I had to say and expressed their desire to be biblical, no matter the cost. I have to be honest, though, and confess that there was one gift that I kept tucked away in the closet.

Praying in the Spirit

My first encounter with the gifts of the Spirit came when I was nineteen years old. In the summer of 1970, after my freshman year at the University of Oklahoma I was living in Lake Tahoe, Nevada, serving with Campus Crusade for Christ on an evangelistic project. We spent the summer witnessing to those who visited the beaches and casinos.

I pumped gas in a Shell station. There wasn't much excitement in that, except for Fridays, when the motorcycle gangs from Sacramento and San Francisco would descend upon that resort city. Their first stop upon entering the outskirts of Tahoe was to fill up at my service station. I thank God for the courage and opportunity to share the gospel with a few of them before the summer ended.

My perspective on the church and Christians as a whole was soundly shaken that summer. This was due, in no small measure, to a visit I made to the campus of the University of California, Berkeley. You must remember that this was the late spring, early summer of 1970. It was a time of hippies, the Viet Nam War and its protestors, hallucinogenic drugs, and the emergence of what came to be known as the Jesus movement. While in Berkeley I spent a couple of days with those who called themselves the Christian World Liberation Front, or CWLF. Let me assure you that nothing in my nineteen years as a Southern Baptist from Oklahoma prepared me for the radical, off-beat approach to Christianity that I encountered there! Although my exposure to the CWLF was brief, I was challenged in a positive way to be a bit more open and tolerant of those who worshiped and lived out their life in Jesus in ways that differed from my own.

Toward the end of that summer I attended a meeting at which Harald Bredesen, one of the early leaders of the charismatic movement, was scheduled to speak. In the course of the evening he mentioned a book by John Sherrill entitled *They Speak with Other Tongues*. The story he told of Sherrill's experience wasn't even remotely similar to my life in God. But he had my attention. I obtained a copy and read it immediately.

The issue of speaking in tongues soon became an obsession with me. As my time of ministry in the beautiful Rocky Mountains concluded, I returned to the University of Oklahoma to continue my studies as a sophomore. During this time I began to pray earnestly that, if the gift were real, God would give it to me. I wasn't exactly sure what I was praying for. Nevertheless, for several weeks I spent each night in a secluded area near my fraternity house pleading with God for some indication of his will for me concerning this gift.

I can't say that I ever expected anything to happen. My skepticism toward spiritual gifts like tongues was deep-seated and pervasive. Having been raised for twenty years in Southern Baptist churches, speaking in tongues was rarely mentioned, and only then with scorn and disdain. One thing is certain: I was not "primed", so to speak, either psychologically or spiritually, for what eventually happened.

One night in October of 1970, quite without warning, my normal, somewhat routine, prayer was radically interrupted. I suddenly began speaking forth words of uncertain sound and form. I didn't start out by consciously muttering a few senseless syllables which then gave way to a more coherent linguistic experience. It was more like a spiritual invasion in which the

Spirit intruded on my life, interrupted my speech patterns and "gave utterance" (Acts 2:4).

There was a profound intensification of my sense of God's nearness and power. I distinctly remember feeling a somewhat detached sensation, as if I were separate from the one speaking. I had never experienced anything remotely similar to that in all my life. While this linguistic flood continued to pour forth I kept thinking to myself, "Sam, what are you saying? Are you speaking in tongues?" It was the first time I had ever experienced the sensation of thinking in one language while speaking in another.

My reaction to something so unfamiliar and new was a strange mixture of both fear and exhilaration. I don't recall precisely how long it lasted, but it couldn't have been more than a couple of minutes. I was confused, but at the same time felt closer to God than ever before. At the time I didn't have theological categories to describe what happened. In hindsight, I'm more inclined to view it as a powerful filling of the Holy Spirit rather than Spirit baptism (although I'm open to being convinced otherwise). Having said that, I must confess that when I look for words to describe it the only thing that comes to mind is immersion and saturation, a sense of being inundated or flooded with the presence of God.

Those who've had a similar experience know why I struggle to describe what happened. My relationship with God to that point had been largely, if not entirely, intellectual. I'm not questioning the reality of my salvation. I'm simply saying that aside from a few emotional moments in church as a young boy, I had no tangible awareness of a dimension of reality beyond what I could encounter through the five senses. But on the night in question it was as though the veil that separated my being from the being of God was lifted. My spirit was engulfed by the Spirit of God. Neither before nor since that day have I felt so directly, empirically, and undeniably in touch with the realm of the supernatural.

I returned to my fraternity house filled with excitement and called a friend who was on staff with Campus Crusade for Christ. I didn't tell him what had happened; only that I needed to speak with him immediately. Thirty minutes later I sat down in his car and said, "You'll never guess what happened tonight."

"You spoke in tongues, didn't you?" he asked, almost deadpan.

"Yes! How did you know? It was great. But I don't understand what it means."

This man cared deeply for me and had no intention of offending me or obstructing my Christian growth. But what he said next affected me for years to come.

"Sam, you do realize, don't you, that you will have to resign your position as student leader and give up any hope of joining staff when you graduate. Campus Crusade doesn't permit people who speak in tongues to hold positions of authority. Of course, if you don't do it again, there's no need for us to tell anyone. Everything can be the same as it was before." [My understanding is that Campus Crusade for Christ reversed their policy on spiritual gifts several years ago.]

I was crushed. I remember feebly and fearfully trying to speak in tongues the next night, but nothing happened. Not wanting to forfeit my position in the ministry on campus, I concluded that it must have been something other than the Holy Spirit. I never thought it was demonic, although many of my friends did. I explained it away as a momentary emotional outburst that I'd be better off forgetting. I rarely spoke of the incident in the years following, fearful of the disdain of my friends who looked with suspicion on anyone remotely associated with or showing interest in the gift of tongues. Needless to say, I didn't speak in tongues again for twenty years!

I think it's important to point out that deep within I always knew that the experience was a genuine encounter with the Spirit of God. My agreement with those who explained it (away) by appealing to psychological factors was prompted less by conviction than by my fear of incurring their ridicule or, worse still, losing their friendship. I also believe that my attempt to write it off as a momentary, one-time phenomenon, better left in the past, was offensive to God and a clear instance of quenching the Holy Spirit.

More than twenty years later, in November of 1990 I attended a theology conference in New Orleans and spent time with Jack Deere, a close friend and former classmate at Dallas Seminary. Jack is the author of *Surprised by the Power of the Spirit* and *Surprised by the Voice of God* (Zondervan), both excellent biblical refutations of cessationism. Jack taught Old Testament and Hebrew at Dallas for twelve years before being dismissed because of his embrace of continuationism. At the time of our visit in New Orleans he was serving as an associate of John Wimber at the Anaheim Vineyard in California.

I shared with him my journey and told him about what had happened back in the fall of 1970, hoping to gain additional insight into the nature of my experience and what God's will for me might be. He then reminded me of something the apostle Paul said to young Timothy: "For this reason I remind you to fan into flame ["kindle afresh"; NASB] the gift of God which is in you through the laying on of my hands" (2 Timothy 1:6). Jack then laid hands on me and asked the Lord to kindle afresh in me this gift he had bestowed so many years before.

This verse in 2 Timothy is important. It tells us that one may receive a spiritual gift only to neglect and ignore it. The imagery Paul uses is helpful. He describes a spiritual gift in terms of a flame that needs to be continually fanned. If it is not understood and nurtured and utilized in the way God intended, the once brightly burning flame can be reduced to a smoldering ember. "Take whatever steps you must: study, pray, seek God's face, put it into practice, but by all means stoke the fire until that gift returns to its original intensity."[1]

I took Paul's advice to Timothy and applied it to my own case. Every day, if only for a few minutes, I prayed that God would renew what he had given but I had quenched. I prayed that, if it were his will, I would once more be able to pray in the Spirit, to speak that heavenly language that would praise and thank and bless him (1 Corinthians 14:2,16,17). I didn't wait for some sort of divine seizure, but in faith began simply to speak forth the syllables and words that he brought to mind.

Some fifteen years have passed now since God renewed his precious gift in my life. Praying in the Spirit is by no means the most important gift. Neither is it a sign of a spirituality or maturity greater than that of those who don't have this particular gift. But if no less a man than the Apostle Paul can say, "I thank God I speak in tongues more than you all" (1 Corinthians 14:18), who am I to despise this blessed gift of God?

Contrary to the caricatures that many have of this gift, it has served only to enhance and deepen my relationship with the Lord Jesus. Believe it or not, I can still tie my shoelaces, balance my checkbook, drive a car, hold down a job, and I rarely ever drool! I don't mean to be sarcastic, but this particular gift of the Spirit has a terrible public image. For me to reveal to you that I speak in tongues is to run the risk of being perceived as a mindless, spiritually flabby fanatic who periodically mumbles while in a convulsive or hypnotic trance. I can't do much about that, except to encourage you to search the Scriptures, seek the face of God, and carefully read chapters eight and nine in my book, *The Beginner's Guide to Spiritual*

Gifts (Regal Books), where I discuss the gift of tongues and how it functions in the life of the Christian.

On the Winds of Worship

Without question, the most powerful catalyst in my personal transformation was the discovery of God and his beauty and power and love during times of worship. I had always worshiped God. I had always loved music, especially the great hymns of the church. But all too frequently worship for me was little more than singing songs about God. Of course, we ought to sing about him. But I rarely had any expectation of meeting God or experiencing his presence or engaging my heart with his or, far less, of *enjoying* him.

I can't recall how it happened or through whom, but late in 1988 I began to listen to new expressions of praise and worship. Tapes produced by Hosanna Integrity as well as the Vineyard somehow made their way into my office cassette player and into the tape-deck in my car. It was more than just a new style of music. I have never stopped loving or singing the traditional hymns of the church. But something was happening in times of worship that had never happened before. It's difficult to describe, but I'll try.[2]

The Birth of a Christian Hedonist

There was a time when I thought the verb "enjoy" and the noun "God" should never be used in the same sentence. I could understand "fearing" God and "obeying" God, even "loving" God. But "enjoying" God struck me as inconsistent with the biblical mandate both to glorify God, on the one hand, and deny myself, on the other. How could I be committed above all else to seeking God's glory if I were concerned about my own joy? My gladness and God's glory seemed to cancel each other out. I had to choose between one or the other, but embracing them both struck me as out of the question. Worse still, enjoying God sounded a bit too lighthearted, almost casual, perhaps even flippant, and I knew that Christianity was serious business.

Then I read Jonathan Edwards (1703-58). Something he said hit me like a bolt of lightning. I'm not a Christian Hedonist because of Jonathan Edwards. Scripture always has and will remain the final authority in my life. But Edwards helped me to see that God's glory and my gladness were not antithetical. He helped me see that at the core of Scripture is the truth that my heart's passion for pleasure (which is God-given and *not* the result of sin) and God's passion for praise converge in a way that alone makes sense of human existence. I should let you read it for yourself. Outside of the Word of God, it's the most significant and life-changing utterance I've ever read:

> "Now what is glorifying God, but a rejoicing at that glory he has displayed? An understanding of the perfections of God, merely, cannot be the end of the creation; for he had as good not understand it, as see it and not be at all moved with joy at the sight. Neither can the highest end of creation be the declaring God's glory to others; for the declaring God's glory is good for nothing otherwise than to raise joy in ourselves and others at what is declared."[3]

Here it is again, in other words:

> "God is glorified not only by his glory's being seen, but by its being rejoiced in. When those that see it delight in it, God is more glorified than if they only see it. God made the world that he might communicate, and the creature receive, his glory . . . both [with] the mind and the heart. He that testifies his having an idea of God's glory [doesn't] glorify God so much as he that testifies also his approbation [i.e., his heartfelt commendation or praise] of it and his delight in it."[4]

Edwards' point is that *passionate and joyful admiration of God, and not merely intellectual apprehension, is the aim of our existence.* If God is to be supremely glorified in us we must be supremely glad in him and in what he has done for us in Jesus. Enjoying God is not a secondary, tangential endeavor. It is central to everything we do, especially worship. We do not do other things hoping that joy in God will emerge as a by-product. Our reason for the pursuit of God and obedience to him is precisely the joy that is found in him alone. To worship him for any reason other than the joy that is found in who he is, is sinful.

I know how strange this sounds the first time one hears it (it can sound strange for a long time thereafter as well!). So permit me to look elsewhere for help in making sense of it. In an article entitled "We Want You To

Be A Christian Hedonist," found on John Piper's website (www.desiring-god.org), the following explanation of Christian Hedonism is found.

A "Christian Hedonist" sounds like a contradiction, doesn't it? If the term makes you squirm, we understand. But don't throw this paper away just yet. We're not heretics (really!). Nor have we invented another prosperity-obsessed theology by twisting the Bible to sanctify our greed or lust. We are simply stating an ancient, orthodox, Biblical truth in a fresh way.

"All men seek happiness," says Blaise Pascal. "This is without exception. Whatever different means they employ, they all tend to this end. The cause of some going to war, and of others avoiding it, is the same desire in both, attended with different views. The will never takes the least step but to this object. This is the motive of every action of every man, even of those who hang themselves." We believe Pascal is right. And, with Pascal, we believe God purposefully designed us to pursue happiness.

Does seeking your own happiness sound self-centered? Aren't Christians supposed to seek God, not their own pleasure? To answer this question we need to understand a crucial truth about pleasure-seeking (hedonism): we value most what we delight in most. Pleasure is not God's competitor, idols are. Pleasure is simply a gauge that measures how valuable someone or something is to us. Pleasure is the measure of our treasure.

We know this intuitively. If a friend says to you, "I really enjoy being with you," you wouldn't accuse him of being self-centered. Why? Because your friend's delight in you is the evidence that you have great value in his heart. In fact, you'd be dishonored if he didn't experience any pleasure in your friendship. The same is true of God. If God is the source of our greatest delight then God is our most precious treasure; which makes us radically God-centered and not self-centered. And if we treasure God most, we glorify Him most.

Does the Bible teach this? Yes. Nowhere in the Bible does God condemn people for longing to be happy. People are condemned for forsaking God and seeking their happiness elsewhere (Jeremiah 2:13). This is the essence of sin. The Bible actually commands us to delight in the Lord (Psalm 37:4). Jesus teaches us to love God more than money because our heart is where our treasure is (Matt. 6:21). Paul wants us to believe that gaining Christ is worth the loss of everything else (Phil 3:8) and the author of Hebrews exhorts us to endure suffering, like Jesus, for the joy set before us (Heb. 12: 1-2). Examine the Scriptures and you'll see this over and over again.

Christian Hedonism is not a contradiction after all. It is desiring the vast, ocean-deep pleasures of God more than the mud-puddle pleasures of wealth, power or lust. We're Christian Hedonists because we believe Psalm 16:11, "You show me the path of life; in Your presence there is fullness of joy, in Your right hand are pleasures for evermore."

Join us in this pursuit of satisfaction in God, because God is most glorified in us when we are most satisfied in him.

The next step is a difficult one for some to take. Here it is: our glad-hearted passion for God is exceeded only by *God's* glad-hearted passion for God. If the chief end of man is to glorify God by enjoying him forever, the chief end of *God* is to glorify *God* and to enjoy *himself* forever!

What is the pre-eminent passion in God's heart? What is *God's* greatest pleasure? In what does *God* take supreme delight? I want to suggest that the pre-eminent passion in God's heart is his own glory. God is at the center of his own affections. The supreme love of God's life is God. God is pre-eminently committed to the fame of his name. God is himself the end for which God created the world. Better, still, God's immediate goal in all he does is his own glory. God relentlessly and unceasingly creates, rules, orders, directs, speaks, judges, saves, destroys and delivers in order to make known who he is and to secure from the whole of the universe the praise, honor and glory of which he and he alone is ultimately and infinitely worthy.

The question I most often hear in response to this is that if God loves himself pre-eminently, how can he love me at all? How can we say that God is for *us* and that he desires *our* happiness if he is primarily for *himself* and his own glory? I want to argue that it is precisely *because* God loves himself that he loves you. Here's how.

I assume you will agree that your greatest good consists of enjoying the most excellent Being in the universe. That Being, of course, is God.

Therefore, the most loving and kind thing that God can do for you is to devote all his energy and effort to elicit from your heart praise of himself. Why? Because praise is the consummation of enjoyment. All enjoyment tends towards praise and adoration as its appointed end. In this way, God's seeking his own glory and God's seeking your good converge.

Listen again. Your greatest good is in the enjoyment of God. God's greatest glory is in being enjoyed. So, for God to seek his glory in your worship of him is the most loving thing he can do for you. Only by seeking his glory pre-eminently can God seek your good passionately. For God to work for your enjoyment of him (that's his love for you) and for his glory in being enjoyed (that's his love for himself) are not properly distinct.

This theological digression is important because it articulates the transformation in my understanding and experience of worship. There's no other way to say it: I suddenly felt the freedom to *enjoy God*. I actually *felt* his presence. I actually *felt* his enjoyment of me in my enjoyment of him (cf. Zephaniah 3:17). I began to sense a *power* and *spiritual intensity* that at first was a bit frightening. Although I have always been a romantic and somewhat emotional, when it came to worship, especially in a public setting, I was always diligent to rein in my emotions. I felt compelled to preserve a measure of so-called "dignity" and "religious sophistication".

But God *visited* me in worship! As I drew near to him, he drew near to me (James 4:8). I began to experience an *intimacy* and *warmth of relationship* with God that reminded me of Paul's prayer for the Ephesians: "(I pray) that according to the riches of his glory he may grant you to be strengthened with power through his Spirit in your inner being, so that Christ may dwell in your hearts through faith – that you, being rooted and grounded in love, may have strength to comprehend with all the saints what is the breadth and length and height and depth and to know the love of Christ that surpasses knowledge, that you may be filled with all the fullness of God" (3:16-19).

David tells us that in God's presence there is "fullness of joy" and at his right hand are "pleasures forevermore" (Psalm 16:11). I began to move beyond the affirmation of this truth to the tangible, experiential enjoyment of it. It suddenly dawned on me that, whereas I had trusted God with my mind, confident that he was sufficiently sovereign to protect my theology, I had not trusted him with my emotions. A few years later I came across a statement in one of Jack Hayford's books that perfectly expresses what I was sensing at that time:

"It began to dawn on me that, given an environment where the Word of God was *foundational* and the Person of Christ the *focus*, the Holy Spirit could be trusted to do *both* – enlighten the intelligence and ignite the emotions. I soon discovered that to allow Him that much space necessitates more a surrender of my senseless fears than a surrender of sensible control. God is not asking any of us to abandon reason or succumb to some euphoric feeling. He is, however, calling us to trust Him – enough to give *Him* control."[5]

Several people played a significant role in my life at this time. I will never forget a particular Sunday morning in our church in Oklahoma when I saw something I had never seen before. A young lady and her husband were visiting our church for the first time. During the singing of one of the hymns, I looked up and saw her. Unlike everyone else in the congregation, whose faces were either bored or buried in the hymnbook, she was gazing toward heaven, her eyes aglow and a smile of "joy inexpressible and full of glory" (1 Peter 1:8) spread across her face. I was deeply moved. I know it sounds odd, but I couldn't get over how much she appeared to be *enjoying God*. There was an openness, a vulnerability, a child-like confidence in her countenance that I couldn't help but envy. I can remember saying to myself: "I wish I felt like that about God. I wish I could be free enough to express my joy like she did." Both wishes (prayers) were to come true.

Not long after that Sunday morning, I obtained a video tape of a worship service led by Jeanne Rogers, who for many years had been associated with the ministry of James Robison. Virtually every night I watched and listened to the hour-long service. I saw people lifting their hands, dancing, weeping, rejoicing, and singing not simply *about* God but *to* God. Each time I was led away from merely watching the video into my own personal worship of the Lord. I sensed God draw near to me. I felt as if he were saying: "Sam, don't be afraid. Open your heart to me. Lift your hands to me. I want you to enjoy me. I want to enjoy you. I want to flood your spirit with mine" (cf. Romans 5:5).

I immediately undertook an in-depth study of the Scriptures. I wasn't about to pursue anything that didn't have the explicit endorsement of the Word. I preached a 12-week series on worship in the Bible. I read every book I could find on the subject. My life has never been the same since.

About this time someone told me of a man named Dennis Jernigan, then worship leader at Western Hills Church in Oklahoma City. Soon many of us in Ardmore began making the short drive each month to the "Night of Praise," a 3-4 hour worship celebration led by Dennis. That may sound a bit excessive for those of you accustomed to, at most, fifteen minutes of singing on Sunday morning. But it was in those services that God enlarged my heart to embrace him, freely and fully, without regard for what people might think. The music and message of Dennis Jernigan have contributed immeasurably to my growth as a Christian. It was Dennis, in fact, who first made me aware of Zephaniah 3:17 and the shocking discovery that God loves me so much that he *sings* over me![6]

Other worship leaders were unwittingly used by God to expand my enjoyment of God and the freedom with which I expressed that delight. On numerous occasions I would find some excuse to drive to Dallas, Texas, only to end up attending a worship celebration that encouraged me to express my joy and satisfaction in God in ways that were as yet unacceptable (or at least extremely unfamiliar) to my church in Ardmore. On more than one occasion I actually traveled to St. Louis, Missouri, to attend a marathon worship service led by Kent Henry, one of the most anointed worship leaders I know. Jack Deere contributed in his own way to my growth by repeatedly sending me every new Vineyard worship tape as soon as it was produced.

I still sing *about* God. I always will. But there's something different in singing *to* God. Yes, I still join with others and sing: "*We* love him." After all, we must never lose sight of the fact that we are a *community* of worshipers. But I much prefer engaging God one-on-one, my heart touching his, and singing: "*I* love *you!*"

I made a discovery about worship that I believe is found repeatedly in Scripture. Unfortunately, whereas I read it, I never experienced the reality of it. I'm referring to the outpouring of divine *power* during times of praise. When God's people exalt and enjoy him, he releases his power to heal them, to encourage them, and to enlighten them, among other things, in a way that is somewhat unique. When God's people worship, he goes to war on their behalf (2 Chronicles 20). When God's people worship, he enthrones himself in their midst (Psalm 22:3). When God's people worship, he speaks to them and guides them (Acts 13:1-3). When God's people worship, he delivers them from their troubles or comforts and sustains them in the midst of hardship (Acts 16:19-40).

Healing on the Home Front

God has blessed me in many ways these fifty-four years on the earth. But few blessings can rival the people and friends at Christ Community Church in Ardmore, Oklahoma. I spent eight years living with these people, loving them, teaching and being taught.

The changes that we began to implement in the worship and ministry model at CCC did not split the church, as has sadly been the case in numerous other congregations around the country. Some people left, but the vast majority stayed, even if they didn't fully understand or agree with what we were doing. I honor those who persevered through my feeble efforts to open the door to the full range of the Spirit's ministry. I didn't always do it well, but I tried. And they loved and supported me through it all.

We began obeying the Scriptures concerning our responsibility to pray for the sick. It wasn't a question of who or how many did or did not get healed. It was a question of whether or not we were going to be obedient. I embraced the perspective of John Wimber who once said, "I would rather pray for one-hundred people and see only one get healed than not to pray for any and none get healed." In other words, I finally reached a point at which I refused to allow the fear of failure to justify my disobedience to the Word.

My expectations concerning divine healing were radically impacted by two unrelated events separated by almost twenty years. The first occurred in 1961 in Midland, Texas. I was only ten years old, having been a Christian for about two years. I was theologically uninformed and knew nothing of the supernatural. I suspect that what I'm about to share may strike some of you as silly, or at best the confusion of an immature kid. Undoubtedly I was immature. What ten-year-old isn't? But I'm confident about the truth of what happened.

One night I lay in bed, suffering from the worst headache I had ever experienced. I didn't have words for it then, but it was something akin to a migraine. The pain was paralyzing and I felt helpless even to call out for the help of my mother or father. I can't say that I had ever asked God for healing before that night, but I was desperate. My prayer was simple and typical for a ten-year-old.

"God, if you're there, would you heal me? Please take this pain away. I'm going to count to three." I know what you're thinking, but isn't that the way you would have done it at that age?

"When I get to three, please take the pain away. One. Two. Three!"

I didn't expect anything to happen. To say I was shocked when something did is quite the understatement. There wasn't a gradual diminishing of pain. Nothing along the lines of, "I'm beginning to feel a little bit better." The healing was sudden, total, and startling. Immediately on saying "Three," all pain disappeared. I remember being so surprised that I lay motionless, fearful that if I moved the pain would come back, fearful that it was all make-believe.

But I went from excruciating pain to complete and empirically undeniable healing in an instant. I'd love to be able to say it happened the next time a headache came along, but I can't. It was a one-off, as they say. But that doesn't make it any less real. It's one of those experiences that, no matter the age when it happens, you never forget it. The moment it occurred is as real to me today, nearly forty-five years later, as it was that night. It was so exceptional and out of the ordinary that I was more scared than relieved. Again, I suspect that's typical for ten-year-old kids.

On countless occasions since that night in 1961 I've reminded myself of what God did for a silly little kid who counted to three. The lesson I learned is as simple now as it was then: there is a God who heals, not every time we count to three, but according to his sovereign and merciful good will.

The second event that alerted me to the reality of healing is what I call an act of *prophetic providence.*[7] It was Friday, October 26th, 1990 and I was busily preparing my Sunday sermon. I was preaching through Acts and had reached the story of the paralytic in chapter three. Here was a forty-year-old man, paralyzed from the womb, who was healed through the ministry of Peter and John. My sermon preparation wasn't going very well. I was literally in mid-sentence, writing the words I would soon speak to my congregation, words that denied or at least cast a long shadow of doubt on the possibility that God might heal someone like that today. Then came a knock at the door.

My secretary entered with the day's mail. I was a little surprised, because the mail didn't normally arrive until well after 1:00. Here it was just after 11:00 a.m. For some reason I put my pen down and opened *the one and only letter* that arrived that day. It was from an elderly lady in Wales, of all places. I certainly didn't know anyone in Wales. I'd never been to Wales. But someone had sent this lady a copy of the book I had written *against* healing. I'm not proud of that book (thankfully, it's out of print).

The letter was short and to the point. She kindly affirmed some of what she read in my book, but went on to humbly suggest that she believed

God would respond with power to our prayers for healing. After reading the letter, I noticed something else in the envelope. It was the written testimony of a lady named Margery Steven. In 1955 she was afflicted with an extraordinarily severe case of multiple sclerosis. She had to be lifted in and out of a wheelchair, her legs having become utterly useless. Straps were used to keep her from falling out of the chair. Her left arm was completely useless, her left eye was closed and vision in her right eye was virtually gone. She would often lose consciousness for hours at a time.

Five years into her illness, on February 4th, 1960, Margery had a powerful dream during the night. She saw herself sitting in a chair beside her bed, completely healed. When she awakened, she heard a voice filling the room, a voice she believed to be that of Jesus. He said: "Tarry a little longer." But she seemed only to get worse from that day on. Eventually her speech became so impaired that it was virtually impossible to understand a word she said. Perhaps it would be better if I let you read in her own words what happened next.

"On Monday, July 4th, exactly five months after God had spoken to me, my Lord healed me, in the very chair of which I had dreamed! I had said goodbye to my husband at five minutes to six on that Monday morning – a helpless woman. At 6:15 my mother gave me a cup of tea. At 6:20 my father and mother lifted me from my bed, strapped me in the chair beside the bed, put a bell in my good hand, to summon aid if needed, and left me alone. Mother went to get my washing water and my father had gone to get a towel from upstairs. *Then in a matter of seconds, when I was all on my own, my Lord Jesus healed me!* I felt a warm glow go over my body. My left foot, which was doubled up, straightened out; my right foot, the toes of which were pointed towards my heel, came back into position. I grasped the handle of my bedroom door which was beside me, undid the straps which were about my body, and said 'By faith I will stand,' which I did. With that I thought of my mother and the shock it would be to her if she came back to find her daughter standing after so many years, so I sat down and called for her. With that both my parents came running to my room, thinking I was in need of them. I said, 'Mum dear, take my hands, please don't be afraid, something wonderful has happened.' I put out my right arm and as I did so my left arm came out from behind me and joined the other! It was so wonderful a few mintues afterwards to find I could wear my own wedding ring which I had not been able to do for years, as my fingers of that hand had got so thin. My mother said, 'Darling, how wonderful, your hand is warm, and is well again.' I said, 'Mum, dear, it's more wonderful than that. *I can stand.*' With that, holding her hands, *I stood once more on my two feet.* Then, gently putting my parents to one side, I said, 'Dears, I do not need your help anymore, I'm walking with God.' Unaided I then walked from my bedroom, through the small dining room to the kitchen, my parents following mutely behind me. When I reached the kitchen I turned and went back into the dining room and taking off my glasses I said, 'Mum, I can trust God for my hands and feet. I can trust Him for my sight.' *With that, in a moment, my left eye opened and my sight was fully restored!* In fact Jesus made such a perfect job I do not need the glasses I had before I was ill and I am now writing dozens of letters a day! To Him be all the glory!"

The Welsh lady who sent me this testimony informed me in her letter that Margery Steven was still alive and well, thirty years after her healing.

I sat at my desk more than a little stunned. It couldn't have been mere coincidence. In the marvelous providence of God, someone had sent my book to this lady at *just the right time* so that she would send to me *at just the right time* a copy of this testimony. *I just so happened* (!) to be writing the very words that would undermine people's faith in God's willingness to heal today when the letter arrived . . . not from someone in my own church who knew what I was preaching or even from someone in the U.S., but from someone I'd never met in Wales!

I try not to read into events more than I should, but no one will ever convince me this was anything less than the providential timing of a God who was determined to put some sense into a preacher's head and some passion into his heart. It worked.

It wasn't long after that when a young couple came to me before the Sunday service and asked that the Elders of the church anoint their infant son and pray for his healing. We were unskilled, but committed to do what James 5 said to do. After the service we gathered in the back room and anointed him with oil. I can't give you the precise medical name for his condition, but

at six months of age he had a serious liver disorder that would require immediate surgery, possibly even a transplant, if something did not change.

As we prayed, something very unusual happened. It has only happened to me twice in these many years that I have prayed for the sick. As we
laid hands on him and prayed, I found myself suddenly filled with an overwhelming and inescapable confidence that he would be healed. It was altogether unexpected. I hadn't made any attempt to create such a feeling.
Nothing was said or done to prepare me for what occurred in the depths of
my soul. I recall actually trying to doubt, fearful that I was on the verge of
acting presumptuously toward God. But I couldn't do it! It was a divinely
induced supernatural surge of faith that was both unshakeable and undeniable. "God," I said to myself, "you really are going to heal him." I prayed confidently. The family left the room unsure. But not me. I was absolutely *certain*
God had healed him. The next morning the doctor agreed. He was totally
healed and is a healthy, happy young boy today.

---

[1] Some would argue that the word translated "fan into flame" (ESV) simply means to "kindle," without any suggestion of a prior diminishing operation.

[2] An excellent defense of contemporary worship written by a highly trained Calvinistic the-
ologian is *Contemporary Worship Music: A Biblical Defense* (Phillipsburg, NJ: P & R
Publishing, 1997), by John Frame. Frame currently teaches theology and apologetics at
Reformed Theological Seminary in Orlando, Florida.

[3] Jonathan Edwards, *The Miscellanies [Entry Nos. a-z, aa-zz, 1-500]*, The Works of Jonathan
Edwards, Volume 13. Edited by Thomas A. Schafer [New Haven: Yale University Press,
1994], no. 3, 200).

[4] Ibid., no. 448, 495.

[5] Jack Hayford, *A Passion for Fulness* (Dallas: Word Books, 1990), 31.

[6] This is a theme I wrote about in my book, *The Singing God: Discover the Joy of Being Enjoyed
by God* (Creation House, 1998).

[7] The substance of this story is taken from chapter four of my book, *The Beginner's Guide to
Spiritual Gifts* (Ventura, CA: Regal Books, 2002).

Chapter THREE

❧

Dreams, Visions and Deliverance

I first met Jack Deere in 1973 while we were students together at Dallas Theological Seminary. Both of us were strict cessationists. Neither of us would ever have envisioned the theological path we would one day walk. After I moved out of Dallas to Ardmore in 1985, we lost contact with each other until one day early in 1988 when I saw Jack on the campus at Dallas. Ironically, I was there to visit a friend in Baylor Hospital, near the seminary campus, who was dying of brain cancer.

Jack shared with me some of what God had been doing in his life. Not long after our conversation, he was dismissed from the faculty because of his views on the ministry of the Holy Spirit and, as I noted earlier, eventually joined the staff of the Vineyard Christian Fellowship in Anaheim, California, where John Wimber was serving as senior pastor. Jack and I maintained close contact with each other as he helped and encouraged me in my own pilgrimage.

During our time together at that theological conference in November of 1990, Jack invited me to attend a large Vineyard conference to be held in Anaheim in January of 1991 (the one I mentioned in the Introduction). I will never forget how I felt as I walked into the Anaheim Convention Center and joined 7,000 other believers in worship. Several things happened that week that forever changed my life. I want to briefly share them with you.

On the second night of the conference, Jack and I went to dinner with several people, one of whom was a British lady who had spent the previous 25 years ministering in Hong Kong (as of the writing of this book she has labored forty years in Hong Kong). Jackie Pullinger, whose remarkable story is told in the book *Chasing the Dragon* (Servant Publications) is, unfortunately, one of a kind. I say "unfortunately" because the kingdom of God could use a thousand more just like her. I had never before, nor have I since, met a Christian like Jackie Pullinger. The depth of her commitment and sacrificial spirit, her zeal for the Lord Jesus Christ, and her compassion for the lost of the world are, at least in terms of my experience, unparalleled in the church. I can only urge you to read her book and pray that God will stir and break your heart through her story the way he did mine. You will be stunned, as I was, by the way God has used the gift of tongues in her ministry with drug addicts. But I'll leave that for you to discover on your own as you read her book.

Another person whom I met for the first time that night was a young pastor from Kansas City named Mike Bickle. I'll have more to say about Mike later on.

On the last day of the conference, Jack invited me to join him in one of the back rooms at the convention center. He encouraged me to sit quietly and listen and learn. Over the next two hours or so I had the opportunity to observe several men pray and minister prophetically to people who were attending the conference from all across the U.S. and abroad. The room slowly emptied, as each took his or her turn, finally leaving me alone, sitting sheepishly at the back. I moved to the front and sat down across from several men whom I had never met.

One of them looked at my name tag, peered deeply into my eyes and rather casually said: "I'd like to tell you what you've been praying in your hotel room this week," which is precisely what he did! People in the Vineyard commonly referred to this phenomenon by saying: "He read my mail!" I hadn't told Jack or anyone about my prayer. I had only told God. But evidently God had told this man! He didn't speak in general or broad terms, but recited to me the very words that I had repeatedly cried out to the Lord the previous three nights.

Shaken, and still a bit uncertain about what had happened, I returned to my hotel room and immediately fell to my knees. No, I wasn't preparing to pray. I started searching for a bugging device! I thought Jack had secretly bugged my room and then passed off the information to this individual in a cruel hoax, all designed to draw me into a world that I might otherwise have forever resisted. The simple explanation, however, was that I had just had my first experience with what I now know as New Testament prophetic ministry. True to Scripture, I was profoundly *edified, consoled, and encouraged* (1 Corinthians 14:3).

Aside from that experience in the fall of 1970, this was my first experience with one of the miraculous gifts of the Holy Spirit. I believed in the gift of prophecy before I ever went to Anaheim. I had just never seen it in operation. Since that day in January of 1991 I have witnessed countless instances of prophetic utterance and, by God's grace, have even been used of the Lord on a few occasions to speak similarly into the lives of other people. I'll share a couple of those instances later on.

My time in Anaheim was incredible. The opportunity to spend time with Jackie Pullinger, Mike Bickle, and Jack Deere was rewarding beyond words. As I sat on the plane back to Oklahoma, I recorded three things that impressed me about the people at the conference. These are by no means the only things characteristic of their Christian walk. I only want to mention what I saw and heard and sensed that created in my heart a cry: "Lord! I want that!"

(1) These people had an *unashamed, extravagant affection for Jesus*. I love Jesus. I have loved Jesus ever since I was a child. But I can't say that my love for Jesus had been *unashamed* or *extravagant*. I had always been careful to keep my love for Jesus private and under control. When in public I was diligent to express my affection for Christ only in ways that conformed to accepted religious tradition. I was careful not to embarrass myself or make other people feel uncomfortable with my devotion to the Son of God. But these people were open and honest and passionate and care-free and proud of their affection and love for the Son of God. I saw it. I heard it. I *wanted* it.

(2) These people manifested a *sense of immediacy in their relationship with God*. I don't know a better term to use than immediacy. By it I mean a sense of God's proximity, his nearness, what theologians call his immanence. They lived and talked and laughed and sang as if God were *right there in and with them*. Their God was not a distant deity or a remote ruler. To use the words of an old hymn, he "walked with them and talked with them and told them they were his own." I believed God was near. But I rarely sensed it. I rarely lived as if it were true. I had become an *evangelical deist*, one who worshiped a God far off, removed from the daily struggles of life. But not these people. Once again, I saw it. I heard it. And once again, I *wanted* it.

(3) These people *prayed anywhere, at any time, for anyone, for any reason.* I was standing in line for a hot dog during the break, eavesdropping on the prayers of the people in front of me. They stopped right there in line, laid hands on a needy friend, and prayed! None of this: "I'll pray for you!" as a Christian way of saying "Good-bye. Have a nice day!" They didn't *say* it. They didn't even *promise* it. They *did* it. Why? Because they had the *spiritual audacity* actually to believe God's Word. They really believed God listened to them. They really believed God would answer them. They took seriously a verse that I had only memorized but failed to practice: "You have not because you ask not" (James 4:2). Yes, I saw it. I heard it, and yes, I *wanted* it.

The Power of the Prophetic

Jack was relentless in his determination to broaden my exposure to the gifts of the Spirit. So he invited me to a conference in Houston, Texas, hosted by Calvary Community Church. It was there, in March of 1993, that I first met Paul Cain. Many of you are aware that Paul recently suffered a personal setback in his life.[1] Because of this I initially hesitated to refer to him in this story. But after much prayer and thought, I decided to describe the events of my life precisely as they happened, including my friendship with Paul and the impact of his ministry on me and my wife. If you find this problematic I encourage you to read the brief addendum titled, "When a Gifted Person Falls" (at the time of this writing Paul has confessed his sin and is seeking counsel and restoration from a group of competent Christian leaders).[2]

On the last night of the conference, Paul called me out of the audience and delivered a ten-minute prophetic word of encouragement. The text he used was from Isaiah 58. In the course of his message, throughout which he had been speaking of my ministry and how God wanted to use me, he paused. He said, "Sam, I know you have thought, 'Who's going to take care of me? If I give my life to pastoral ministry, if I deny myself and take up my cross, who will watch over me?' Sam, the Lord says to you, '*I* will guide *you* personally. I *will* guide you personally; I will take care of you. I will guide thee continually.'" This very pointed application of the first phrase in Isa. 58:11 was then followed by Paul quoting the rest of the verse: ". . . and satisfy your desire in scorched places, and make your bones strong; and you shall be like a watered garden, like a spring of water, whose waters do not fail."[3]

At the time, I didn't fully appreciate Paul's words. I thought it was nice. But I couldn't make much sense of its application. After all, this was March of 1993. I was committed to the ministry in Ardmore. I had no intention of leaving. Our family was happy and the church was prospering. Joining a Vineyard church was the farthest thing from my mind. Immediately after the meeting, Jack came to me and said, "Sam, you may not understand fully what Paul said, but get a videotape of it and write it down. It will probably take on new meaning in five months." As it turned out, Jack's advice was right on target, almost to the very day!

Let me jump forward to August of 1993. Later on I will explain the events that led to our leaving Ardmore for Kansas City, but for now I want to tell you what happened on the day we moved.

Moving day was August 18, 1993. It was one of the most demanding and depressing days of my life. Making the decision to leave our church family in Ardmore was among the most difficult I had ever made. When the time finally arrived for us to say good-bye, it was almost more than I could bear. We had spent the day before helping the movers load our belongings and saying our farewells to family and friends. We were scheduled to meet the movers at our new residence in Kansas City at three in the afternoon. It was very early Wednesday morning, August 18th. I was depressed and worried that I had made a terrible mistake. I was fearful of the new responsibilities, both financial and occupational, that I was to assume upon our arrival in Kansas City. Ann was tired and apprehensive. Our daughters were just tired.

Melanie was in the car with me. Ann and Joanna were in the mini-van. As Melanie rubbed the sleep from her eyes, she opened a going-away gift she had received from the principal of her school. It was one of those verse-a-day calendars that people set on their kitchen counters or on their bedstand. Needing more than a little encouragement, but with no expectation I'd receive any, I said, "Well, Melanie, this is as big a day as we've ever had. We're moving to Kansas City. What's our verse for today?" She opened the calendar and turned to August 18th.

If you haven't figured it out yet, the verse for that day was . . . Isaiah 58:11! This was the precise verse the Lord had given Paul Cain as a special promise to me at the conference in Houston, virtually five months to the day (as Jack Deere had "unwittingly prophesied").

I felt like I had been hit with a bolt of lightning. Slamming on the brakes, I jumped out of the car and ran back on the shoulder of the highway to Ann who was probably thinking that I had changed my mind about the move. I shouted, "Ann, you'll never guess what has happened. Today is the day. We're moving. We're stepping out in faith. And look at what verse is for today!"

I have no idea how many thousands of verses there are in the Bible. But I do know there are 365 days in the year. You tell me: What are the odds of that *one* verse appearing on that *one* day? They are astronomical, no doubt. But to a God who controls the universe and speaks through his people whom he has gifted prophetically, it is a mere trifle. To me, it was stunning, supernatural confirmation that indeed we had heard the Lord correctly and were doing his will.

The next time we run into each other, I'll show you the original page from that calendar. I carry it with me everywhere as a small token of God's faithfulness and power.

Isaiah 58:11 Again

Before I move on, I need to share one other incident involving this passage of Scripture and how God continued to use it in providential ways.

In 1997 Ann and I were struggling over a major decision related to her job. From the time of our move there in 1993, Ann had served as the receptionist at our church in Kansas City, Metro Christian Fellowship (we withdrew from the Association of Vineyard Churches in 1996 and changed the name accordingly). She loved her job and everyone was thrilled to know that she was, so to speak, the "gatekeeper" for the ministry of our local fellowship. But another opportunity had come along.

The Headmaster at our church school, Dominion Christian, had approached Ann about a teaching position. The possibility of returning to the classroom was quite appealing. Ann had taught school for several years at Trinity Christian Academy when we lived in Dallas. This job would give her the summers free, a higher salary, and also make it possible for her to spend more time with Joanna, our younger daughter, who was a student at Dominion.

I can't begin to tell you how much turmoil and inner anguish this decision created for both of us. It may sound like a simple decision, but anyone who has faced a choice such as this in which both options appear equally rewarding knows how difficult it can be. We prayed for weeks and sought the advice of friends and family. We were about at our wit's end when the Headmaster called and said he needed a final decision by Wednesday at 11:00 a.m. It was Tuesday evening.

Ann and I prayed yet again for some clear indication of God's will in the matter and then went to bed, hoping for an answer by the next morning. I decided to attend the prayer meeting that we regularly conducted on Wednesdays from 10:00 a.m. to 12:00 noon. It was about 10:15 and I was deeply immersed in prayer, pleading with God for clarity so that our decision at 11:00 would reflect his best for Ann and everyone concerned.

Suddenly I had what felt like a random thought race through my head. Perhaps you know what I mean. One of those "out of the blue" ideas that just seems to pop into your head without cause or warning.

"Go check your mail."

That's what I heard in my head. I don't know how else to explain it. What made it so odd is that not only had I not been thinking about the mail, but it typically didn't arrive until around 1:00 p.m. Still, it was so unexpected that I decided I should "obey". I walked into the office where Ann worked and the mail boxes were located.

"Hey," shouted Ann, "the mail came early today. That's weird." I could tell from the sound of her voice that she was as uptight as I, worrying about what we were going to tell the school in about 45 minutes.

I looked into my box and there sat one item, and one item only. It was a letter from Jean Raborg. For those of you who don't recognize that name, I strongly encourage you to obtain Jack Deere's book, *Surprised by the Voice of God* (Zondervan) and read the story of a remarkable miracle of healing that occurred in her life. Trust me, you'll never forget it. Jean had shared her testimony at one of our conferences just a few weeks earlier, but I hadn't expected to hear from her. There was no special occasion to warrant her writing me. Yet, there it was.

I opened the envelope to find a brief word of encouragement from Jean written on what appeared to be a fairly typical greeting card. But pasted to the card was a short article she evidently had cut out from another publication. The title of it was "The Graciousness of Uncertainty." I can't begin to tell you what happened in my soul as I read the three paragraphs in the article. I gave it to Ann and she read it too. Nothing could have spoken more clearly to Ann and me about what decision we needed to make. It was as if a huge burden simultaneously lifted from our hearts. We looked at each other and said, "Well, that settles it."

Then I saw it. At the bottom of the card was a biblical text. Jean hadn't written it. It was printed as part of the card itself. You guessed it! "The Lord shall guide thee continually . . . ." Isaiah 58:11 KJV.

Incidents like this understandably don't have the impact on others that they do on the people for whom they are intended. I certainly don't expect you to respond as Ann and I did. But given the magnitude of the decision we were facing, the deadline that had been given us for making it, the prompting in my spirit to check the mail, the fact that Jean's letter came on *that* day rather than Tuesday or Thursday, its bizarre and almost unprecedented early arrival at 10:15 a.m., the singularly appropriate message it contained, and what I can only call the divine imprimatur of Isaiah 58:11 staring us in the face, nothing could have been clearer that God had once again spoken in a powerful and loving way.

Ann's Journey

People have often asked, "What did your wife think about all these changes in your life and theology? Was she on board with you?" Initially, no. Ann thought I was caught up in some fad that would soon pass. She had been raised in an Episcopal church but didn't come to know Jesus as her savior until the beginning of her sophomore year at the University of Oklahoma.

As I noted earlier, we were married in 1972. What a blessing she has been these many years! But she is quick to point out that my beliefs and behavior, beginning in 1988, were more than a little confusing to her. I was finally able to persuade her to join me in one of my many trips to Dallas for a worship service. In the van, as we returned, I made the mistake of asking those who had joined us in the trip, "Well, what did you think?" No one spoke up immediately. Finally, Ann broke the silence: "I don't know what the rest of you are thinking, but if that's the direction you're going, you can count me out!"

When I asked her later why she felt that way, it came down to the freedom and open display of affection for Jesus she observed in those in attendance. She was especially offended by what she referred to as the "free-lance" worship of a number of people. This was her way of describing "singing in the Spirit," or singing in tongues, something she had never seen except through a momentary glance at a charismatic service on television.

But the music and ministry of Dennis Jernigan were beginning to pry open cracks in her otherwise closed and suspicious heart. Or, more accurately, the Spirit used his music and lyrics to effect the transformation. The first inklings of change came in the summer of 1992 as we made the long drive from Ardmore to Estes Park, Colorado, for a few weeks of vacation. I brought with me the tape series, recorded by Mike Bickle, of the prophetic history of his church in Kansas City. It took a little persuasive pressure on my part, but she finally conceded to listen. It wasn't long before she was, quite literally, leaning forward with her ear virtually pressed against the tape player. She'd never heard anything quite like it before. Neither have you, if this is your first exposure to these ideas, in which case I encourage you to obtain the series, recently taught yet again by Bickle (it is titled "Encountering Jesus" and may be purchased via his website at www.ihop.org). As we arrived in Estes Park, and the last tape concluded, she sat up in the car and said: "Wow! I feel like I've just visited the early church in the Book of Acts!"

That very night Ann had her first supernatural dream. In it, she found herself standing in the presence of what appeared to be a burning bush. She was holding high a large cup, not unlike those immense golden trophies or "loving cups" given to the winner of a Nascar race. As she extended it toward the presence of God in the bush, she heard a thundering voice declare: "When you obey, I will fill your cup." Ann's interpretation of this word was that when we, together with our church, committed ourselves fully to the pursuit of God's power in our midst, he would quickly hear our prayers and respond.

Almost immediately in the dream Ann's attention was directed to the right of the bush, where she saw an individual who happened to be a faithful and fervent member of our church in Ardmore. The voice spoke yet again: "Two weeks after she's gone, . . ." We took it to mean that God's answer to our prayers would come two weeks after this person was "gone". We had no idea what this "going" entailed. Would this person leave our church? Would she die? Or did it simply refer to a trip she planned on taking? We had no desire that she depart as she was one of the most godly and devoted members of our fellowship. After nearly seven months had passed, we gave little thought to the dream and had long since given up on trying to interpret its meaning.

Then, on my birthday, a Saturday, this individual died. We were devastated, but as yet made no connection between her passing and the dream in Colorado.

Much to our surprise, and delight, two weeks later we witnessed the first public prophetic utterance in our church! It was a powerful word that brought encouragement to a great many people, if for no other reason than it appeared to signal an open door from God to pursue his presence and power in a more fervent manner.

So there it was: two weeks after "she's gone" the Lord fulfilled his promise. But that was only the beginning for Ann, as you'll see momentarily.

Broken Windows, Healed Hearts

We need to return to late March in 1993. Not long after I had returned from that conference in Houston, I received a phone call from a young man named Brock Bingaman. Brock was in his first year of study at Trinity Evangelical Divinity School near Chicago. His voice was cautious. I knew that Brock was wonderfully gifted in the area of prophetic revelation, but he was reluctant to share with others what God would frequently reveal to him. This time, however, he felt compelled to tell me about a dream he had.

In this dream Brock had five separate visions. As it turned out, each of them proved true, but I will here mention only two. Brock said that he saw our house in Ardmore and a pick-up baseball game taking place in our yard. Brock had been to our home once before, but in the eight years we lived there nothing remotely similar to a baseball game had occurred. He said that he also saw foul balls being hit, and that one of them broke a window high up in the second story of our house. Our home in Ardmore was over 70 years old at the time (1993) and had been remodeled just before we purchased it in 1985. It is considerably taller than the average two-story home. In the eight years we lived there we had not witnessed so much as a scratch in a window, much less a shattered pane.

I wasn't overly impressed by Brock's dream. I didn't understand it. But I knew Brock and I trusted his integrity as well as his gifting. So I wrote down what he said and stuck it in the desk drawer.

About a month later Ann's three nephews came to stay with us for a few days while their parents vacationed in Florida. The oldest was eight, the others six and two. On Saturday, the third day of their visit, I worked at the church all morning. By this time Ann's parents had also come to town to join in visiting with the boys. When I walked into the backyard, Ann's father was standing there with a sheepish look on his face.

"What's going on?" I asked.

"Oh, nothing much," he said. "We're just surveying the damage."

"What damage?" I asked. He then directed my attention to the highest window in the second story of our home, where I immediately saw it: a baseball, having shattered the outer storm-window, was lodged between the inner pane and what was left of the outer one.

Evidently, in my absence my younger daughter, Joanna, and her three nephews had started a baseball game in the backyard. From the far end of the yard Daniel, the eight-year-old, had hit the ball that did the damage. Note well: this was not a regular baseball. It was a Tee-ball, one of those soft, cushioned balls that are safe for children to play with. Yet from twenty yards away an eight-year-old had hit it and shattered what was otherwise a sturdy storm-window!

Showing my sin nature, I never once thought about Brock's dream. All I thought about was the $150 it would take to repair the damage! Three days later, at 4:00 a.m., Ann suddenly awakened and sat up straight in bed. As if the proverbial light-bulb had just lit up over her head, the Lord reminds her: "Of course! Brock's dream! The pick-up baseball game! The foul ball! The shattered window!" Although she was tempted to wake me up, Ann waited until the next morning to tell me. I quite literally slumped against the wall with shock. How dull could we have been! How slow to see! I envisioned God, loving and longsuffering, waiting three days as if saying: "Come on. Figure it out. O. K. Enough is enough. Boom!" Ann is awakened and makes the connection.

What is the point of it all? Aside from the second vision in the dream that I'll mention later, I believe it was God's way of alerting us to the fact that he was speaking and would speak yet again in a supernatural way. We soon learned that often God confirms in the natural what he is doing in the supernatural. It was his way of saying, "Look! Listen! Pay attention when I speak to you in dreams and visions. These were not merely for the first century. They are for today. They are for you." This time we listened. What we heard next was life-changing.

The Conference
and
the Call

Needless to say, the first six months of 1993 were filled with events that to this day leave me breathless. Little did we know that June of that year would be the most astounding time of all.

In early April a close friend of mind had stopped in Ardmore for a short visit. As he was about to leave, he asked me if I planned on attending any conferences in Kansas City. I mentioned that a weekend seminar in April was scheduled, but finances were a bit tight. He immediately reached in his pocket and handed me three crisp $100 bills and insisted that I go.

It was at this weekend seminar at Metro Vineyard Fellowship in Kansas City that Mike Bickle, MVF's senior pastor, suggested that I consider joining the staff as President of Grace Training Center. I was surprised by his invitation. He said that he wanted me to return with Ann for the summer conference in June so that he could make the offer official to both of us. When I told Ann what Mike had said, she sensed that perhaps in the distant future it might come about, but not anytime soon.

The conference began on Tuesday night. On Wednesday morning Mike did indeed issue a formal invitation. "I know you're the man for the job. You can have it in three weeks or three years. I'll wait." Ann thought it might be three years. She was wrong.

On Wednesday night, Ann's life was forever changed. So, too, was our marriage. Mike was scheduled to preach part two of a message on Psalm 2 that he had begun the previous evening. Five minutes into his message he stopped and said: "I can't do this. God has something else in mind. I want the worship team to come back up on stage and let's wait and see what God has for us." There were two-thousand people in attendance, but it was as if what God had in store next was for Ann in particular.

The same individual who had delivered that powerful prophetic word to me two and half years earlier in Anaheim, joined Mike on the platform. They both discerned that the Lord wanted to minister to those in the audience who were oppressed by and in bondage to a spirit that evoked the fear of failing God. They asked for anyone to stand who wanted healing and deliverance from a spirit of failure and the shame it brings.

Ann instantly stood to her feet, as did several others. To say I was shocked wouldn't remotely capture the essence of my reaction. To be honest, I was somewhat embarrassed. After all, I was a pastor and a leader. My pride led me to think that my stature in the church and value as a husband were dependent on my wife and me being free from any such spiritual struggles. How wrong I was!

As the worship team sang, two ladies that neither Ann nor I had ever seen before laid hands on her and began singing in tongues. What I saw happening before my eyes was the spiritual transformation of my wife of twenty-three years. Intense sensations began in her temples and then gradually coursed throughout her body. She struggled to remain standing as the ladies lovingly continued their ministry to her. At one point, Ann reached up and patted their hands and said, "I'm o.k. That's enough," all the while saying to herself, "But I'm a pastor's wife. I'm supposed to be o.k." Thank God, the ladies knew better. "No," they said, "let's stay with this a while longer and see what God will do."

Ann and I have been married thirty-three years. We've had a really good marriage. We love and respect each other. God has blessed us with two wonderful daughters, a tremendous son-in-law, and two grandsons. But in our third year of marriage, which was my second year of seminary, I deeply wounded my wife. No, I have always been faithful. It wasn't immorality. But in my insensitivity and selfishness I had deeply hurt her. To make it worse, I was too naive to recognize what I'd done. Ann never told me. But from that day on, until that night in June in Kansas City in 1993, Ann had shut both God and me out of a part of her life. She loved God. His steadfast faithfulness towards her all those years made her want to serve him wholeheartedly. But there was a part of her soul, deep down, hidden, and carefully guarded, that she kept for herself. She loved me, too. She had been a wonderfully faithful wife and mother. But there was a part of her that didn't trust either one of us.

In her bitterness and fearful self-protective reaction to my sin against her, she had opened the door to the enemy. As she describes it, "I let the sun go down on my anger and thereby gave the enemy a foothold" (Ephesians 4:26-27) She said she made an inner vow never again to be that vulnerable to God or me. Truly, the enemy used this opportunity to gain a *foothold* in her life that could only be overcome by the power of the Holy Spirit. Virtually every day for the next seventeen years, she listened to the voice in her head that said: "Sam hasn't made you happy. God hasn't made you happy. Come with me. *I will make you happy.*" She described it to me as if the Enemy was wooing her by waving his finger in a beckoning manner.

For all those many years Ann lived with what she calls a hole in her soul filled with black goo. It crippled her relationship with the Lord. It adversely affected her intimacy with me. It daily tormented her with guilt and frustration and shame. At night she often had dreams that left her feeling defiled. She blamed herself for being such a failure as a Christian that those kinds of dreams would invade her soul. Ann never revealed her struggles to me for all those years because of the shame she felt.

Do you remember Brock's dream about the baseball? One other vision he had at the same time was of a woman sitting alone in a rocking chair, held captive, wanting to be set free but unable to get up. Brock couldn't see her face, but felt confident in the dream that her prayer for healing and deliverance would be answered. When I told Ann about the dream she said nothing. But she knew instantly the woman was her. The very night before Brock had called, Ann found herself in precisely that position, crying out to God and experiencing and saying precisely what Brock had seen. Still, she could not share what she thought to be God's revelation of her own soul because of the embarrassment and feelings of hopelessness. At this stage in her spiritual growth she was still unaware of the dynamics of spiritual warfare. She still believed only weird people could come under such intense demonic attack.

But then it happened. As the ladies prayed and sang in the Spirit over Ann, the cleansing power of the Holy Spirit was released in her body and the invisible black goo came out. I know it sounds strange, but that's the only way Ann knows how to explain it. The ugly mass began to explode upward from her toes through her heart and out her mouth. The tears flowed as she was carried into a new revelation of Christ's love for her. The deep dark hole was suddenly filled with the light of forgiveness and freedom and cleanness.

At that very moment, Ann herself had a vision she would never have anticipated. She saw herself as a pure, spotless bride in a radiant and gloriously white wedding gown, walking down the aisle as her groom, the Lord Jesus himself, waited at the altar. David Ruis, who was then the worship leader at MVF, began singing a song ("It is Done") that he had received from the Lord only the day before. David didn't know Ann, but it was as if the lyrics were just for her, especially the first two lines of verse two:

"It is done,
It's complete,
By your blood You paid my price.
Only grace,
Given free,
My boast in the cross of Christ.

I am clean,
I am free,
Through Your perfect sacrifice.
No more fear,
I'm redeemed,
I will enter paradise.

I am yours,
You are mine,
No power can come between.
When I fall,
You are there,
To bring me back to liberty.

(Chorus)
It's your mercy,
Your healing,
Forgiveness,
Your grace.
Your cleansing,
Your freedom,
As I gaze into your face."[4]

The next day as Ann and I were heading to the airport in the car, trying to make sense of what had happened the night before, she suddenly grasped her head with her hands and exclaimed:

"It's gone! It's gone!"

"What's gone?" I asked.

"The voice is gone," she said. "The voice that I've heard and fought against every day for years is gone!"

What a change it has made. Our marriage isn't perfect, but it's great. Our relationship, spiritually and physically, is now on an entirely different plane. Yes, we do believe it was a demonic being, a tormenting spirit that oppressed Ann for all those many years. No, we're not ashamed to talk about *deliverance*. Oh, what a glorious word! Set free by the mercy and cleansing grace of Jesus! Praise God! I got a new wife. Together we got a new marriage! Don't hesitate to ask her. She'd love nothing more than to tell you all about it.

That's only the beginning. Wednesday night, after her deliverance, Ann had a spiritual dream. She found herself scaling a high concrete wall that she knew in the dream represented our move to Kansas City. Melanie was on the wall with her, as was Joanna. But when she looked for me, I was still on the ground. My body was wrapped with bands that pinned my arms to my side and prevented me from doing anything but hopping up and down. She knew instinctively that it symbolized the struggle that I would have, more than anyone else, in making the move.

On Friday of that same week, I had the opportunity to receive ministry from several prophetically gifted people. None of us knew each other. The first to speak was a man named Phil Elston. He looked at me and said, "Your father is not living. He died several years ago and is now with the Lord. Your relationship with him was very special. Your love and respect for him were unusually deep and personal. In fact, since his death you have tried hard to carry on his reputation. He was an honorable man and you are proud to be known as his son." I can't begin to tell you how accurate that word was. Phil shared a few other things about my relationship with my dad, all of which were remarkably on target.

Next a young lady with a Canadian accent spoke to me. I later learned that it was Anita Ruis, wife of David Ruis, whose song quoted above had ministered so powerfully to Ann. Anita said: "I just had a vision of you. You were wrapped from head to toe with bands, holding your arms at your side. All you could do was hop up and down. But then I saw this huge pair of scissors suddenly snip the bands and set you free."

Wow! How could she know what Ann had dreamed about me only two days earlier? Well, I know how. What do you think?

That very night Paul Cain arrived in town. Mike Bickle and I were very careful to make certain that Paul knew nothing of Mike's invitation that I become President of Grace Training Center. We both wanted an independent confirmation of what we felt was the leading of the Lord. I wondered how God would provide the needed confirmation.

Toward the conclusion of Paul's time of prophetic ministry, he asked me to stand up. He said: "Sam, God spoke to me very clearly about you being *trained for training*. Promotion comes from the Lord, and it looks like it is coming from the *north*. And yes, you will be moving soon." Grace *Training* Center in *Kansas City* was very much in my heart before Paul ever spoke. In fact, I had already made the decision to move. Paul's word was a welcome confirmation to both me and Mike.

An Unwelcome Intruder

When I returned to the hotel I immediately called Ann, who had returned to Oklahoma the day before.

"You'll never guess what happened today," I shouted over the phone. I then proceeded to tell her about the prophetic words from Phil, Anita, and Paul.

"Well," she replied, *"you'll* never guess what happened here. You'd better sit down first."

The night before, on Thursday, Ann and our oldest daughter Melanie were up late packing for Melanie's departure to cheerleading camp. Ann noticed that Melanie was extraordinarily jumpy and nervous before bed, but she insisted that everything was o.k. The next day as they were driving to Oklahoma City, Melanie said: "Mom, something happened last night. I didn't tell you then because I didn't think you'd believe me. But when I went downstairs to the dining room, I saw a man sitting on our love seat. I saw his reflection in the mirror and turned to look. He was sitting with his legs crossed. He had a scarf wrapped around his neck and sat with his chin in his hand. When I looked at him, he extended his hand, as if to invite me forward, waving his finger in a beckoning manner!"

In case you are wondering, No, we had not told Melanie anything about Ann's experience in Kansas City, or the visual image in her mind that she had faced every day for those seventeen years of a demonic being wooing her to come, waving his finger in a beckoning manner.

Ann was stunned.

"Melanie, do you think it was Jesus or an angel?"

"No, Mom," she said. "It was evil. I got scared and ran back upstairs."

Most of you don't know Melanie and need to understand that she is not the sort of person to be duped or easily deceived. She had never had any experience remotely similar to that before. Nothing had prepared her or created expectations in her mind that something of that nature might occur. She was as stable and mature as any teen-ager I know.

What did she see? First of all, understand that she did not experience a vision. She saw this "man" with her physical eyes. You can do with this what you wish, but Ann and I are convinced we know who and what it was. As I was driving Ann to the airport in Kansas City on Thursday morning (Melanie saw "him/it" on Thursday night), she said:

"I'm a little afraid to go home."

"Why?" I asked.

"Because I'm afraid it will be there waiting for me."

I initially thought she was being a bit melodramatic about it all. But not anymore.

We believe that the demonic spirit that had oppressed Ann for so many years was making an attempt to jump generations, to the first-born in our family. We thank God that he gave Melanie the maturity and discernment to see the evil in this being and refuse it a place in her life.

On the following Monday, five days after Mike had offered me the position on his staff in Kansas City, I faxed him my response: "Yes! Amen!"

The Demonic, Once More

While I'm on the subject of demonic manifestations, I want to share one other experience that alerted me to the reality of the supernatural realm. Certain details concerning the people involved have been modified to protect their identities. Still, the essence of what occurred remains true to fact.

We had been in Kansas City for only a few months when I found myself hosting a weekend conference at our church. Everything had gone well the first day and a half, but that was soon to change. As I entered the auditorium on the afternoon of the second day, nothing seemed out of the ordinary or a reason for concern. I was then informed that a man had "set up shop", so to speak, in the back of the auditorium. When I approached him I noticed that he had constructed something of an altar, around which he continually walked while chanting, speaking, or occasionally singing. That some form of witchcraft was involved seemed obvious. What I was to do about it didn't!

I immediately consulted with a few of my associates, at which time I noticed that the man had left his "altar" and was now sitting on the back row of the auditorium. Before I could take any action, a lady from our church entered the building and sat down within a couple of seats of the man in question. I knew this lady fairly well and was aware that she often proved to be quite discerning in spiritual matters. I said to myself, "I'll let Susie (not her real name) see if there's anything amiss. If anyone can discern the activity of the enemy, she's the one."

No more than thirty seconds later, I watched as Susie stood up and walked briskly toward me, her eyes blazing with concern.

"Sam," she blurted out, "that man over there is seriously demonized."

Before I could respond, one of the women attending the conference was walking toward me with the man in question following close behind.

"Sam," she said, "would you please tell this gentleman to leave me alone. He's chanting curses at me!"

What happened next is, to this day, difficult to describe. But I'll do my best. As the lady positioned herself behind me, evidently thinking that I would protect her from this strange intruder, the man walked up and stood about three feet in front of me. I immediately felt what I can only describe as an invisible "force" or "energy" enveloping me. It was like "liquid air," if that makes any sense. I'm not talking about sensing in my heart some spiritual phenomenon. This wasn't a case of a mental or psychological awareness. I *physically* felt something *non-physical*. This was something altogether new to me. There had been instances in the past where I "discerned" or "sensed" in my spirit that demonic forces were present. But this was the first time I had tangibly and concretely and physically felt their presence.

We often laugh at Luke Skywalker of Star Wars fame when he speaks of "The Force" and its abiding presence in and through all elements of the universe. But in a sense, this is the best language I have for what "touched" me. As I said, the man never made physical contact with me. He never came closer than three to four feet from my body. But a "wall" of energy or power or, as I said, what felt like "liquid air", engulfed me. It actually pushed me backwards a step or two.

Immediately I began to feel dizzy and lightheaded. I feared that I might faint. My thoughts were jumbled and chaotic. I quite simply couldn't think straight. That's hard for a Ph.D. to admit! We pride ourselves (sadly) on our intellectual capacities. But on this occasion I couldn't connect two thoughts. Worse still, I couldn't speak. It was as if my tongue weighed a ton and my lips were glued shut. I felt utterly helpless to do or say anything.

If that weren't enough, a wave of nausea suddenly swept through my body. It was a sickening feeling worse than any stomach ache I had ever experienced. If I had been able to think coherently I probably would have run for the men's room. After all, it wouldn't bode well for my future at the church if I was found vomiting in the auditorium during a conference!

But just as I felt at my worst, "Susie" grabbed my arm and pulled me away. She spoke first.

"Did you feel that," she asked? "When I sat down next to him I got dizzy and lightheaded and thought I was going to throw up."

I was at least glad to know that I wasn't alone in this experience. With the help of others we regained our composure and escorted the man into a back room where we made an attempt to ask a few questions and get some idea of what he was up to. We weren't very successful! The situation worsened until we had to call the police to have the man escorted out of the building.

If you are wondering, as I often have, why God would have permitted this experience, there are at least two reasons. First, it was an especially effective way of confirming in my heart the reality of the supernatural realm. What had always been a staple of my theological convictions suddenly invaded my experience in an undeniably tangible way. But second, and perhaps even more important, it was God's way of alerting me to the consequences of entering spiritual battle unprepared. Ephesians 6:12-18 and its emphasis on the necessity of adorning ourselves with the full armor of God suddenly became more relevant and urgent than I had ever imagined. Now, back to our story.

Two days later, on Monday morning, fifty or so people were gathered at our office building for our regular intercessory prayer meeting. My wife, Ann, was sitting at the front desk serving as the church receptionist. Suddenly, in walked the man in question. Ann was immediately overwhelmed with what she described as the worst stench she had ever had the displeasure of smelling. Without a word, the man walked past her and into the prayer room. Before I even saw him, I was overcome by the smell. Please understand. I'm not trying to be humorous. This wasn't a case of body odor. Anyone who was there would tell you that this was more than a failure to take a shower and apply sufficient quantities of Right Guard.

The smell literally filled the room. It permeated through the halls of the office building and even up to the second floor. I had never before nor have I since smelled anything so putrid or revolting. It quite simply defies description. If you had asked me before that day, "Do demons have an odor?" I probably would have laughed and written you off as some sort of charismatic quack. But the answer to the question is most assuredly, Yes, they do! And it is far from pleasant!

We didn't waste any time, but immediately escorted the man into one of our pastoral offices. I and two others on our pastoral staff began investigating who this man was and what he wanted from us. And yes, in case you are wondering, the odor made it extremely difficult to concentrate. But as his story unfolded, it turned out that he had been involved for several years in a vast array of occultic practices, from witchcraft to earth worship. We carefully and prayerfully explained the gospel of Jesus Christ to him and watched in amazement as his countenance changed. We took authority in the name of Christ over every demonic spirit and commanded, in that same name, that every demon leave and be consigned to the abyss.

This ministry of deliverance lasted for at least an hour, perhaps longer. Surprisingly, there was little resistance from either the man himself or the demons he carried. No shouting, no physical convulsions, no obscenities. The power of the Holy Spirit pierced his heart and awakened his soul to the beauty and glory of Jesus Christ, crucified and raised from the dead.

It's hard to say whether either the deliverance or conversion of this man was finalized that day. Perhaps it was the beginning of both, but of this I can testify with all sincerity. This man was set free of demonic bondage and darkness and was transferred into the kingdom of the Son of God! Not long after his conversion he joined our church where he and his family became faithful and supportive members. He eventually became the leader of a home group! Such is the demon-defeating, Christ-exalting power of the Holy Spirit, to the glory of God the Father.

---

[1] You can read the details of what happened by going to www.morningstarministries.org and clicking on the Special Bulletins icon. The information is found in numbers 6,7, and 9 for 2004 and number 4 in 2005.

[2] You can find information about Paul's confession and progress in restoration on his website, www.PaulCain.org.

[3] Yes, I'm very much aware of the context of this passage. The focus is God's appeal to Israel concerning the sort of fast that pleases him, as well as their responsibility to minister sacrificially to the hungry and homeless. But I also believe there is a principle underlying its original intent that applied to me in the present day.

[4] Used by permission of David Ruis.

Chapter Four

✤

Angels, Anglicans, and Prophetic Poetry

Those first few months in Kansas City were incredibly difficult. Ann's dream which indicated that I would have a particularly hard time of it was all too painfully true. I knew we were supposed to be at Metro Vineyard Fellowship. I never doubted the clarity of God's call. In those days I would often rehearse in my mind the events that I've been sharing with you. Each time I was encouraged. But it still hurt to leave family and friends in Ardmore. My affection for the people at Christ Community Church was deep and remains so to this day. I experienced a lot of guilt, feeling as if I had abandoned them in a time of special need. I needed encouragement. I got it.

I'm not suggesting that what I'm about to describe is normative for every believer. All I know is what God graciously did for Ann and me in a time of desperation.

One night in early November, 1993, I had gone to bed about 11:00. I'm an especially sound sleeper. Virtually nothing can wake me up. Ann had unintentionally fallen asleep in Joanna's room after having put her to bed. At about 1:00 a.m. Ann woke up and walked back into our bedroom. There above the headboard, as she describes it, was the outline of what looked like an angel. Since Ann had never seen an angel before, she quickly dismissed the possibility and got in bed.

You must understand, of course, that I only know this because she later told me. I was sound asleep. But I was dreaming. In my dream I heard the unmistakable and distinctive sound of four chimes. The melody was clear and pristine. The experience was so profound that, uncharacteristically, I woke up. Just as I was coming out of my sleep, I felt Ann's fingernails digging into my arm.

"Did you hear the chimes?" she asked in a quivering voice.

"Yeah. But how could *you* hear what *I* was dreaming?" By this time we were both *wide* awake!

The idea that Ann had heard with her physical ears what I heard only in my mind was enough to bring me completely out of my slumber. I immediately said:

"Did the chimes sound like this . . . ?" at which point I quietly repeated for her the brief melody. Her fingernails dug even deeper into my flesh.

"Yes! What do we do now?"

Being the theologian that I am, I said: "I don't know. What do you think?" "I think we ought to pray," she responded with great profundity. We did. Later Ann told me that the chimes sounded as if they were coming from over by the door to our bedroom, some twenty feet away. As for me, they were in my head.

Skeptics will try to dismiss it all as just so much hyper-spirituality. I can't do anything about that. I can only tell you in the integrity of my heart what we experienced. You have to make up your own mind. But Ann and I are convinced beyond doubt that we were the recipients of an angelic visitation. No words were spoken, but the room and our hearts were filled with awe and fear and an increased awareness of God's presence and power.

A few months later, Ann was still wondering why it all happened. So she asked the Lord. His answer was simple and to the point: "To give you courage." Of course! If we needed anything at that time it was the courage to persevere, the courage to press on, the courage to hold fast to what we knew was God's leading in our move to Kansas City.

We don't live each day with the expectation of an angelic visitation. We don't make our decisions based on supernatural experiences like the ones I've described. We look first and fundamentally to the written Word of God. But we do bow before the God of heaven and earth and say, "Thank you, we love you. We praise you for these tokens of your presence and the encouragement they bring."

The Prophetic Once More

For years I never really understood why the Apostle Paul repeatedly exhorted the Christians at Corinth to desire and zealously pursue the gift of prophecy (see 1 Corinthians 12:31; 14:1,5,24-25,39). This was primarily due to my misconception of the prophetic gift. I don't claim to know everything about it now, but I believe I've grown in my appreciation for what it can accomplish in the body of Christ. Let me share with you just a couple of examples.

In the fall of 1994 a young couple from out of town attended one of the weekend seminars conducted by the Grace Training Center. I knew nothing about them, other than that they were acquaintances of friends of ours in Oklahoma City. I met them for the first time on Saturday of the seminar, and invited them to join several other people who would be coming to our home for fellowship and worship later that evening.

There were about 30 people crammed into our living room that night as we sang and prayed and enjoyed the presence of the Lord. About fifteen minutes into worship, something unusual happened to me. Without warning, the word *endometriosis* sprang into my mind. *You* think it sounds strange! You should have been in *my* shoes! Absolutely nothing had been said to trigger that word in my mind. Absolutely nothing had been done to incline me to think along those lines. I'm not the sort of guy who sits around and casually meditates on the subject of endometriosis!

I was a bit perplexed by it, but the impression was so strong that I simply asked the Lord to help me understand why and for whom the word had come. Immediately he directed my attention to the visiting couple. "She's the one," I sensed the Lord saying. I was in something of a pickle. That particular subject is very personal and not the sort of thing you bring up in a crowd of 30 people. It has the potential to be both embarrassing and hurtful. I tried to put it out of my mind altogether and focus again on the worship that was continuing among the others present.

But the Lord wouldn't let me. Finally, I got up and quietly went back to my bedroom. I took one of my business cards and wrote the young lady's name on it along with the word "endometriosis". I returned to the living room and took my seat. After worship ended, I tentatively said:

"I want to be careful and sensitive about this, but I believe God has given me a word for someone here. The last thing I want to do is embarrass anyone, so I'm not asking you to identify yourself. In fact, I think I know who it is. But I'll leave it up to you whether or not you want to say so. I think the Lord has told me that a lady here has endometriosis."

No sooner had the words come out of my mouth than the lady whom I suspected thrust her hand into the air and said, "That's for me!" I told her that I thought she was the one. I then took the card from my pocket and gave it to her. She was overwhelmed. But more important, she was profoundly encouraged and consoled. I told her that I didn't know if God had given me this word because he wanted to heal her. I certainly wasn't about to make any promises that God himself hadn't made. Perhaps he revealed this to me simply to tell her in a powerfully undeniable way, "Yes, I know who you are and where you are. I know about your condition. I have indeed heard your prayers and your cries." If that alone was God's purpose, it worked. We proceeded to pray for, asking the Lord to heal her and to bless her and her husband with the children for which they had been praying for several years. She left with renewed faith, renewed confidence, renewed hope, and "joy inexpressible and full of glory" (1 Peter 1:8). She later underwent surgery and not long thereafter gave birth to twins!

I've shared this next example in my book, *The Beginner's Guide to Spiritual Gifts,* but it so perfectly illustrates the point that I want to cite it yet again.

It showed no signs of being anything other than a routine day, until a strange car pulled up outside our church. A distraught father escorted into my office his twenty-year old son who appeared to be struggling with numerous psychological problems that some thought was the result of demonic oppression. He was unable to perform the routine tasks of daily life and was desperate for insight and help into what the source of his problem might be.

As we were praying, the name "Megan" popped into my head. [I've taken the liberty to alter the names of those involved in this story.] The inescapable impression on my heart was that this lady was the cause of his problem and that in some way through his questionable involvement with her, she had exposed him to demonic influence.

A few moments later, as he was telling me his story, I asked him the name of his girlfriend. He had referred to her several times (but not by name) and it was obvious she played a crucial role in his life. "Megan," he said. As it turned out, "Megan", who was heavily involved in the occult, had seduced him into an immoral relationship. The sexual encounter had taken place in her mother's home, who also was deeply immersed in occultic practices. Taking this as being from the Lord, I was able to pray for him more intelligibly and with greater fruit.

About thirty minutes later, it happened again. The name "Derek" sprang into my mind with no less clarity than had "Megan." This time, though, I didn't feel as if "Derek" was a part of the problem, but rather of the solution. Unlike before, I didn't hesitate on this one.

"Does the name 'Derek' mean anything special to you?" I asked.

His eyes widened and his face lit up: "Oh my, yes! He is my dearest friend; a man older than myself who has been praying for me through this entire mess. In fact, we were on our way to his house to get his advice when we stopped off to talk with you."

Both of these words were used by God to help this young man deal with his problems. I'm still not sure what to call it. Some prefer to identify them as *the word of knowledge* (1 Corinthians 12:8) whereas others call it *prophecy*. Whatever the case, the Holy Spirit can use anyone at anytime to minister in power to those in pain.

There have been other occasions when God used me prophetically without any sense on my part that such was the case. I've had several incidents where I was praying for someone, often a student of mine, and a single biblical text would suddenly come to mind. I would then quote it in the prayer and try to make application of it to their need. Afterwards, I would look up to find them in tears, asking: "How did you know that I had been meditating on that one verse before I walked in here? I was asking God to confirm his will to me through that verse and suddenly you spoke it into my life."

I took the time to describe for you just these instances so that you might see what it means to experience the power ministry of the Holy Spirit. We must always preach the Word of God. We must always cultivate the fruit of the Spirit. We must always proclaim the gospel to the lost. But we must also always be available for the miraculous work of the Spirit, whose power resides within each of us who know and love the Lord Jesus Christ.

A Vicar's Vision

The first time you read it, you'd think it was a script from Star Trek: bizarre creatures with four faces and four wings (Ezekiel 1:6), celestial beings with blazing eyes (Daniel 10:6), a dream about fat and skinny cows that changed the destiny of nations (Genesis 41:18-19), a holy man marrying a whore (Hosea 1), supernatural swarms of devouring locusts (Joel 2), a prediction of famine (Acts 11:28), and a man struck blind through a spoken word (Acts 13:11). The weird world of biblical prophets and their prophecies is almost more than some people can take.

I now want to share with you one prophetic event that served to forever put my doubts and fears to rest. I trust you will find it encouraging and instructive.

It was March of 1995. I was standing in the living room of the vicarage of St. Andrews Anglican Church in Cullompton, England. I had traveled to England to speak at a weeklong conference hosted by a church in Chorleywood where Bishop David Pytches served as vicar. At the close of the week, Bishop Pytches informed me that a man named David Saunders, who pastored the church in Cullompton, had telephoned him asking if I might be available to preach there on Sunday morning. Although I had never met David Saunders, nor knew anything of him, I happily said yes. We made the short journey from Chorleywood to Collumpton and went to bed without the slightest sense of what would occur the next day.

On Saturday morning a member of David's church appeared at the front door with a burden on his heart to pray for his senior pastor. So this man, whose name I've long since forgotten, David's wife, Lin, and I began praying for him. Suddenly, the prayer meeting took an interesting turn.

"I'm having a vision," David announced. The three of us became silent as he began to narrate what he "saw":

"I see a large house with a sign out front. It reads: 'Betty Jane's Boarding House.' As I enter the house I notice a table with a blue gingham table cloth immediately on my left. The room is quite large with a high ceiling. Off to the right the room leads in to yet another room that is white. There are old signs on the walls as well as a long white countertop, perhaps fifteen feet long. It's obviously the kitchen, but it's extremely bright, almost as if the sun were shining in directly from above. The appliances in the kitchen are all new, and everything is perfectly clean and in place. My sense is that there's a great deal of activity in the kitchen, but it's all incredibly clean and tidy. Betty Jane is herself there. But her husband is in a room back beyond the kitchen where he seems to stay most of the time. I see him in an office. He's an attorney. I also see a fire station and many firefighters in close proximity to their house. Something significant is going on with these firefighters."

He paused, and asked the three of us if any of this meant anything to anyone. No one said a thing. Twenty-four hours earlier this man had been a complete stranger to me. I knew nothing about him, other than his name, and that's all he knew about me. But my insides were trembling with holy fear. I kept a straight face, not wanting to give anyone the slightest hint at what had just happened.

I asked them:

"Is the name 'Betty Jane' a common one in England?"

"No," they all replied, with something of a laugh. In fact, not only did none of them know anyone by that name, they had never even heard that name before.

I said, "My reason for asking is that I have only one sibling, a sister. Her name is Betty Jane! She lives in Ardmore, Oklahoma, a small city in the south central part of the state. And you have perfectly described the shape and color of her living room and kitchen. Her kitchen is always spotlessly clean (even when she's cooking in it!) and has a countertop some fifteen feet long. There's a skylight that makes it the brightest room in the house. And, yes, her husband was a lawyer!"

David turned and looked at me and said, "Two children, both of whom are older, that is, in their late teens or early twenties."

"Right again," I replied.

Some of you may wonder why God might choose to reveal to an Anglican vicar, in the remote town of Cullompton, England, the name of a woman from a small town in Oklahoma half way around the globe, together with the appearance of the inside of her home. The reason is found in certain details of the vision I omitted. In the course of describing Betty Jane and her home, David had several words of instruction and encouragement concerning my sister and her family. The revelation of her name and the details of her home were a token from God that David was indeed hearing him speak and therefore an inducement for Betty Jane and her family to be careful to heed what David was to say.

The only part of the vision that didn't seem to make sense concerned the fire station and the firefighters.

"As far as I know," I said, "they have no connection with anything or anyone like that."

"Perhaps so," said David, "but it is very clear." We decided that the best thing to do would be for me to return to the U.S. and find out if anything of a related nature was going on.

When I returned home the next day I told my wife about the vision.

She was stunned. I then told her about the one part that didn't seem to make sense. Ann's face turned white and her mouth fell open.

"You'll never guess what's going on in Ardmore!" She then explained how there had erupted a major dispute over whether or not the fire department should be privatized. All of this had taken place just after my departure for England. Mike (Betty Jane's husband) was directly involved in the negotiations, which unfortunately had become quite volatile and divisive.

The next morning the final installment of this prophetic word arrived on our doorstep. We had lived in Oklahoma for eight years and I continued to subscribe to the *Daily Oklahoman*, the newspaper of Oklahoma City, for a couple of years after we had moved to Kansas City. The next day, when the paper arrived, I couldn't believe my eyes. There on page one was a lead article devoted to this very dispute going on in that small Oklahoma town.[1]

The Mundane and the Miraculous:
Our Move to and from Wheaton

God has used a variety of means to guide and direct me and my family these many years. I don't live in expectation of constant prophetic words or dreams and visions. In fact, our decision to leave Wheaton College and move back to Kansas City was unaccompanied by any overt supernatural activity. I was neither prompted to resign my position at Wheaton because of a revelation, dream, or manifestation of a spiritual gift, nor was any confirmation provided through such means.

I don't believe God was any less active in my life during this time. Nor do I have less confidence that it was the correct decision simply because God appeared to lead us through more mundane and natural means than he did at other stages in life. While at Wheaton I became increasingly unsatisfied with spending so much time in a classroom setting teaching the same course material semester after semester. As I reflected on the fact that I have, perhaps, twenty years of public ministry remaining, I asked myself if I wanted to use that time and the gifts God has given me in an academic context. The answer that repeatedly echoed in my soul was: "No."

Many of our closest friends in life were in Kansas City, not to mention our older daughter and her husband and our two grandsons. And living there would put us within reasonable driving distance of our parents and other family members who live in Oklahoma.

The bottom line is that the decision to return to Kansas City was based more on personal preferences, common sense, the exercise of what I trust was godly wisdom, the counsel of others, an evaluation of how best to utilize my gifts for the sake of the kingdom of God, and perhaps most of all, the desire of my wife to return. My point is simply that there were no angels appearing in our bedroom, no miracles pointing us in that direction, no prophetic words of confirmation, nothing. But God was not for that reason absent or inactive in the decision making process. I believe he was guiding my thoughts and transforming the desires of both my heart and that of my wife. I never concluded from the absence of supernatural guidance that God was angry with me or that I had missed his "perfect" will for my life. Nor did I think that this was a form of divine discipline for some sin(s) I may have inadvertently committed.

In fact, I can honestly say that this move has been attended with greater confidence in my heart and subjective assurance that this was the right decision at the right time than any of the other life-moves that were attended with considerable supernatural activity.

Having said all that, I do want to share some of the events that transpired in late 1999 and through the first half of 2000 that convinced us that God was leading us to Wheaton College in the first place. I have already described a number of events from the last twenty years that no doubt caused more than a few upraised eyebrows, perhaps even a scoffing laugh here and there. Well, prepare yourself for more!

The means God employed on this occasion to guide us and confirm his will in our hearts were of a different nature than what occurred in earlier years. Some of you may struggle with a few of them, and I can certainly understand why. But our God is not only sovereign over every detail of life, he is remarkably creative and innovative. Just when we think we've got him figured out, he surprises us! We pride ourselves in discerning his ways and means, only to discover again and again that his ways are not our ways, his means are not our means. So, here goes.

In November of 1998, Wheaton College wasn't even a blip on my radar screen. I knew of Wheaton, had attended a conference there in 1984, and was pleased that my nephew had chosen to attend a school of such high academic and spiritual reputation. But the thought of teaching there was nowhere to be found. I was happy in Kansas City and entertained no thoughts of leaving.

During a conference sponsored by our church, a rather strange prophetic word was uttered, in my absence no less. I had flown to Florida to attend the annual meeting of the Evangelical Theological Society, my custom every year. While away, Michael Sullivant, one of the pastors of our church and very prophetically gifted, stood up during the course of the conference and began ministering to those in attendance who had come from the Chicago area (Wheaton is 25 miles west of downtown Chicago). During the course of this word, Michael referred to several interesting and accurate details concerning both Wheaton and the work of the Spirit there. As he concluded his prayer for the expansion of the kingdom he blurted out (we don't know how else to describe it; it was so utterly unexpected): "Send your servant Sam Storms and people like him. Amen."

Upon returning home several days later I was told of Michael's "word". People wanted to know if it meant I was leaving. "Not as far as I'm concerned," was my standard response. Honestly, I thought that perhaps it meant that at some future time I would be invited to deliver a lecture there or perhaps preach in a church close to the campus. But leave Kansas City and join Wheaton's faculty? No way.

Almost a year later I became aware of several openings in the faculty of the Bible department at Wheaton while visiting the campus to watch my nephew play in his final home football game. While we were standing in the parking lot of the Billy Graham Center after the game, there suddenly descended upon me or rose up within me, I don't know which, an overwhelming sense of peace and assurance that my future was at Wheaton College. I turned to Ann even as she turned to me. Simultaneously we both spoke: "God is calling us to Wheaton." Yes, it was stunning. But we didn't feel it was profoundly supernatural, although the simultaneity of our responses did seem a bit odd. After much prayer and discussion with my family, I decided to submit my *curriculum vitae* and see what would happen.

Sometime later, on November 3rd, I was attending a prayer meeting and made the focus of my intercession the question of whether God wanted us to move to Wheaton. I can't recall a more intense time of prayer in my life. I was desperate to know if God was leading us there, primarily out of concern for our younger daughter, Joanna, who at the time was a freshman in high school. "Please, O Lord, I need to hear from you. For the sake of my daughter, if I move I have to know that she'll be o.k." After nearly two hours of prayer, often prostrate before God, I got up and drove home.

What happened next was strange, even by my standards! I walked in the door of our home and suddenly stopped. An overwhelming urge came over me to turn on the television. I picked up the remote control device, clicked on the power button, and watched as the picture gradually took shape. Quite literally, the first words that I heard coming from the TV were: "So, I see that you're an accountant from Wheaton, Illinois." I hadn't changed channels, nor did I have any idea why I felt so compelled to turn it on. But it was an episode of the game show, "Wheel of Fortune." Pat Sajak, the show's host, was introducing the most recent contestant. Yes, I was more than a little stunned. So I sat down.

Immediately after taking my seat, as I tried to figure out if what I had heard was anything more than a grand coincidence, I felt another inexplicable urge to open my copy of that day's U.S.A. Today newspaper and turn to the sports page. It was November, and professional football was in full swing. At that time I was still very much a Dallas Cowboys fan. So I turned to the page on which brief capsule summaries of events related to each team were found. I literally hadn't read another word in the paper before my eyes fell on the paragraph that updated the latest news with the Cowboys. It featured one and only one player, a defensive back by the name of Kenny Wheaton! By this time the Lord had my attention. I could only sit and wonder what it meant.

The next morning, on November 4th, as I was studying, Ann called me on the office intercom. She was serving as the church receptionist at the time.

"Go downstairs to the prayer room," she shouted, with an obvious tone of urgency in her voice.

"I'm really busy, honey. Do I have to right now?"

"Yes," right now, she insisted.

"Why?"

"Just do it," she said, somewhat impatiently.

I walked into the prayer room that also served as one of our classrooms at Grace Training Center. No one was present. And then I saw it. There was a huge whiteboard that we used for classes. It was entirely blank, except for one thing: www.Wheaton.edu., the web address for Wheaton College. Neither my wife nor I have any idea why it was there or who wrote it. One thing we did know for sure is that not one person in Kansas City had the slightest hint that we were thinking about Wheaton or that I had submitted an application. We were diligent to maintain utter secrecy until we had some sense that this was indeed God's purpose for us.

A few weeks later, on November 24th, I felt it necessary to revise my CV and include reference to an article I wrote but had inadvertently omitted from the first version I had submitted with my application. It was the day before the Thanksgiving holiday and I was sitting in my office at the church. After sealing the revised CV in an envelope, I laid my hands on it and asked God yet again for some confirmation of his leading and will. Within three seconds of that prayer, a loud knock on my door jolted me out of prayer.

"Come in."

Standing in the hallway were two young ladies, one of whom, from Oklahoma, I knew quite well. I hadn't seen her in some time and was shocked that she was in Kansas City. So, what's the point? Both young ladies were students at Wheaton College! They were on their way south for Thanksgiving and decided to stop in to say hello to old friends. While there, "it dawned on them" to check and see if I might be around.

About a week later, on December 1st, while in my church office, I had a random thought race through my head. Nothing profound had pro-voked it, nor did it "feel" in any way supernatural. It was, quite simply, a "ran-dom thought". I went downstairs where Ann was faithfully answering phone calls and said: "I just had a strange thought enter my head. I think my appli-cation to Wheaton is going to get 'lost', so to speak, in a pile of other appli-cations. I'll probably get the standard form letter thanking me for my interest but hear absolutely nothing else from them. Then, in five months, they'll call and ask me to come up for an interview."

As I said, it seemed utterly random and unprovoked. But, you guessed it, on May 1st, precisely five months to the day I had the thought, I received a phone call from the chairman of the department at Wheaton ask-ing me if I would like to schedule a time to visit the campus and interview for a position. The interview didn't happen for another four weeks, but the invitation came at precisely the time I anticipated it would.

In addition to these admittedly strange happenings, several of our friends who had absolutely no knowledge of what was going on, came to us and reported dreams they had experienced in which we were seen as moving to the Chicago area. We played dumb and thanked them for their interest, but could not admit at this time that we had plans for leaving Kansas City. After we announced to the church that we would be leaving, at least a half dozen others came with the news that they, too, had experienced dreams indicating our move to Wheaton, but they had refrained from telling us lest they put the idea in our heads!

On several occasions, as I would travel to conferences or be introduced to someone in a restaurant, they were invariably from Wheaton!

Coincidences? Chance happenings? Meaningless serendipities? I suppose some, perhaps many, may be led to conclude precisely that. That's usually the case with such events until they happen to you. It's easy to be skeptical until such incidents touch your own life at an especially needy moment. No, I can assure you we did not base our decision to move solely, or even largely, on such considerations. But they were undoubtedly seen by me and my wife as gracious confirmations of what we had decided on other grounds was the leading of God.

Does God really utilize television programs and newspapers and seemingly random encounters and otherwise mundane events to speak to his people? Yes. I don't want to endorse a form of hyper-spirituality that looks for divine significance in everything, but neither am I willing to dismiss the hand of God in such matters. Let me give you one illustration that comes from the early days of the church in Kansas City where I ministered for seven years.

Prophetic Poetry

I'm convinced that our world is filled with what I call *the prophetic poetry of God*. By *prophetic poetry* I'm referring to the countless ways in which God communicates and reveals himself to us even in the seemingly mundane affairs of life. Again, I'm not suggesting that we go to such an extreme that we find in *everything* something of spiritual significance. But let's not forget that every blade of grass that grows (Psalm 104:14) and every drop of rain that falls (Psalm 104:10-13) and every flake of snow that drifts earthward (Psalm 147:16) and every breeze that blows (Psalm 147:18) is the handiwork of God! The God who turns the heart of the king to accomplish His purpose (Proverbs 21:1) and works all things according to the counsel of His will (Ephesians 1:11) is more than able to take both the small and great things of His world and use them to make known His heart and ways.

One rather surprising example of this occurred in 1985. On a Sunday morning in June, a prophetically gifted man named Bob Jones came to Mike Bickle (senior pastor of the Kansas City church) and said, "God is going to speak to us through the baseball game." Your reaction to that is probably much like that of most who were in church that day. It seemed strange, to say the least. Mike especially struggled with it, in part because he knows so little about baseball: he's a football fan!

But Bob wasn't finished. "The Lord said that He would speak to this church through the baseball game, and that for a time it would appear that Kansas City would lose, but suddenly they will win." At least one thing was clear from this word: the experience of the Kansas City Royals major league baseball team was to be a prophetic parable for what would happen to the kingdom of God in Kansas City.

The season was well under way when this word was given. It was June and the Royals were struggling. By the time of the All-Star break in July they were seven games out of first place. When September arrived, it didn't appear as if the Royals would make the playoffs. But a sudden winning surge late in the month catapulted them into the playoffs. They faced the Toronto Blue Jays for the privilege of going to the World Series. Just as had been predicted, it appeared as if Kansas City would lose, only to win suddenly. The Royals fell behind three games to one but staged a remarkable rally to win the best-of-seven series 4-3. Game Six looked to be the end of the road for Kansas City, but a two-run ninth inning pulled out a victory for the underdogs.

The Royals were matched in the World Series against their cross-state rival, the St. Louis Cardinals. The media referred to it as the I-70 Series because Kansas City and St. Louis are connected by interstate 70 in Missouri.

No one gave the Royals much of a chance against the more talented Cardinals. The Series did not start well for the Royals. They began by losing the first two games at home. It may interest you to know that prior to 1985 no team in World Series history had *ever* lost the first two games at home and come back to win. It only got worse, as after four games they found themselves on the short end of a three-games-to-one deficit. Those of you who are baseball fans know that virtually no one recovers from a 3-1 deficit in a best-of-seven series. In fact, it had only been accomplished six times prior to 1985. In the sixth game the Cardinals should have won, but a controversial call at first base allowed the Royals to stay alive for the drama of a seventh and deciding game.

Those who witnessed that sixth game will never forget it. It was the bottom of the ninth inning and the Royals trailed 1-0. Jorge Orta hit a ground ball to the right side of the infield, forcing the St. Louis pitcher, Todd Worrell, to cover first. Umpire Don Denkinger called Orta safe. However, the television replay clearly showed that he was out. His foot actually landed on top of Worrell's. The fact that he was safe totally changed the complexion of the inning and catapulted Kansas City to a comeback victory, 3-2. One other interesting baseball fact is that this was the *only* time all year that the St. Louis Cardinals blew a lead in the ninth inning![2]

Game seven was scheduled for Sunday night, October 27th. On Saturday, Bob Jones came once again to Mike and said, "The Lord is going to speak to us through the number 11 in the game tomorrow." No one knew exactly what this meant, but so far everything else seemed to be panning out just as Bob had prophesied. Certainly the part about Kansas City on the verge of losing when suddenly they win seemed to be happening. Numerous people who heard the "11" word were anxious for Sunday night to arrive. In case you may have forgotten, unlike most final games of the World Series, this one was a rout. The Kansas City Royals won by a score of 11-0! The newspapers dubbed it the "Miracle Series". They had their reasons for calling it that, and we had ours!

I am still not sure how this will all work out in terms of the kingdom of God in Kansas City. Perhaps the fulfillment of this prophecy is yet to come. No one is quite sure how, but you can rest assured we're watching.

Prophetic Dreams

I'll have more to say about the role of revelatory dreams in a later chapter, but at this point I want to relate two incidents that are illustrative of what life was like for us during this season in Kansas City prior to our move to Wheaton.

The first incident occurred in our second year in Kansas City. Our younger daughter Joanna, nine years old at the time, invited a friend over to spend the night. There was no indication that anything dangerous was at hand; nothing to alert us to an impending spiritual encounter. That night Ann had a frightening dream. She saw a hideous demonic spirit kick in the front door of our house and begin to make its way down the hall toward the bedrooms. This "spirit" had long flowing and disheveled hair and flailed its arms wildly, as if preparing to harm someone.

Instead of entering our bedroom it made its way into Joanna's room where she and her friend were sound asleep. Ann knew instinctively in the dream that a spiritual attack of some sort was being launched against the girls. The spirit proceeded to bite both girls, and then disappeared. Ann woke up, trembling, and immediately began to pray for protection over the girls as well as our entire family.

The next morning she went in to awaken the girls, both of whom were not feeling well. Joanna's friend complained of a pain on her rib cage. Ann lifted her shirt and discovered a large, swelling bite mark, much like one would receive from a black widow spider or brown recluse. Joanna also complained of not feeling well. When Ann lifted up her shirt she discovered on her shoulder and rib cage what we would later be told was a case of shingles. The doctor who examined her was more than a little surprised, insofar as shingles was not common in nine year-old girls.

Perhaps some will say that we were not justified in drawing a direct cause and effect relationship between Ann's dream of the demonic spirit and the girls' physical condition. But as we prayed and processed the meaning of it all, it became increasingly clear that the dream was a call for us to intercede in prayer for the young girls of our church. There were circumstances in our local fellowship that I cannot divulge in this book which alerted us to the fact that a number of young girls were under spiritual attack from the enemy. Needless to say, we prayed fervently and are confident that this was God's way of averting further problems.

The second incident occurred in late 1998. I've not had many dreams that I consider revelatory, but on occasion God has spoken with great clarity when I needed it most. One such occurrence came on the eve of my decision concerning which of two publishers (I'll call them "A" and "B") to use for one of my books. All things considered, they seemed to be equally worthy and suitable for what I hoped the book would accomplish. But I simply couldn't come to a decision on which one was better.

On the night after I received a letter from publisher "A" indicating their desire to work with me, I had an explicit dream that clearly related to the choice I must soon make. I dreamed that the book was released in hardback by publisher "B" with an excessively glossy cover and raised lettering. Across the top of the front cover was the name of a well-known Christian author who wrote exclusively works of fiction. I had never met the man, nor have I to this day. It was clearly my book, but his name was featured prominently. It's important you know that I had never read one of his books nor did I have any knowledge of what publisher, if any, he typically used for his works.

At the bottom of the front cover was a reference to the Foreword, but it was misspelled as "Forward." My name, together with the title, did appear on the cover but in extremely small and obscure type. When I opened the book I immediately noticed that the first half was devoted entirely to advertising and sensationalistic hype concerning magazines and ministries and other products of publisher "B". Half way through the book, where the material I had written finally began, there were somewhat flashy and ostentatious pictures of me in a variety of poses. I remember feeling offended in the dream that so much space was devoted to self-promotion rather than focusing on the theme of the book itself.

Those who are better skilled at dream interpretation than I will undoubtedly have their opinions as to its meaning. But I recall thinking in the dream, as I'm looking at the book, that if I were to sign a contract with publisher "B" the book would contain errors (such as the misspelling of Foreword) and would not truly represent what I had hoped to communicate. My particular theological perspective would be obscured by the advertising hype and manipulative marketing strategies this specific publisher would employ. But it didn't stop there.

The editor of a prominent Christian magazine regularly forwarded to me dozens of books that had been sent to him for review in his magazine. Once he had removed whatever books were destined for review, the remainder were to be used to expand the library of Grace Training Center, the Bible school at our church, where I taught theology. Five days after this strange dream, a shipment of six or seven boxes arrived at my door. I opened the first box, with no idea or expectations of what I might find. The first book I removed from the first box was the latest release of Christian fiction by the author who appeared in my dream. His name was sprawled in huge letters across the top of the front cover, precisely as I had seen it in my dream! I opened the book and immediately noticed that the publisher ("B"!) was the very one that had been highlighted in my dream, the one that I had sensed would make unwarranted changes to my manuscript and eventually obscure the message God had given me. Needless to say, I signed a contract that very day with publisher "A" and never regretted my decision.

The Practical Power of Prophecy

The gift of prophecy is worth fighting for. I say that in response to those who either have grown to "despise" prophetic utterances (contra Paul's counsel in 1 Thess. 5:20) or are weary of cleaning up the mess they so often produce. If you value "upbuilding and encouragement and consolation" (1 Corinthians 14:3) you can hardly afford to ignore or neglect the operation of this gift in the body of Christ.

But there is yet another reason why prophecy is worth fighting for. Prophecy itself is one of the most powerful and reassuring tools God has given us by which we are to wage war in a world run amok. A much-neglected passage in Paul's first letter to Timothy makes the point with unmistakable clarity. "This charge I entrust to you, Timothy, my child, in accordance with the prophecies previously made about you, that *by them* you may wage the good warfare, holding faith and a good conscience" (1 Timothy 1:18-19a; emphasis mine).

I hardly need remind you that the Christian life is a never-ending battle, a struggle, a war with the world, flesh, and the devil. Our enemies are many and varied and committed to the destruction of our souls. The weapons of our warfare are delineated in Ephesians 6:12-18. But there is one additional implement of battle that we can ill afford to ignore: prophecy!

Paul's appeal to young Timothy resounds with ear-shattering clarity: "Timothy, please, I implore you as my spiritual son, don't even think about trying to fight Satan, the enemy of our faith, without drawing strength and encouragement and power from the prophetic words delivered to you! Never attempt to face opposition in the church apart from the reassurance that flows from those revelatory words you received. Timothy, there is strength and confidence for you in the truth and certitude of those Spirit-prompted utterances that came to you at your ordination. By all means fight. Never fear. But fight fearlessly through the power of those prophetic words!"

How do you wage a good war? How does one fight and resist the seductive allure of the passing pleasures of sin? By "holding faith and a good conscience." Paul has in mind both theological and ethical integrity, both right belief and right behavior, both orthodoxy and orthopraxy, both truth in our doctrinal affirmations and purity in our lives. This is no easy task! We are assaulted daily by those who would undermine our confidence in God and his Word. We struggle with anxiety, with provocations to lust, with greed, with despair and doubt and the temptation to quit. With what shall we fight? What shall we bring to bear against the deceitful promises of sin? Paul is clear: It is by means of the prophecies made about you that strength to stand firm is found.

We don't know what these prophetic utterances were, but there is no shortage of possibilities. Paul may have in mind certain spiritual gifts that were promised to young Timothy, gifts on which he could rely and should now draw strength to fulfill his calling. Perhaps there were prophetic words spoken over Timothy related to ministry opportunities or open doors that would expand his influence. There may well have been simple affirmations of Timothy in terms of his identity in Christ and God's purpose for his life. I've known people who received unique prophetic promises of God's presence and protection in the face of unusual danger. In Timothy's case, perhaps someone spoke powerfully of a biblical promise, drawn from a particular biblical text, that applied directly to him. Someone may have had a vision or dream that reinforced to Timothy his fitness and giftedness for ministry which would prove especially helpful when those older than he began to question his qualifications. We could speculate further, but no need. Timothy obviously would have known what Paul meant, even if we don't.

How does one appeal to such prophetic words to wage a good war? By constantly reminding oneself of God's commitment and presence and unshakable purpose to enable Timothy (and us) to fight doubt and anxiety and fear and despair. It is incredibly reassuring to recall tangible, empirically verifiable evidence of God's existence and power and presence communicated through a prophetic utterance.

I suspect that, perhaps long ago, many of you reading this book received words you believed were of God. But for whatever reason you've lost confidence in his promise. You've begun to wonder if it was really the Spirit who spoke. I encourage you to dig up those words, rehearse them in your mind, meditate on them, put legs under them to see if God intended all along for you to be the means by which they are fulfilled. Pray them back to God (as did David in the Psalms), and hold him to his word. But whatever you do, never attempt to fight the battles of faith apart from the strength such words provide.

In conclusion, and on a personal note, I think often of the story I shared earlier concerning how God has used Isaiah 58:11 in my life. On that August day in 1993 when I was on the verge of emotional collapse and spiritual despair, the prophetic word of God's abiding presence and protection sustained me and equipped me to fight despondency and to hold firmly to the hand of my heavenly Father. I was empowered to press on in the face of uncertainty by holding fast to the prophecies made concerning me. I can't imagine how I would have won that battle apart from the reassurance of the spoken word of God.

---

[1] What follows is the full text of the newspaper article chronicling the events that were unfolding in Ardmore. The title to the article was: "Ardmore Petition Aimed at Halting Privatization Move." The date was March 21, 1995, and the reporter's name was Lillie-Beth Sanger.

"ARDMORE - An Ardmore citizens' group has turned over an initiative petition with more than 3,600 signatures seeking a 1 charter amendment to prevent the city from privatizing its fire department.

The city also has received notice a similar citizens' group intends to circulate a petition asking for the recall of Ardmore's four city commission members and its mayor because of their privatization efforts that began last month.

On Monday, city officials finished counting the 3,612 signatures on the initiative petition and have turned the matter over to the city attorneys, City Clerk Penny Long said.

Her office must verify about 1,800 signatures of registered voters to bring the issue to a vote.

The city's move to turn its fire service to a private company has provoked controversy, much of it from union representatives and their supporters, since the announcement last month after officials studied the issue for more than a year.

Don Lewis, one of the petitioners with Concerned Citizens for Ardmore, said he got involved when he heard the commissioners' vote could not be reversed.

'It's certainly not in the interest of the majority of citizens,' he said.

'The citizens have spoken loud and clear. They don't want a private company using the equipment the taxpayers have paid for.' City Manager Kevin Evans has spent the last month defending the privatization move and telling opponents the city would require a private company to hire most of its firefighters locally.

'Most of the information on the streets is of very much an uninformed nature,' Evans said. 'We're certainly trying to get some correct information out.'

'Quite frankly, the contracting out of the fire department stands to be a very, very cost-effective measure for the community, and I have a hard time understanding why (there is) so much controversy over getting government out of business,' he added.

The recall petition, also filed last week, seeks to remove the commissioners from office because they have 'indicated the city will terminate the employment of the current firefighters of the city . . . and (they) have indicated they will resist placing the fire department initiative petition . . . on a ballot,' the petition states.

The petition also questions the city's desire to pay out-of-state companies for fire protection.

Evans said he has never heard city officials say they wouldn't place the petition on a ballot if ordered to do so."

---

[2] Those of you who are sports fans are probably aware of the television show called The Sports List on Fox Sports Network. Recently they presented their list of the top ten most Outrageous Officiating Mistakes in the last twenty-five years. Yes, you guessed it: number one was the mistaken call of Don Denkinger that may well have cost the St. Louis Cardinals the World Series.

PART TWO

The Wedding of Word and Spirit

Chapter Five

*B*ridging or *B*roadening the *C*hasm?

As noted earlier, in January, 1991, I attended my first Vineyard conference, soon after which I found myself in the cerebral atmosphere of Reformed Presbyterianism. To all appearances, no two venues could have represented more contrasting perspectives on Christian life and ministry than these.

A growing number of theologians, pastors, and informed observers have contributed in a variety of ways to shed light on this unfortunate divide. To be honest, not all consider it unfortunate. They see the "other side" as deceived, perhaps even dangerous, and consider it a divine mandate to warn the body of Christ to steer clear of even a remote association with those they regard as borderline heretics.

In this chapter I want to highlight the efforts of a few who have written on the subject, whether in an attempt to bridge the chasm or, in some cases, to broaden it. At the close, I have compiled an extensive list of contrasting emphases found in cessationist and charismatic churches, the significance of which I will unpack in the two chapters that follow.

Is there Hope for Healing?

In his book, *Evangelicalism and the Future of Christianity*, Oxford theologian Alister McGrath comments on the divisive debate that rages between evangelicals oriented to the Word and those whose principal emphasis is the Spirit. "In practice," notes McGrath, "Word and Spirit are perhaps easier to reconcile than the polarization of the debate might suggest. . . . There are excellent reasons," he concludes, "for hoping that the next generation of evangelicalism may see an increasing maturity in both camps."[1] McGrath does not himself explore those reasons, but in the past twenty or so years a number of scholars on both sides of the divide have attempted to heal the breach.

Among the first into the fray was Donald A. Carson and the book that had such a profound influence on me, *Showing the Spirit: A Theological Exposition of 1 Corinthians 12-14* (Grand Rapids: Baker Book House, 1987). As I indicated, when I picked up Carson's book in 1987 I was a Calvinistic, evangelical cessationist. When I put it down I was well on my way to becoming a Calvinistic, evangelical charismatic.

Carson put his finger on one reason for the lack of unity, indeed, the deep-seated suspicion that exists between charismatics and non-charismatics when he spoke of the "neat stereotypes" that each has of the other party. He begins with how the former often view the latter:

> "As judged by the charismatics, noncharismatics tend to be stodgy traditionalists who do not really believe the Bible and who are not really hungry for the Lord. They are afraid of profound spiritual experience, too proud to give themselves wholeheartedly to God, more concerned for ritual than for reality, and more in love with propositional truth than with the truth incarnate. They are better at writing theological tomes than at evangelism; they are defeatist in outlook, defensive in stance, dull in worship, and devoid of the Spirit's power in their personal experience."[2]

If this seems unfair, which, of course, it is, things don't improve much when cessationists take their turn in describing their charismatic cousins. Needless to say, they see things differently:

> "The charismatics, they think, have succumbed to the modern love of 'experience,' even at the expense of truth. Charismatics are thought to be profoundly unbiblical, especially when they elevate their experience of tongues to the level of theological and spiritual shibboleth. If they are growing, no small part of their strength can be ascribed to their raw triumphalism, their populist elitism, their promise of short cuts to holiness and power. They are better

at splitting churches and stealing sheep than they are at evangelism, more accomplished in spiritual one-upmanship before other believers than in faithful, humble service. They are imperialistic in outlook (only they have the 'full gospel'), abrasive in stance, uncontrolled in worship, and devoid of any real grasp of the Bible that goes beyond mere proof-texting."[3]

Duke University historian Grant Wacker describes much the same phenomenon that characterizes the relationship between what he calls "mainliners" (traditional denominations such as Lutheran, Presbyterian, Methodist, etc.) and "Pentecostals." The two, notes Wacker, "generally glide around each other like icebergs passing in the night. Over the years, Pentecostals have viewed mainliners with deep skepticism, judging them theologically lax and culturally spineless. Mainliners, for their part, have viewed Pentecostals – when they viewed them at all – with disdain, judging them theologically primitive and culturally unwashed. No one took prisoners."[4]

Such caricatures serve only to deepen the suspicion that each party has of the other and to drive a wedge between them that makes any reasonable hope of meaningful unity a fast-fading dream. Carson concludes that we are left with one of three options: "one side or the other is right in its interpretation of Scripture on these points, and the other is correspondingly wrong; both sides are to some degree wrong, and some better way of understanding Scripture must be found; or the Bible simply does not speak clearly and unequivocally to these issues, and both sides of the dispute have extrapolated the Bible's teachings to entrenched positions not themselves defensible in Scripture."[5] What follows here in Part Two of this book is decidedly influenced by the second of these options.

Subsequent to Carson's excellent exposition of 1 Corinthians 12-14, others have ventured into the darkness of the chasm that separates these two evangelical groups.[6] Wayne Grudem, for many years Carson's colleague at Trinity Evangelical Divinity School, and Jack Deere, former professor of Old Testament at Dallas Theological Seminary, both made contributions to the dialogue as evangelicals, like myself, who have abandoned the traditional cessationist model. Grudem's *The Gift of Prophecy in the New Testament and Today*, recently reissued in a revised edition by Crossway Books (2000), and Deere's *Surprised by the Power of the Spirit* (Zondervan, 1993) and *Surprised by the Voice of God* (Zondervan, 1996), were attempts to maintain a fidelity to

Scripture while embracing the full range of charismatic phenomena described in the New Testament. Although not one to call himself a charismatic, no less a defender of the Reformed faith than John Piper wrote a series of articles for his denomination's magazine, *The Standard*, in which he argued for the continuation of the charismata and their proper functioning in the life of the church.[7]

For similar efforts, see my book, *The Beginner's Guide to Spiritual Gifts* (Ventura, CA: Regal Books, 2002), as well as my contribution to *Are Miraculous Gifts for Today? Four Views*, edited by Wayne Grudem (Zondervan, 1996). Other excellent books in this regard are Max Turner's, *The Holy Spirit and Spiritual Gifts in the New Testament Church and Today* (Peabody: Hendrikson Publishers, 1998); Craig S. Keener's, *Gift & Giver: The Holy Spirit for Today* (Grand Rapids: Baker Book House, 2001); Gordon D. Fee's, *God's Empowering Presence: The Holy Spirit in the Letters of Paul* (Peabody: Hendrikson Publishers, 1994); William W. Menzies' and Robert P. Menzies', *Spirit and Power: Foundations of Pentecostal Experience* (Grand Rapids: Zondervan, 2000); Jon Ruthven's, *On the Cessation of the Charismata: The Protestant Polemic on Postbiblical Miracles* (Sheffield: Sheffield Academic Press, 1993); and Gary S. Greig and Kevin N. Springer, editors, *The Kingdom and the Power: Are Healing and the Spiritual Gifts Used by Jesus and the Early Church Meant for the Church Today?* (Ventura: Regal Books, 1993). Cessationists may certainly disagree with these authors but they cannot casually dismiss their work as exegetically shallow or "theologically primitive."

Two works with a more pastoral orientation were written with high hopes that evangelicals might abandon the destructive caricatures noted by Carson and begin to forge a unified front that draws from the strengths of both biblical Word and charismatic Spirit. Vineyard pastors Rich Nathan and Ken Wilson offered us *Empowered Evangelicals* (Ann Arbor: Vine Books, 1995), whose subtitle admirably expressed their aim: *Bringing Together the Best of the Evangelical and Charismatic Worlds*. Although widely known for his penchant for writing Forewords, I find it instructive that J. I. Packer describes the book as seeking "to lead polarized people out of some tangles of negative and impoverishing opinion in which they are currently caught. One group [noncharismatics] sees the other as weak in the head, while the second [charismatics] rates the first as weak in the heart. Each forfeits some wisdom and maturity," notes Packer, "by declining to learn from the other."[8] Packer had no illusions about the book, but he did express hope that "following their lead will be a big step forward toward the unity in truth and power that our times oblige us to seek."[9]

A similar and somewhat more popular treatment of the issue is Doug Banister's book, *The Word & Power Church: What Happens When a Church Experiences All God Has to Offer?* (Grand Rapids: Zondervan, 1999). Would that Jack Deere were right when he wrote on the dustcover: "This book may signal the end of the battle between charismatics and evangelicals." My sense, however, is that the battle will continue to rage, though perhaps with less vitriolic heat and more theological light than has heretofore been characteristic of the respective combatants.

A more recent contribution to the convergence between Word and Spirit comes from the pen of Ian Stackhouse, as found in his book, *The Gospel-Driven Church: Retrieving Classical Ministry for Contemporary Revivalism* (Waynesboro, GA: Paternoster Press, 2004). Stackhouse is Pastoral Leader of Guildford Baptist Church in England. This volume, a revision of his Ph.D. dissertation, is the first in a series devoted to an ecumenical conversation known as "Deep Church" (the latter is attributed to a letter by C. S. Lewis in *Church Times*, February 8, 952). "Deep Church" is a "recapitulation and restoration of the historic Christian faith as reflected in the scriptures, creeds and councils of the early church, and in the lives of the community of saints."[10] Again, it is best described as "an adherence to the apostolic faith of the New Testament as it was received, expounded and explicated in the patristic tradition of the early Christian centuries."[11]

As for Stackhouse's contribution to this series of studies, he attempts to call the contemporary charismatic church back to the stability and centrality of the gospel of a dying and rising savior. He's not suggesting that charismatics deny the cross or diminish its significance for Christian faith and life, but he does believe that many suffer from a severe and debilitating case of "theological amnesia." In their occasional hankering for what is new and sensational and effective in promoting church growth they have lost contact with the only thing that will truly bring renewal and the kind of qualitative growth that honors Christ: the gospel itself, embodied and expressed in the believing community.

Later on in the book, Stackhouse identifies specifically what he has been arguing for throughout: "a more robust theological basis for charismatic revivalism in order to counter the faddish nature of its praxis."[12] Don't be put off by this. Walker concedes that "it is possible that some will interpret

The Gospel-Driven Church as a turning away from both evangelism and charismatic renewal, and regressing to a staid liturgical fastidiousness and a discredited and discarded formalism."[13] To do so, however, would be to miss Stackhouse's point. Yes, this book "is certainly a rebuke to the excesses of revivalism, but it is not a rejection of evangelism or charismata per se. Rather, it is a plea from a pastor for a more rounded and deeper understanding of renewal – one that is ever open to the Holy Spirit's leading, but also one that remembers all that God has already achieved for us on the cross and in his resurrection."[14]

In a word, Stackhouse firmly believes that the future of charismatic renewal, to which he is wholeheartedly committed, lies in the retrieval of the *classical tradition*, what Lewis called "Deep Church". This flies in the face of much in the charismatic world which has typically assumed that renewal is dependent, at least in part, on the abandoning of those classical disciplines of church life that many feel have stifled and formalized the passions of the heart. Moreover, "theology and tradition are viewed [by many in the charismatic world] as symptomatic of the unpopularity and irrelevance of the church" and thus "ought to be abandoned."[15] [I will have considerably more to say about Stackhouse's proposal in the next two chapters.]

There are others, however, who are persuaded that there is little hope for reconciliation and cooperative activity. Indeed, the tone of their writings is that such unity would require theological concessions they are unwilling to make. It is certainly not my recommendation that for the sake of "unity" we settle for some insipid, inoffensive "golden mean" between two extremes. Often times the apparently noble attempt to steer carefully between the Scylla and Charybdis of opposing views yields a cowardly and unbiblical compromise that is devoid of either conviction or passion. I have no desire to "err on the side of caution". By all means, whatever the truth, passionately pursue it, and whatever the error, fervently shun it. My aim is simply to identify tendencies in both camps as well as strengths in each from which we should draw and weaknesses we should avoid.

Balance?

I've often been told that what we need is neither an emphasis on the Word or the Spirit but some sort of nebulous, elusive thing called "balance". If by that one has in mind an avoidance of destructive extremes, it would be hard to disagree. But I have frequently found that in the name of "balance" people have justified a theologically spineless "gospel" that bears little resemblance to what we read in the New Testament. So, perhaps an attempt to define this word is in order.

Some think a "balanced" person is the one who is neither hot nor cold but lukewarm (in the good sense of that term, if there is one). They think God is most pleased with the one who is "somewhat" a student of the Word and "somewhat" compassionate and "somewhat" evangelistic and "somewhat" into worship and "somewhat" a servant. They are careful not to let themselves get too excited about any one ministry venture lest others suffer by neglect. The result is invariably a form of Christianity that gets along well enough in the world but makes little long term impact on it.

I hope we can agree that if a biblical command is worth obeying it is worth obeying wholeheartedly and with abandon. One cannot be "somewhat" committed to the Spirit and "somewhat" committed to the Word. One must be *wholly* and *radically* committed to both. Otherwise, both Spirit and Word will end up being diluted and underemphasized. Spirit and Word were never meant to be "balanced" with each other, far less played off against each other, but "wedded" to each other!

Being "balanced" does not mean you lack conviction or the courage to speak up in defense of your beliefs lest someone get offended or you be perceived as dogmatic. On the other hand, I'm not advocating that anyone be deliberately abrasive or rude. Biblical truth has a way of stepping on certain toes no matter how it is presented. Clearly, we must look elsewhere for a more helpful definition of the term.

Others think a "balanced" person is one who believes that unity is more important than truth and is thus willing to compromise on essential Christian doctrines. But there can never be justification for the latter. In the absence of foundational truth, such "unity" often degenerates into a mushy and overly subjective form of "fellowship" that accomplishes little for Christ and his kingdom.

Perhaps a "balanced" person is one who fears that selected teachings or commandments in Scripture have the potential for canceling each other out. They suspect that certain things in Scripture are intrinsically incompatible with each other and one must be sacrificed for the sake of the other. Somewhat related is the view that a "balanced" person is one who believes that fully obeying what Scripture teaches is potentially dangerous and excessive. They seek a moderate approach to the Word that acknowledges its complete truthfulness but put a definite limit on how thoroughly or extensively one may actually implement what it says and obey what it commands. In this scheme, "imbalanced" is a synonym for "fanatical". The mistake is in thinking that if I'm going to properly exalt God's love I can't be too fervent about his wrath. Or if I'm going to be characterized by "self-control" I can't be too exuberant in worship.

We should also reject "balance" if it means being half-heartedly committed to a lot of things rather than whole-heartedly committed to only a few, or that you work hard at keeping a lid on your zeal, not letting yourself get carried away with what you believe. Sadly, for some the "balanced" Christian is the one who keeps tight reins on his/her emotions and is careful not to be extravagant in the display of either joy or displeasure. People tend to measure your "balance" by the degree to which you express or suppress the urge to get excited about biblical truth. It's almost as if "balance" and "imbalance" are issues of personality type.

Some think a "balanced" person is one who thinks that if a church is falling short in implementing principle "A" but is excelling in implementing principle "B", the remedy is to diminish the practice of "B". No. The answer is to increase the practice of "A". A church is never justified in disobeying one command of Scripture as a way of compensating or making up for its failure to follow another command. If the church is lagging behind in full complicity to "A", the solution is not found in de-emphasizing "B".

Being "balanced" does not mean you believe that all doctrines in Scripture are equally important or that all commands are equally imperative. Unfortunately, many think being balanced means not giving priority or greater emphasis to certain truths above others. The fact is, not all things commanded in Scripture are equally important. All are equally true, but some truths and principles and practices are more crucial and important than others. Prioritizing in accordance with biblical teaching is not a compromise or a failure to be wholly devoted and passionate.

The problem, though, is that people in a church often differ in their opinion as to what is comparatively more important. They perceive "imbalance" to be when a *less* important truth or command or principle is given greater emphasis in the sermon, more money out of the budget, more time, more resources, more staff, more space in the bulletin, allowed to dominate the service, etc. than a *more* important truth or command or principle.

When it comes to worship some think a "balanced" church is the one that schedules a traditional service at 8:30 a.m. and a contemporary one at 10:30! Or, if there is only one Sunday service, it must be "blended": half hymns and half contemporary music; or half celebration and half contemplation. When this is applied to preaching and teaching a "balanced" church is thought to be the one where equal time is given to all the themes in Scripture and no one theme is emphasized more than any other. On this latter point there may well be a measure of truth.

Every church has a distinct calling and mission that entails an emphasis on distinct aspects of the faith that other churches may not emphasize as much. Certainly there is a base, common body of shared truths and obligations and ministries that all churches must share to qualify as a Christian or biblical church: sacraments, training in the truth of the Word, worship, evangelism, discipline, etc. But each church also has a unique calling, dependent on location, culture, constituency, resources, giftings, passions, and other factors.

To put it simply and shortly, biblical balance is pursuing everything the Bible demands with the degree of emphasis and energy that the Bible commands. Nothing in Scripture is to be pursued or obeyed half-heartedly. Every truth is to be passionately embraced. Every activity is to be implemented without hesitation or qualification. That doesn't mean everything will be spoken of as frequently or given as much time and receive as much money or be as fully staffed as everything else. Thus being "balanced", both as an individual Christian and as a church, means that you embrace with appropriate fervor and emphasis all the priorities of Scripture.

In this regard, I have come to appreciate the perspective embraced by British pastor and theologian David Pawson. In his book, *Fourth Wave: Charismatics and Evangelicals, are we ready to come together?* (London: Hodder & Stoughton, 1988), he argues that in this proposed "convergence" between evangelical and charismatic "something like a Hegelian dialectic is involved, in which the solution to the gap between the evangelical thesis and the charismatic antithesis will not be found at some mid-point of 'balance' *between* them, but in a new synthesis *above* them both."[16] I can only hope that my small contribution in this book is a step in that direction.

The Grounds for Unity

One cannot help but notice that those who are writing with a view to convergence are virtually all on the charismatic side of the divide. A number of cessationists would argue that this is precisely the problem: charismatics, they contend, generally lack the depth of theological insight and conviction that ought to make them reticent to join hands with those with whom they differ.[17] The problem, according to J. I. Packer, is that charismatics appear to "trust in the unitive power of shared feelings and expression," whereas cessationists seek "to ground believers in a rational, disciplined piety."[18] If true, the possibility of more than a token oneness remains seriously in doubt. Although Packer's point must be noted, I generally find charismatics more devoted to the authority of Scripture and theological precision than most cessationists would allow.

Among those who embrace a rigorous cessationism and seem less inclined to hope that such unity, at any level, is a realistic expectation include John MacArthur (*Charismatic Chaos* [Grand Rapids: Zondervan, 1992]), Thomas R. Edgar (*Satisfied by the Promise of the Spirit* [Kregel, 1996]), O. Palmer Robertson (*The Final Word: A Biblical Response to the Case for Tongues and Prophecy Today* [Carlisle, PA: Banner of Truth Trust, 1993]); and Eric E. Wright (*Strange Fire? Assessing the Vineyard Movement and the Toronto Blessing* [Durham, England: Evangelical Press, 1996]), just to mention a few.[19]

This latter group of authors would argue, and not without good reason, that either you believe God speaks today and you facilitate the exercise of prophecy in your church, or you don't. Either you believe speaking in tongues is a valid form of prayer and praise and you encourage its use, or you don't. Either you believe God imparts gifts of healing today and provide opportunities for such supernatural power to operate in the life of the local assembly, or you don't. It is difficult to envision what a cooperative church effort between cessationists and charismatics would look like. I personally don't know of a church that has successfully endorsed both positions and survived to tell of it. Indeed, how could they without being guilty of speaking out of both sides of their mouth?

Those who practice such gifts are generally more inclined to worship side-by-side with those who don't than are those who don't with those who do. Cessationists struggle to justify fellowship with those whose Christian experience in their opinion is, at best, the fruit of emotional excess and theological naiveté and, at worst, energized by the devil. Perhaps more than anything else is the discomfort cessationists feel (yes, contrary to popular opinion, cessationists *do* have feelings) with the informality and exuberance of charismatic worship, as well as what they perceive to be theologically shallow sermonizing. Charismatics, on the other hand, are no less suspicious of cessationists, often believing them guilty of quenching the Holy Spirit and reducing Christianity to little more than a theological fastidiousness that breeds a joyless arrogance.

Given the polarities as they exist, what unity, if any, might we expect and aim for? Is there any meaningful common ground between Orlando and Anaheim? That obviously depends on what kind of unity we have in mind. If our expectations are of ecclesiastical oneness in which cessationists and charismatics worship and serve together in the same local church, the chances are slim. But that need not be a bad thing, if the unity for which we strive is the acknowledgement and celebration of foundational theological conviction, as well as mutual affirmation and loving cooperation. Cessationist and charismatic churches need not merge organizationally in order to experience a depth of unity that will testify to the saving presence of Christ in both.

A Blurring of Boundaries

It must also be noted that in certain arenas the boundaries between mainstream evangelicalism and the charismatic world have grown increasingly fuzzy. There are today countless evangelical churches that have adopted mildly charismatic forms of worship, yet retain explicitly cessationist assertions in their doctrinal statements. Churches that would never permit prophecy or speaking in tongues, whether in public or private, now openly encourage the lifting of hands during extended and often deeply emotional times of worship (most often to the tune of contemporary music produced by the likes of the Vineyard and Hosanna Integrity). Yet, while keyboards and drums may have replaced Baldwin pianos and robed choirs, suspicion remains when it comes to the practice of the charismata.

To what might we attribute these changes? Some may take offense, but I'm persuaded that in many cases it is clearly the fruit of financial pressure created by the threatened departure of young adults who long for a more intimate, personally relevant, and spiritually authentic worship experience. In other words, the so-called "contemporary" or "blended" service in evangelical churches is often less the product of theological conviction and a passion for God's presence than a pragmatic concession on the part of leadership to the otherwise inevitable loss of members and the obvious programmatic and financial problems this would create for the church itself.

Of course there are some who are simply drawn either to the aesthetic qualities of contemporary music or the atmosphere it generates or perhaps the psychologically soothing mood it evokes.[20] One can only hope that, whatever "style" or aesthetic form our corporate services assume, they are consistent with biblical truth and the expression of whole-hearted devotion to God and a hunger for his glory to be seen and his presence to be enjoyed.

Sola Scriptura vs. Sola Experientia?

The respective emphases on either Word or Spirit is sadly illustrated in a somewhat extreme way through the encounter of the 16th century reformer Martin Luther with the radicalism of the Zwickau Prophets. While in exile at the Wartburg Castle following his condemnation at the Diet of Worms (1521), two of Luther's disciples were left in charge of affairs back home in Wittenburg: Philip Melancthon and Andreas Carlstadt, the latter of whom forced his way into leadership. Bard Thompson explains the crisis:

> "By Christmas, 1521, the cradle of the Reformation was engulfed in wild iconoclasm under Carlstadt's management. The Catholic Mass was undone and redone. The monks and nuns poured out of the convents and got married. Churches and monastic chapels were scenes of desecration. In the midst of the turmoil, the Zwickau Prophets arrived – three so-called prophets lately expelled from the town of Zwickau [Nicholas Storch, Thomas Drechsel, Marcus Thomae]. They were enthusiasts in the technical sense of the word; that is, they professed to have received new revelations from God quite apart from the Bible, *whose relevance exceeded that of the Bible* [emphasis mine]. They proceeded to deride Martin Luther for his slavish dependence upon the Scriptures. *Bibel, Babel, Babbel*, they taunted – 'Bible, Babel, Bubble' – in derision of Luther's biblical interest."[21]

According to Lindberg, the three men "arrived in Wittenberg soon after Christmas claiming divinely inspired dreams and visions of a great

Turkish invasion, the elimination of all priests, and the imminent end of the world. They further claimed that people are to be taught by God's Spirit alone who has no connection to Christ and the Bible."[22] Thomas Munzer (1489-1525) also claimed extra-biblical revelation in a way that undermined the authority of Scripture. According to Munzer, the true and living word of God must be heard directly from God's mouth and not indirectly from any book, not even the Bible. He appealed to an inner Word to justify belief that the last days were at hand and that the church should take up arms against both the civil authorities and the medieval papacy. Luther, he said, "knows nothing of God, even though he may have swallowed one hundred Bibles." To which Luther replied (in characteristic fashion!), "I wouldn't listen to Thomas Munzer if he swallowed the Holy Ghost, feathers and all!" Lindberg identifies the principal theological difference between the two men. In Munzer's theology,

> "*Sola scriptura* is displaced by *sola experientia*. Scriptural faith is a dead faith which worships a mute God. The God who speaks is the God who is experienced directly in the heart. In a letter to Melancthon dated 29 March 1522, Munzer wrote: 'What I disapprove of is this: that it is a dumb God whom you adore. . . . Man does not live by bread alone but by every word which proceeds from the mouth of God; note that it proceeds from the mouth of God and not from books.'"[23]

Needless to say, both Luther and Munzer were guilty of creating a caricature of the other, not unlike what we see today. Cessationists loudly insist that they both believe in and long for the power of the Spirit. I have no reason to doubt their sincerity. It isn't a question of whether they truly desire the fullness of the Spirit's work. They do. It is more an issue of what they believe the Bible says is legitimate for us to expect the Spirit to do in today's church.

A Comparative Analysis

Neither evangelical cessationism nor the charismatic movement is theologically monolithic. I earlier referred to many evangelicals who concede that the exegetical and theological evidence for cessationism is negligible, if not non-existent, yet make no concerted effort to cultivate the charismata either individually or corporately. There is an even wider variety among those who affirm the validity of these gifts: classical Pentecostals (e.g., Assemblies of God[24]), Oneness Pentecostals (e.g., the United Pentecostal Church, whose evangelical credentials are suspect, given their anti-Trinitarianism[25]), independent charismatic churches,[26] those involved in the burgeoning apostolic-prophetic movement,[27] the word of faith / prosperity movement,[28] and evangelical Third Wavers, among whom I include myself.

Since I personally identify with the Third Wave,[29] a brief word of explanation is in order. The Third Wave refers to the growing, and increasingly organized, numbers of conservative evangelicals who have experienced a fresh empowering or infilling of the Spirit and now embrace the full range of spiritual gifts. Typical of, but by no means restricted to, the Third Wave is the Association of Vineyard Churches.

According to this typology, the "first wave" of the Holy Spirit was the classical Pentecostal movement that began in 1906 with the Azusa Street revival and birthed such denominations as the Assemblies of God. The "second wave" was the charismatic movement that saw traditional denominations embrace the ministry of the Holy Spirit. Although there were isolated instances of this in the 1950's, the beginning of the movement is generally dated on Passion Sunday, April 3, 1960, when Dennis Bennett, rector of St. Mark's Episcopal Church in Van Nuys, California (1953-1961), announced to his church that he had been baptized in the Spirit and spoken in tongues.

Although Third-Wavers embrace the full range of the charismata, they generally distance themselves from classical Pentecostalism and charismatics. An especially helpful discussion of the variety within protestant Pentecostal and charismatic circles is the collection of articles in *Pentecostal Currents in American Protestantism*, edited by Edith L. Blumhoffer, Russel P. Spittler, and Grant A. Wacker (Chicago: University of Illinois Press, 1999). Aside from their lack of denominational affiliation, Third-Wavers typically differ from their Pentecostal brethren on two fronts: (1) not all of them insist that Spirit-baptism is separate from and subsequent to conversion, and (2) few of them argue that tongues is the initial physical evidence of Spirit-baptism or that it is normative for all believers. The Third Wave has also distanced itself from the excesses of the Word of Faith movement as well as other forms of the so-called "Health and Wealth" or "Prosperity" gospel.

In spite of the obvious fluidity that exists among these many movements, it is possible to identify certain emphases, involving both praxis and principle, that shed light on the reasons for the theological as well as relational distance that so often obtains. I should point out that a number of the "distinctives" listed below, and explained in the next two chapters, are less what each side openly affirms of itself and more what each side believes and says of the other (which often reduces to sinful caricature). Nevertheless, thinking about these distinctives requires a healthy dose of humility from everyone, for many, if not most, are painfully accurate, as much as we might wish they were not. Space does not allow me to comment extensively on each pair, so I will focus attention in the next two chapters on those areas that are most influential in the shaping of the life and theology of each group.

I quite expect to incur the anger of both parties. Many will insist they do not recognize themselves in my portrayal, although they are just as certain that I have accurately described the other side! I simply ask you to keep in mind that these are envisioned as *tendencies, potential emphases, and underlying assumptions, not rigid categories from which neither group ever parts company.* My hope is that as we think through these characteristics we will recognize that much is to be gained by everyone concerned from acknowledging our own errors as well as drawing on the insights of the other. Perhaps our enhanced understanding of what each believes might also serve to minimize the division that is so often the fruit of a lack of informed dialogue in the body of Christ.

Word (Cessationist)	Spirit (Continuationist)
Centrality of Sermon	Centrality of Worship
Predictability	Spontaneity
Principles	Power
Prizes knowledge	Prizes experience
Focus on the Intellect	Focus on the Affections
The Bible: emphasis on meaning	The Bible: emphasis on significance
Explanation of what God has done/said; focus on past achievements (preserve them)	Expectation of what God will do/say; focus on future purposes (pursue them)
Penchant for the archaic	Penchant for the novel
Insists on biblical precedent	Insists on biblical prohibition

Process oriented	Event oriented
Christian life is the progressive outworking of an original deposit	Christian life is the repetitive experience of a fresh power
Reformation	Revival
Biblically informed wisdom	Spiritually imparted discernment
Observation	Intuition
Guidance: confidence in objective principles	Guidance: confidence in subjective promptings
Focus on the "Not Yet"	Focus on the "Already"
Potential for defeatism	Potential for triumphalism
A focus on quality; a desire for better	A focus on quantity; a desire for more
Tendency to embrace suffering	Tendency to expect healing
Struggle with Flesh	Struggle with Demons
Mundane	Miraculous
The seen	The unseen
Tendency to deify tradition	Tendency to demonize tradition
God has spoken	God is speaking
Prayer is monologue	Prayer is dialogue
Reliance on natural talents	Reliance on spiritual gifts
Lack of appreciation for the supernatural and surprising	Lack of appreciation for the natural and routine
If a natural explanation is possible, it's probable	If a supernatural explanation is possible, it's probable
Tendency to be skeptical	Tendency to be gullible
Proclamation evangelism	Power evangelism
Focus on the NT	Focus on the OT
Focus on the Epistles	Focus on the Gospels
Emphasis: God's sovereignty	Emphasis: man's responsibility
Stresses Christ's Deity	Stresses Christ's Humanity
Worship = proclamation of biblical truth	Worship = personal encounter with God
Worship: focus on understanding God (worship is theological)	Worship: focus on enjoying God (worship is relational)
Worship: God's presence is a theological assumption to be extolled	Worship: God's presence is a tangible reality to be experienced
Worship: focus on God's transcendence	Worship: focus on God's immanence

Worship: fear & reverence	Worship: joy & love
Worship: concern with form	Worship: focus on freedom
Worship: controlled & restricted	Worship: emotionally & physically expressive
Worship: sing about God	Worship: sing to God
Sacramental	Non-sacramental
Emphasis: "Instrumentality"	Emphasis: "Immediacy"
Faith in God	Love for God
Obedience to God	Intimacy with God
Focus on Justification	Focus on Sanctification
Lower expectations of prayer	Higher expectations of prayer
Angels: a theological belief	Angels: a functional reality
Emphasis on intellectual impact of divine principles	Emphasis on emotional impact of divine presence
Fearful of emotionalism	Fearful of intellectualism
Tendency to draw the boundaries of orthodoxy more narrowly	Tendency to draw the boundaries of orthodoxy more broadly
Potential for arrogant exclusivism	Potential for naïve sentimentalism
Grounds for unity: theological agreement	Grounds for unity: shared experience

In the next two chapters I'll try to unpack the significance of these different points of emphasis in hopes of moving us forward in our pursuit of a genuinely biblical convergence.

---

[1] Alister McGrath, *Evangelicalism and the Future of Christianity* (Downers Grove: IVP, 1995), 172.

[2] Carson, *Showing the Spirit*, 11-12.

[3] Ibid.

[4] Grant Wacker, "Hand-Clapping in a Gothic Nave: What Pentecostals and mainliners can learn from each other," *Christianity Today*, Vol. 49, No. 3 (March 2005):58.

[5] Ibid., 12.

[6] According to J. I. Packer, "the charismatic movement appears as evangelicalism's half-sister, which helps to explain why self-conscious evangelical reactions to the phenomena of charis-

matic renewal sometimes seem to smack of sibling rivalry" (*Keep in Step with the Spirit* [Old Tappan, NJ: Fleming H. Revell, 1984], 173).

[7] See especially his series of sermons entitled, "Compassion, Power and the Kingdom of God," preached during January-April, 1990, and available on the website, desiringgod.org.

[8] Packer, Foreword to *Empowered Evangelicals*, 7.

[9] Ibid., 8.

[10] Andrew Walker, Foreword to *The Gospel-Driven Church*, xiii.

[11] Ibid.

[12] Stackhouse, *The Gospel-Driven Church*, 201.

[13] Walker, Foreword to *The Gospel-Driven Church*, xvi.

[14] Ibid., xvii.

[15] Stackhouse, *The Gospel-Driven Church*, 21.

[16] Pawson, *Fourth Wave*, 12.

[17] Some have argued that nothing is more indicative of this than the inescapable fact that until recently one would be hard-pressed to identify a substantive and biblically grounded systematic theology text written by a Pentecostal or charismatic believer (although see Douglas Jacobsen, "Knowing the Doctrines of Pentecostals: The Scholastic Theology of the Assemblies of God, 1930-55," in *Pentecostal Currents in American Protestantism*, edited by Edith L. Blumhofer, Russell P. Spittler, and Grant A. Wacker [Urbana: University of Illinois Press, 1999], 90-107). There are signs of change, however, most notably J. Rodman Williams, *Renewal Theology: Systematic Theology From a Charismatic Perspective*, 3 volumes (Grand Rapids: Zondervan, 1988-92), and Wayne Grudem, *Systematic Theology: An Introduction to Biblical Doctrine* (Grand Rapids: Zondervan, 1994). See also Larry D. Hart, *Truth Aflame: A Balanced Theology for Evangelicals and Charismatics* (Nashville: Thomas Nelson Publishers, 1999), and Simon Chan, *Spiritual Theology: A Systematic Study of the Christian Life* (Downers Grove: IVP, 1998). Notwithstanding the paucity of such texts, there is an undeniable and steady growth in both biblical and theological reflection among pentecostal and charismatic scholars. One need only consult the work being produced in *The Journal of Pentecostal Theology*, *Pneuma: The Journal of the Society for Pentecostal Studies*, and the *Asian Journal of Pentecostal Studies*, as well as the Journal of Pentecostal Theology Supplement Series, now at twenty-one volumes, published by Sheffield Academic Press. See also Wonsuk Ma, "Biblical Studies in the Pentecostal Tradition: Yesterday, Today and Tomorrow," in *The Globalization of Pentecostalism: A Religion Made to Travel*, edited by Murray W. Dempster, Byron D. Klaus, Douglas Petersen (Oxford: Regnum Books International, 1999), pp. 52-69; and John

Christopher Thomas, "Pentecostal Theology in the Twenty-First Century," *Pneuma* 20.1 (Spring 1998):3-19.

[18] Packer, *Keep in Step with the Spirit*, 172.

[19] There are countless other critics of charismatic phenomena, among which are Michael G. Moriarty, *The New Charismatics: A Concerned Voice Responds to Dangerous New Trends* (Grand Rapids: Zondervan, 1992), John Napier, *Charismatic Challenge: Four Key Questions* (Homebush West, Australia: Lancer Books, 1991), Norman Geisler, *Signs and Wonders* (Wheaton: Tyndale House, 1988), Victor Budgen, *The Charismatics and the Word of God* (Hertfordshire, England: Evangelical Press, 1985), Peter Masters and John C. Whitcomb, *The Charismatic Phenomenon* (London: The Wakeman Trust, 1982), and Leith Samuel, *Time to Wake Up! Evangelical fantasy vs. biblical realism* (Durham, England: Evangelical Press, 1992).

[20] David Wells (*Losing our Virtue: Why the Church Must Recover Its Moral Vision* [Grand Rapids: Eerdmans, 1998]) is especially critical of contemporary charismatic hymnody and worship. It is, he argues, "deeply privatized" (44), "more therapeutic than moral" (44), in which "the thought of loving God, and occasionally being in love with God . . . has replaced the emphasis on consecration and commitment that was so characteristic of classic hymnody" (45). He thus concludes that contemporary charismatic worship "is less about ascribing praise to God for who he is than it is celebrating what we know of him from within our own experience" (46). A similar emphasis is found in Marva J. Dawn, *Reaching Out without Dumbing Down: A Theology of Worship for the Turn-of-the-Century Culture* (Grand Rapids: Eerdmans, 1995). Whereas I have profited immensely from both Wells and Dawn in other respects, I find their criticisms of contemporary worship seriously misinformed and bordering on caricature. I encourage all to read John M. Frame's careful and, in my opinion, convincing analysis in *Contemporary Worship Music: A Biblical Defense* (Phillipsburg: P & R Publishing, 1997). See especially his review of Dawn's book on pp. 155-174.

[21] Bard Thompson, *Humanists and Reformers: A History of the Renaissance and Reformation* (Grand Rapids: Eerdmans, 1996), 405-06.

[22] Carter Lindberg, *The European Reformations* (Oxford: Blackwell Publishers, 1996), 104.

[23] Ibid., 151.

[24] Especially insightful into both the theology and sociology of the Assemblies is Margaret Poloma's work, *The Assemblies of God at the Crossroads: Charisma and Institutional Dilemmas* (Knoxville: The University of Tennessee Press, 1989). The standard text on the Assemblies remains that of Edith W. Blumhofer, *Restoring the Faith: The Assemblies of God, Pentecostalism, and American Culture* (Urbana: University of Illinois Press, 1993).

[25] See Gregory A. Boyd, *Oneness Pentecostals & the Trinity* (Grand Rapids: Baker, 1992).

[26] An insightful treatment of the independent charismatic movement is Charles Hummel's *Fire*

in the Fireplace: Charismatic Renewal in the Nineties, 2ⁿᵈ edition (Downers Grove: IVP, 1993). See also Peter D. Hocken, "A Survey of Independent Charismatic Churches," in *Pneuma* 18.1 (Spring 1996):93-105.

[27] See *The New Apostolic Churches*, edited by C. Peter Wagner (Ventura: Regal, 1998), and Wagner, *Apostles and Prophets: The Foundation of the Church* (Ventura: Regal, 2000).

[28] The most incisive critique of this variation of charismatic theology is still that of D. R. McConnell, *A Different Gospel: Biblical and Historical Insights into the Word of Faith Movement* (Peabody: Hendrickson Publishers, 1995). See also *Faith, Health and Prosperity: A Report on 'Word of Faith' and 'Positive Confession' Theologies by ACUTE (the Evangelical Alliance Commission on Unity and Truth among Evangelicals)*, edited by Andrew Perriman (Carlisle: Paternoster Press, 2003), 316 pp., Charles Farah, *From the Pinnacle of the Temple* (Plainfield, NJ: Logos, 1978), Gordon Fee, *The Disease of the Health & Wealth Gospels* (Beverly, Mass: Frontline Publishing, 1985), and Curtis I. Crenshaw, *Man as God: The Word of Faith Movement* (Memphis: Footstool Publications, 1994).

[29] The phrase "Third Wave" was evidently coined by C. Peter Wagner (see his *The Third Wave of the Holy Spirit: Encountering the Power of Signs and Wonders Today* [Ann Arbor: Servant Publications, 1988]).

Chapter Six

Exploring the Divide (1)

I've never been comfortable in drawing a rigid distinction between Word and Spirit, as if everyone falls neatly on one side of the fence or the other. The "boundary" between them is too fuzzy and fluid and is less an impenetrable "wall" than a broken white line that is often easily crossed over. It would be terribly misleading, therefore, as well as overly simplistic, to suggest that charismatics are soft on Scripture or that cessationists long for anything less than what they believe the Bible says about the ministry of the Spirit. Nevertheless, the categories are probably here to stay, so I will do my best to work with them.

One more word of introduction is in order. Nothing in what follows should be taken as a judgment that either cessationists or charismatics love God more than the other or that one is more fervently committed to the glory of God and the expansion of the kingdom than the other. Of course it's true that some Christians do love God more than others, but I don't believe this difference is due to any particular belief about the relationship between Word and Spirit or mind and affection. These latter elements may well affect how that love is expressed in worship or articulated in doctrinal formulations, but there is nothing intrinsic to the theological principles of either cessationism or continuationism that issues in a more sincere or greater passion for Jesus or a more courageous witness on his behalf.

If each of us were to consider those great men and women of God, past and present, who we believe love(d) God more than we do, however painful it may be to make that concession, I suspect they would be equally distributed among cessationists and continuationists. At least the ones on my list are. So resist the temptation to conclude from what follows that these dynamics and patterns of ministry and theological convictions are either the result of greater love for God or will necessarily issue in it.

Biblical Interpretation

As I said, continuationists are quite vocal in their affirmation of biblical authority. I would venture to say that charismatic Christians are equally as fervent in their confidence in the inspiration of the biblical text as are their cessationist brethren. What is unsettling to the latter, however, is the apparent theological gullibility of the former and their somewhat ill-informed and simplistic interpretation and application of the text. All too often charismatics will find in a biblical passage a word or image or literary allusion that sounds analogous to their immediate circumstances and claim it as a promise, or use it to justify a novel practice, without regard for its original context or authorial intent.

I suggest, however, that this is due more to a lack of hermeneutical sophistication than to any conscious diminishing of the text's inspiration and authority. Charismatics could do with a bit more education in the principles of biblical interpretation and the nature of biblical language and how it functions. They also need to recognize that not all cessationists are motivated by a desire to confine the Holy Spirit to a distant past. In most cases they are moved by their high regard for Scripture and their concern lest it be trivialized by unwarranted and flippant applications.

Consider, as an example, the comments of famous Word-Faith pastor Frederick Price, as found in an article for *Ministries Today* magazine. According to the article, "while critics quibble over hermeneutical nuances, at the core of Price's theology is a view of Scripture itself that accepts the text on its face value."[1] Price is then quoted as saying, "Scriptures in the Bible on healing and prosperity require no interpretation – they are what they are. . . . You don't have to interpret them."[2]

My initial reaction is to ask, "O.K., if they are what they are, *precisely what are they*?" Any response is, by definition, an interpretation, or an attempt to ascertain the meaning of a text. But aside from that, perhaps we should give Price the benefit of the doubt. I suspect what he means is that the Bible is true, relevant, and applicable to the contemporary Christian, the meaning of which is accessible without a Ph.D. in Literary Theory or Biblical Hermeneutics.

Price's words resonate with many in the charismatic community who view themselves as average Bible-believing Christians who want to be faithful to embrace whatever Scripture affirms and to do whatever it commands. They are somewhat suspicious of "scholars" who, to their way of thinking, appeal to sophisticated hermeneutical theories and technical grammatical and etymological insights not simply to "explain" the text but to "explain it away." Thus, in-depth historical analysis, sensitivity to contextual setting, together with an awareness of cultural dynamics operative in the time of both original author and audience strike them as potentially arrogant and cynical ways of evading the text's normative authority. Scholarship of this sort is often viewed as a threat to the purity and urgency of simple devotion to Jesus.

Honesty demands that we acknowledge such folk exist. Academic training (or perhaps I should say the "intellectual pride" it occasionally generates) can indeed become a clever way to justify keeping the claims of the text at arm's length. But there are just as many, perhaps far more, moderately educated Christians who view advanced biblical scholarship with disdain and whose consequent theological naiveté can lead to a flippant and baseless use of the inspired text. If the former are potentially prone to undermine the Bible's authority and practicality, the latter are no less prone to draw overly simplistic and doctrinally ridiculous conclusions from the text.

To a considerable degree this dilemma is due to the anti-intellectual tendencies among many in the charismatic world, where all too often the mind is perceived as the enemy. I will take up this issue in more detail later on.

What Happens on Sunday

When it comes to corporate gatherings on Sunday, evangelical cessationists orchestrate their gatherings around the sermon whereas charismatics view congregational singing as central. The former often treat worship[3] as little more than an unavoidable prelude to the exposition of Scripture, after which the service is considered over. Charismatics will often put the sermon before worship as an entrance into praise. Whatever truth is learned is preparation for heartfelt celebration in singing and dancing.

The reason for this difference is found in their respective beliefs concerning where God has pledged to meet his people. Cessationists define their "experience" of God primarily in terms of intellectual growth and what they learn of him in Scripture, when it is preached and taught. They are driven by the conviction, and with this I would agree, that Scripture is God's primary means for making himself known to us. Throughout biblical history we see that God's standard way of first establishing and then sustaining personal and intimate communication with the redeemed is through individuals whom he commissions as his messengers, whether prophets, apostles, pastors, or teachers (cf. Ephesians 4:11).

Thus, cessationists would testify to having "encountered" God, assuming they would even use such language, when their knowledge of his character and ways expands and deepens. They feel confident that God has been honored and his presence affirmed when his truth has been expounded in preaching, sacrament, confession, and creed. Often they will question the need to "experience" God if only the revealed truth about him is accurately understood and proclaimed in sermon and song.

Little, if anything, more is to be expected by the believer in terms of "sensing" God's nearness or seeing his power or feeling his love. In fact, excessive concern with these latter elements or time devoted to their pursuit is often viewed as, at best, secondary, and, at worst, dangerous. Such desires for subjective engagement with God have the potential to distract the Christian from serious and rigorous intellectual grappling with the biblical text.

But, and all Christians need to listen closely, the written word does more than merely communicate truth *about* God: it also *mediates the very person and power of God*. We would not be amiss in viewing preaching as sacramental in nature. That is to say, God draws near to his people *in preaching* to comfort and encourage and strengthen them. As Packer says, "the proper aim of preaching is to mediate meetings with God."[4] The Bible is not a dead letter! It is living and active and sharper than any two-edged sword that convicts and reveals and enlivens and rebukes and awakens the heart and mind to both the ugliness of sin and the beauty and splendor of God (see Hebrews 4:12-13).

As we will see below, whereas charismatics don't dismiss the authority of the word, they do tend to minimize, if not in theory at least in practice, its capacity to bring them into authentic experience of God. Worship, on the other hand, is viewed as an *unmediated closure* with God that is unencumbered by what they perceive to be potentially divisive and often complex dogmas. Clearly, both groups have much to learn from the other.

Cessationists are generally reluctant to allow into a service what isn't in the bulletin. Those accustomed to "high church" traditions or who embrace the regulative principle[5] of worship are opposed to any violation or disruption of prescribed liturgy. They find comfort and a measure of emotional security in predictability and procedures that strike a familiar chord. Anything less is typically viewed as violating the requirement that all be conducted "decently and in order." They tend to be suspicious of spontaneity and often view the latter as a way of justifying either laziness or emotionalism. The last thing they want on Sunday morning is to be surprised by something novel or unexpected. What charismatics view as freedom and sensitivity to the Spirit's leading is often viewed by cessationists as irreverence and an excuse to cover up a lack of studied preparation.

Charismatics tend to associate spirituality with flexibility or an openness to sovereign interruptions by the Spirit. If cessationists fear spiritual surprises, charismatics are terrified of the boredom that so easily comes with repetition. They are reticent to impose a structure on their gatherings that might, in their words, "quench the Spirit." God must be allowed the freedom to shorten the service, extend it, or re-direct its focus in ways unanticipated and unannounced by the pastoral leadership.

This difference is due in large part, as will be noted below, to the expectation by charismatics of hearing what they call God's "present tense voice." What is God saying *now*? What is his Spirit leading us to do *today*? Is the "cloud" moving? Cessationists, on the other hand, typically see their responsibility as providing a venue for the explanation of God's "past tense voice," i.e., his "word" as it is found in the canonical text.

My own experience has been that both approaches can be embraced without sacrificing the intent and integrity of either. I see no insurmountable obstacles, other than stubbornness and pride, to the integration of structure and spontaneity. The Spirit can lead the advanced planning of a service as easily as he can break in, unannounced, during the course of liturgy. It's true that a rigid and inflexible commitment to "order" can breed lifeless ritual. But it's equally possible for an agenda lacking shape or direction to breed chaos and an absence of theological substance. A preacher can experience a powerful anointing on Thursday afternoon, while prayerfully writing a sermon, no less than he can on Sunday morning as the Spirit imparts insights heretofore unseen.

Principles or Power?

Evangelical cessationists tend to emphasize principles over power, understanding over experience, in which maturity is measured by theological expertise. This often entails a corresponding focus on the intellect and rational inquiry. Knowledge becomes the index of spirituality. The kingdom of God is advanced by the understanding, explication, and whole-hearted embrace of truth. The question most often heard following their services is: "Did you *understand* the sermon today? Do you agree with it?"

Charismatics, conversely, subordinate principle to power,[6] tend to gauge growth by the depth of spiritual experience (often, the more bizarre the better), and emphasize the affections above the mind. The kingdom of God is advanced by the visible defeat of Satan, often seen in physical healings and other overt displays of divine power. In the absence of such phenomena during the course of a corporate service, some would doubt whether God had truly "shown up". The question most often heard following their services is: "Did you *feel* the Lord's presence today? Did He touch you?"

Is it too much to believe that one can *feel* God's tender touch in the sermon and *learn* more of his ways and means during worship? Is it too much to expect that one might return home on Sunday afternoon having both learned and loved, having been stretched both mentally and emotionally, having been both edified by a biblical text and healed of a physical affliction? Dare we hope and strive and settle for anything less than *both* the thrill of theological insight *and* deliverance from demonic oppression?

Sadly, though, many on both sides are persuaded that the emphases of the other are detrimental, in the final analysis, to what they believe most honors God. Charismatics are willing to think, but not if rational inquiry impedes the activity of the Spirit. Too much doctrine, they fear, threatens to kill "the anointing". They are often heard to say, "How can I be entirely open to the work of the Spirit in an attitude of humility and receptivity if I'm busy critiquing every syllable spoken by the preacher or if I'm constantly obsessed with the accuracy of every doctrinal assertion?" Or, "We don't want a theological Gestapo in our church spying out every misstep in the interpretation of Scripture."

Cessationists, on the other hand, are skeptical of the authenticity of any alleged "supernatural" ministry if it emerges in the context of theological error, often no matter how infrequent and ultimately insignificant that error may be. If some charismatics are inclined to disparage the mind, some cessationists are nigh unto deifying it. Yes, that's an exaggeration, but the fact remains that an otherwise admirable love for theological accuracy has the potential for hardening one's spiritual arteries.

Let me illustrate this from an incident involving a former student of mine at Wheaton College. "Mary" (not her real name) was an especially gifted and highly intellectual young lady who had taken a number of my courses in various aspects of theology. She was extremely well read and knew the Bible better than most adults.

Mary and I were both present at a conference where the primary speaker was openly and decidedly charismatic. His message on the night in question was quite good, but he was guilty of a couple of minor theological foibles, neither of which, in my opinion, were deserving of a second thought. Mary had a different opinion.

After the meeting she approached me, obviously quite upset. Upon hearing what she believed (correctly) to be a misinterpretation of a particular biblical text, she in essence "shut down". She found it almost impossible to concentrate on anything else the speaker had to say. Her face was wrinkled with anxiety and concern, and even a measure of sadness. As far as she was concerned, the speaker had disqualified himself as worthy of being heard because of his failure to carefully articulate this one particular point of doctrine. Needless to say, Mary wasn't in the least interested in or open to his appeals concerning the ministry of the Holy Spirit. His theological indiscretions had virtually incapacitated her. If anything, she was worried that others present would open their hearts to what she was convinced may well be the influence of a false teacher.

People like Mary believe that the slightest exegetical error or theological misstatement invalidates whatever other ministry a person may fulfill. "Surely God would not bless with power or miracles those who are so careless with his Word!" It's as if they think that God is so offended by the lack of absolute precision that he would withhold his favor from those guilty of it.

Charismatics, on the other hand, are impatient with what they perceive to be excessive and fastidious concern with accuracy in the interpretation of texts and theological concepts that bear little practical fruit. It's not uncommon to hear them say: "I don't want to be slowed down or distracted from what God is doing by ultimately abstruse doctrinal squabbles." They would point to "Mary" as an example of what happens when the human intellect is elevated above the divine Spirit.

Praying with the Spirit AND with the Mind

A good example of both the suspicion that many cessationists have for the charismatic emphasis on the Spirit and the charismatic fear that cessationists have unduly elevated the mind is found in how they respond to Paul's teaching on the gift of tongues in 1 Corinthians 14.

In describing his own gift of speaking in tongues, Paul says "my spirit prays but my mind is unfruitful" (v. 14). I don't think it's necessary to determine whether this refers exclusively to the Holy Spirit or to Paul's own human spirit. It's more likely he has in view a simultaneous and cooperative manifestation of both, which in effect constitutes the essence of a spiritual gift: the Holy Spirit energizing and enabling my spirit to do what otherwise I couldn't do. The important point, however, is that when Paul prays in tongues his mind is "unfruitful". By this he means either, "*I* don't understand what I am saying," or "*other people* don't understand what I'm saying," or perhaps both (with the primary emphasis on the former).

Cessationists, however, are uncomfortable with reading Paul this way. They insist that if one's mind is unfruitful, that is to say, if one's mind is not engaged in such a way that the believer can rationally and cognitively grasp what is occurring, the experience, whatever its nature may be, is useless, perhaps even dangerous. After all, if our minds are not engaged what safeguards do we have against the encroachment of heresy? Subjectivism of this sort will serve only to diminish the centrality of Scripture in the life of the believing community.

The charismatic strongly disagrees. If Paul were fearful of *transrational experience* (which, by the way, is far and away different from being *irrational*), would not his next step be to repudiate the use of tongues altogether, or at minimum to warn us of its dangers? After all, what possible benefit can there be in a spiritual experience that one's mind can't comprehend? At the very least the cessationist should expect Paul to say something to minimize its importance so as to render it trite, at least in comparison with other gifts. But he does no such thing.

Look closely at Paul's conclusion. He even introduces it by asking the question, in view of what has just been said in v. 14, "What is the outcome then?" (NASB; v. 15a), or "What am I to do?" (ESV). His answer may come as a shock to you.

According to v. 15, he is determined to do both! "I *will* pray with my spirit," i.e., I will pray in tongues, and "I *will* pray with the mind also," i.e., I will pray in Greek so that others who speak and understand Greek can prof-it from what I say." Clearly, *Paul believed that a spiritual experience beyond the grasp of his mind, which is what I mean by "transrational", was yet profoundly profitable. He believed that it wasn't absolutely necessary for an experience to be rationally cognitive for it to be spiritually beneficial and glorifying to God.* This isn't in any way to denigrate or impugn the crucial importance of one's intel-lect in the Christian life. Paul insists that we submit to the renewal of our minds, not their repression (Romans 12:1ff.). All I'm saying, what I believe Paul is saying, is that praying in tongues is eminently beneficial and glorify-ing to God even though it exceeds or transcends the capacity of our minds to decipher.

Furthermore, if Paul is determined to pray with the spirit, i.e., pray in uninterpreted tongues, where and when will he do it? Since he has ruled out doing it in the public meeting he must be referring to his private, devo-tional prayer life. Paul's private prayer experience was also characterized by "singing in" or "with the spirit", an obvious reference to singing in tongues, what must have constituted a free and more melodious and musical form of tongues-speech.

What Paul proceeds to say in vv. 18-19 becomes ammunition for both sides. The charismatic appeals to v. 18 while the cessationist points a finger at v. 19:

> "I thank God I speak in tongues more than all of you" (v. 18).
> "Nevertheless, in church I would rather speak five words with
> my mind in order to instruct others, than ten thousand words
> in a tongue" (v. 19).

In v. 18 it's as if Paul pulls back the veil and allows us a brief peek into his private devotional life with God. His "quiet times" with the Lord were anything but, as they featured praying and singing and praising in tongues, an experience for which he is profoundly grateful to God.

"But wait a minute," responds the cessationist. "The crucial issue with Paul isn't whether he speaks in tongues, but what is appropriate in the public assembly of the church. Paul is determined only to do what is cogni-tively rational and thus edifying to others in the meeting of the church."

So, how do we resolve this problem? It's really not that difficult. Paul has said that tongues-speech in the public gathering of the church is prohibited, unless there is an interpretation. Since the purpose of such meetings is the edification of other believers, Paul prefers to speak in a language all can understand. Consequently, he rarely speaks in tongues in a public setting.

However, if Paul speaks in tongues more frequently and fervently than anyone else, yet in church almost never does (preferring there to speak in a way all can understand), where does he speak in tongues? In what context would the affirmation of v. 18 take shape? The only possible answer is that Paul exercised his remarkable gift in private, in the context of his personal, devotional intimacy with God. Again, the only grounds I can see for objecting to this scenario is the reluctance that many cessationists have for spiritual experiences that bypass or transcend the mind.

Let's remember, this is the man who wrote Romans. This is the man whose incomparable mind and power of logical argumentation rendered helpless his theological opponents. This is the man who is known to history as the greatest theologian outside of Jesus himself. This is the man who took on and took out the philosophers in Athens (Acts 17)! Yes, logical, reasonable, highly-educated Paul prayed in tongues more than anyone! So, too, by the way, did all the other apostles. Therefore, I agree with Gordon Fee who said,

> "contrary to the opinion of many, spiritual edification can take place in ways other than through the cortex of the brain. Paul believed in an immediate communing with God by means of the S/spirit that sometimes bypassed the mind; and in verses 14-15 he argues that for his own edification he will have both."[7]

O. Palmer Robertson, an avid and articulate cessationist, refuses to concede that someone can be edified apart from rational understanding.[8] He therefore insists that God not only enables a person to speak in a language not previously learned, but also enables him to understand what he is speaking (contrary to 1 Corinthians 14:14). But why, then, would there be a need for the distinct gift of interpretation? Each person speaking in tongues would already know what he is saying and, in turn, could communicate such to the congregation. Why forbid a person to speak in tongues in the absence of an interpreter (1 Corinthians 14:27-28) if every tongues-speaker is his *own* interpreter? And if the tongues-speaker can understand what he is saying, why encourage him to pray that he might interpret (v. 13)?

My conclusion is that, notwithstanding the critical importance of loving God with our minds and pursuing the edification of others in the church, the charismatic exegesis of this passage in Paul is on the mark.

Anti-Intellectualism?

A brief word is in order here concerning what I noted above as a perceived "anti-intellectual" tendency among many charismatics. If, as it is alleged, charismatics tend to be suspicious of too great an emphasis on doctrine, it's important that we know why. Being a charismatic who happens to love doctrine, I've given considerable thought to this problem. Several points are worthy of note.

Many in the charismatic world fear that too much emphasis on theology and the precise distinctions and definitions that come with it may lead to what they call a "Pharisaical" spirit. Whereas the cessationist's greatest fear is emotionalism, or fervor run amok, the charismatic's greatest fear is a dead orthodoxy. This is illustrated by a comment I once heard in a charismatic church: "If the price for an orthodox mind is a distant heart, I refuse to pay it." I certainly understand that sentiment. Jesus spoke of it in Matthew 15:8-9 by citing the prophet Isaiah: "This people honors me with their lips, but their heart is far from me; in vain do they worship me, teaching as doctrines the commandments of men."

There's no escaping the fact that when knowledge is made an end in itself it can easily become a source of intellectual pride that diminishes one's passion for Jesus and compassion for people. I can personally testify to countless hours debating the ultimately unfruitful intricacies of theological minutia all the while men and women around me were hurting and dying. At the end of the day I often felt smug and self-satisfied for having "won" yet another debate. But my love for God and brokenness for a lost and dying world were unaffected.

But good theology should never diminish zeal. God never meant it to. When truth is searched for, discovered, and defined it has the power to inflame the heart and empower the soul and energize the will to do what otherwise may seem burdensome and boring. **Theological truth is not the problem. Arrogance is.** Contrary to what some charismatics have suggested, **the flesh is the enemy, not the "mind".** God gave us brains to employ in service of the kingdom and to enjoy him and all that he is for us in Jesus. People can be just as arrogant and proud of their intellectual simplicity as others are of their brilliance.

Others fear depth of theological study from a desire to avoid contributing to a divisive spirit. Often they have personally witnessed the schism that zealous commitment to truth can bring. Perhaps they themselves have been cut off, ridiculed, even ostracized over doctrinal disagreements that ultimately prove to be, at best, of secondary importance.

I've heard all sorts of excuses why some people choose not to dig deeply into God's Word:

"I'm not smart enough," as if to suggest that only those with a high I.Q. are responsible for thinking deeply about the things of God. We would do well to remember that those who "turned the world upside down" were, largely, uneducated Galileans (Acts 4:13).

"I don't like those 'theological' types. They're cold and argumentative and distant." Yes, some of them are! But wouldn't it be wonderful if we committed ourselves to the pursuit of theological integrity wedded to a spirit of warmth, compassion, and a heart to engage people in the midst of their hurt and greatest need? Why must we think that these cancel each other out, or that something intrinsic to one will invariably diminish the other?

"Doctrine divides." This is often uttered from the pain of personal experience, perhaps stemming from a church split in which precious brothers and sisters were trampled upon and humiliated.

"Theology takes too much time. There's a world disintegrating all around me, and you want me to read a 300 page volume on the Trinity? I'd rather use what little time I have in service of the people of God and sharing my faith with the homeless."

"If I get too caught up in learning doctrine, I'll lose my zeal for prayer and worship and evangelism. Doctrine just doesn't seem very practical."

"I'm a simple person, just a plain Christian trying to do my best to please God. Theology complicates life. It's so technical and tedious. Why can't I just devote myself to loving others and serving those in need?"

At the same time, we must acknowledge that certain people *are* uniquely gifted and called to serve God through professional theological inquiry while others are no less anointed for ministries of mercy and outreach. What I object to is the suggestion that these necessarily cannot co-exist in the same soul or church or denomination. To argue otherwise is to fall prey to the Corinthian error of thinking that the ear hath no need of the eye or the foot hath no need of the hand (1 Corinthians 12:14-20).

Preaching the Word

There is a corresponding difference in how each group looks at Scripture. Cessationists emphasize what the Bible meant in its original context, often without moving to contemporary application except by way of an appendix to the sermon that feels artificial and contrived. When it comes to justifying contemporary practices, they often insist on an explicit biblical precedent in the absence of which the issue is forbidden (or, at least approached with extreme caution). Thus we see cessationists devoting considerable time to research of biblical backgrounds, historical context, ancient literary customs, and other issues that will illumine both the intent of the original author and the circumstances of his audience.

Charismatics tend to focus less on what the Bible meant and more on its immediate significance. They often treat the Bible as if it were written yesterday by a contemporary who speaks their language, wears their clothes, and drives an SUV. When it comes to what is purported to be a "new work of God" they are more inclined to follow the counsel of Jonathan Edwards (who, ironically, was himself a cessationist):

> "What the church has been used to, is not a rule by which we are to judge; because there may be new and extraordinary works of God, and he has heretofore evidently wrought in an extraordinary manner. He has brought to pass new things, strange works; and has wrought in such a manner as to surprise both men and angels. And as God has done thus in times past, so we have no reason to think but that he will do so still. The prophecies of Scripture give us reason to think that God has things to accomplish, which have never yet been seen. No deviation from what has hitherto been usual, let it be never so great, is an argument that a work is not from the Spirit of God, if it be no deviation from his prescribed rule. The Holy Spirit is sovereign in his operation; and we know that he uses a great variety; and we cannot tell how great a variety he may use, within the compass of the rules he himself has fixed. We ought not to limit God where he has not limited himself."[9]

One can see their distinctive approaches to Scripture in what they preach. Cessationists feel obligated to provide well-structured explanations (often with elaborate alliteration) of what God has done and said within the parameters of biblical history. Their sermons focus on God's *past* redemptive activity, and they regard it a sacred calling to preserve its theological integrity and to expound its meaning. Success is measured in terms of exegetical accuracy (not to suggest for a moment that the latter is a bad thing!).

Charismatics don't disagree with this emphasis, but would also come to church with lively expectations of hearing what God is saying to his people *now* or what God will do in the immediate future. They long to be informed of God's impending redemptive purposes (which they assume can be known even though the biblical text may be silent) and to align themselves with them. Although they do not disregard the written record of God's saving activity, they seem more concerned with whether and when and how God will act on their behalf in the present.

A dinner conversation with an evangelical cessationist will soon turn to a discussion (and sometimes a debate) on the meaning of a text or the logical coherence of a disputed doctrine. It isn't often that probing questions of one's own life and struggles and fears are raised. Charismatics, on the other hand, might grow impatient with that scenario and redirect the focus of the conversation by asking: "So, do you have any insight from the Spirit concerning what God is up to these days? I'm especially interested in what He's doing in *your* life." If cessationists fixate on what the biblical text meant to Paul or Peter or John, charismatics are more inclined to ask: "So what does that text mean to *you*?"

Deep Church

Unfortunately, this often exposes the charismatic to faddism, or yielding to whatever is theologically fashionable. Perhaps this is a good time to return to the proposals made by British charismatic pastor, Ian Stackhouse, in his book *The Gospel-Driven Church*. If nothing else, this volume indicates that charismatics are capable of self-criticism. What I would like to do is employ Stackhouse as something of a dialogue partner in this and the next chapter as we zero in on the strengths and weaknesses of both the evangelical cessationist and charismatic.

Stackhouse begins his proposal with a chapter on the crisis in preaching in our churches. As simplistic (and, for some, boring) as it may sound, he contends that as we faithfully teach the Word of God, the combination of a biblically based theology and the presence of the Holy Spirit will facilitate church growth. Sadly, though, what constitutes the "presence" of the Spirit is a subject on which there is considerable disagreement. For the cessationist it may be little more than affirming the Spirit's role in illuminating the text and empowering mortification of the flesh. For the charismatic it may entail prophetic words, healing of the sick, deliverance from demonic bondage and other expressions of overt power.

He has some harsh words for those who elevate "relevancy" as the standard by which preaching is to be measured (both charismatics and cessationists are guilty on this count). This reflects an obsession for growth, which may be an indication that a church has succumbed to the world's criteria for success. Instead, "the main business of the church is to ensure that the gospel finds a home within its worshipping life. It is this gospel, rather than the church's relevancy or contemporaneity, which determines its identity and mission."[10] One should not be surprised, then, that he also targets anecdotal preaching and an excessive reliance on the visual, as over against oral, presentation of the gospel.

It's also important that we not overlook his emphasis, as also mine above, on the preached word as *sacramental*. The charismatic penchant for immediacy has contributed to the loss of emphasis on the power of the spoken Word. "Don't give me the *word* of God," said one charismatic extremist. "Give me *God*!" Need I say that this is a horribly unbiblical dichotomy? Preaching is not simply a word *about* Christ. Rather, Christ himself enters the congregation *through* the words the preacher proclaims from Scripture. We must never close our Bibles feeling smug for having "conquered" another text (as is a tendency among some cessationists). Nor should we marginalize the Bible as if God will "show up" independently of it (as some charismatics contend). *Our goal is a life-changing **encounter** with Christ as he comes to us by means of the **text***.

Christian Growth

As for their respective approaches to the Christian life, cessationists are generally more process oriented. They are quite leery of a proposed "quick fix" to their problems. Change comes through a focused and consistent study of the Word and submission to the rigors of traditional disciplines. Gradual transformation of character is the result of the power of the Spirit whom they have from the moment of conversion as a permanent deposit. They view their primary enemy as the flesh and its promptings and explain their spiritual failures in terms of a moral or volitional lapse.

Charismatics emphasize event, perhaps a prophetic word or other supernatural encounter that catapults them forward into deeper intimacy with Jesus or empowers them for ministry. If cessationists emphasize the permanent indwelling of the Spirit as the source of growth, charismatics emphasize the repetitive infilling or anointing of the third person of the Trinity. Whereas they would by no means deny the existence of the flesh, charismatics are just as likely to attribute their failures to the dynamics of spiritual warfare, believing that much of their internal struggle is the result of demonic attack. If the latter does not cause the former, it certainly aggravates and intensifies it.

I particularly like the way Grant Wacker describes this phenomenon. Cessationists, or what he calls "mainliners", know "that Rome was not built in a day, and neither is a Christian faith. Mainliners, especially Lutherans and Reformed Confessionalists, seriously catechize the young and reproduce the faith in denominational schools and seminaries. They use the lectionary systematically to present (and re-present) the whole of the Christian theological tradition. Mainliners understand, in other words, that the Christian God is a slow God who builds the edifice of faith one brick at a time."[11]

Charismatics and Pentecostals, on the other hand, often approach Christian growth and nurture the way the producers of the popular TV show, Extreme Makeover, undertake to construct a new home. They take the existing, often dilapidated, structure and assign countless workers and sub-contractors to work literally around the clock. What normally might take six months is completed in less than a week! Charismatics, likewise, can be impatient with the rigors and routine of process and much prefer an immediate turn-around.

A Case Study: The "Toronto Blessing"

Again, turning to Stackhouse will help us focus more clearly on this issue. He points specifically to the so-called "Toronto Blessing" as illustrative of problems endemic to many charismatics when it comes to the subject of sanctification.

He faults the Toronto phenomenon on several counts, only four of which I'll note. First, although it must be said that Stackhouse doesn't regard Toronto in entirely negative terms, he does suggest that it has a decidedly "romantic" slant that seeks to avoid the encumbrance of excessive concern for words and doctrines. Second, it has contributed to "the development of a pneumatology in which experiences of the Spirit, evidenced at the level of phenomenology, become the sole means of legitimising the truth claims of the gospel. The long-term repercussions of this is [sic] a renewal movement detached from the central doctrines of salvation in Christ, but also a revivalism that requires ever more outpourings of the Spirit to secure its place in the world."[12]

Third, "Toronto has severed the link between pneumatology, christology and ecclesiology, and further undermined the confidence of the church in its essential rites."[13] And fourth, "contrary to the Toronto notion of resting and soaking in the Spirit, holiness is not simply a matter of letting go or resting, but of active appropriation of the power of the indwelling Spirit, who conspires to effect radical and ethical change in the world of the ordinary and the mundane."[14]

I have problems with each of these criticisms. First, Stackhouse fails to see precisely for whom, in my opinion, Toronto was intended. The people most powerfully impacted were those who had become burdened with the lifeless and divisive dogmatism of a ministry that was exclusively (or primarily) word-based. [Again, this is not to suggest that *all* word-based ministries are lifeless and dogmatic.] The leadership of Toronto was not opposed to propositional truth or Christian dogma or to reasoned dialogue on the elements of biblical faith, but only to an intellectual arrogance or doctrinal legalism that tends to measure one's spiritual maturity solely in terms of one's theological precision. That some reveled in the subjectivity associated with the renewal (and what renewal or revival in history has entirely escaped this problem?) is undoubtedly true. But that's not the same as saying that Toronto was designed to diminish the centrality or life-changing power of biblical truth.

There is perhaps more a measure of truth in Stackhouse's second criticism. I suppose my objection is with his use of the adjective "sole". Experiences with the Spirit, when grounded in and consistent with the written word do have a measure of apologetic value. But I don't recall many (if any) claiming that Christianity is true based "solely" on what they experienced at Toronto. Perhaps we would be better served to say that such experiences "confirm" or "bear witness" to one's convictions concerning the gospel.

Third, I suppose what Stackhouse has in mind here is the focus in the renewal meetings on experiencing an encounter with the Spirit that *appeared* to be detached from the preaching of the cross or the corporate life of the church. But why should that necessarily undermine the "confidence of the church in its essential rites"? Most of those with whom I spoke during the heightened season of renewal testified to being refreshed and re-energized to return to their local churches with a new and exciting commitment to live out the truths of the gospel. People were drawn to the power of Toronto not as an excuse to ignore the routine responsibilities of church life (O.K., perhaps some were), but to receive a fresh infilling of the Spirit and a new vision for how they can better and more joyfully fulfill them.

In regard to these last two points, yes, it must be admitted, there are always people who rely solely or primarily on experience and who irresponsibly shirk the biblical mandate for community life in the body. But I think it's unfair to suggest that Toronto *consciously* intended to empower such folk in their sin (although it may have inadvertently contributed to this problem). People who are inclined in this way will find an excuse to justify their ill behavior irrespective of renewal or seasons of revival.

Fourth, and finally, no one of whom I know who was part of leadership in the Toronto phenomenon taught or teaches that "resting" in the Spirit is a substitute for "active appropriation" of his power or for commitment to the classical disciplines of the faith. Far from it. Resting or soaking was encouraged precisely for its capacity to renew and refresh and empower weak souls to get up off the floor and get back in the fight against the world, the flesh, and the devil.

Stackhouse here falls prey to the "either/or" syndrome, as if to suggest that a season of "soaking" under the power of the Spirit's work in the inner man negates or is inconsistent with a focused and energetic pursuit of holiness in the grace of God. I would suggest that this phenomenon of "resting" or "soaking" was perhaps Toronto's greatest contribution, not because it was being recommended as a new model of sanctification or an antidote to the rigors of Christian living, but precisely because it was used of the Spirit to heal, refresh, cleanse, empower, and re-ignite in countless weary souls a love for Jesus and his Word and his church.

Could it be that this objection is again related to the suspicion many have concerning the value of "non-cognitive" or "transrational" experiences? Although not a cessationist, perhaps Stackhouse is reluctant to acknowledge that the Spirit can produce significant and lasting change in a person in the absence of conscious cognitive engagement.

So, yes, Toronto had its flaws, some of them quite serious. The pressure to find biblical warrant for bizarre physical manifestations was more than its apologists could resist. Many simply "overinterpreted" the significance of what was happening. Others felt compelled to artificially prop up and perpetuate the renewal when it was obviously (and by God's design) on the wane. And critics are right in pointing out that the Scriptures did not play as central a role as they should have.

But I cannot easily dismiss the countless pastors who told me how the Spirit of God reversed ministry burnout and restored zeal for their calling and to the church while at Toronto. I cannot easily dismiss the hundreds, if not thousands, of people who testified to having their affection for Jesus intensified, their courage for evangelism built up, their wounds from past abuse healed, their capacity to feel God's love enlarged, their marriages restored and addictions shattered and their worship enlivened. So, let's not fault Toronto, or better still, what the Spirit of God accomplished through Toronto, simply because it did not fulfill the expectations of what it never proposed to be.

Reformation or Revival?

When asked, "What does the church need most?" cessationists and charismatics offer differing remedies. The former see the church in desperate need of reformation, which typically would take the form of greater clarity of theological conviction, a renewed commitment to the purity of the apostolic gospel, ethical and moral transformation, and other related matters.

Charismatics, on the other hand, long for revival, by which they most often mean a tangible and definitive invasion of the Holy Spirit that results in unprecedented evangelistic success, physical healing, increased spiritual power and a general restoration of spiritual gifts to the life of the church. In other words, what each group desires fairly accurately reflects the values they embrace as essential for "successful" church life.

Stackhouse argues that the "revivalism" of charismatic renewal is beset with potential landmines. In a chapter titled, "Revivalism, Faddism and

the Gospel," he points to competitiveness among churches and, more significantly, a general weariness that the delay of success engenders. His fear is
that "basic spirituality is [often] subsumed by revival. Indeed, revivalism has
a tendency to cultivate a sub-culture of its own, strangely detached from the
person of Christ."[15]

Stackhouse believes that revivalism, or the orientation of church life
based on an ever-present expectation of an instantaneous surge in spiritual
power and numerical growth, breeds incessant discontent with the status
quo. Indeed, "one of the deleterious features of a revivalist mentality is that
short of what might be termed a surprising manifestation of God there is very
little else to be getting on with. Whole sections of legitimate church activity
are held in suspense, and, moreover, deemed a failure, simply because they
fall short of revival criteria. Commitment to spiritual formation, on the other
hand, takes seriously the fact that there are indeed seasons in the Christian
journey, both personal and corporate, and that intense fervour is not sus-
tainable, nor even necessarily required, in order for Christian living to occur.
It is simply enough to commit oneself to 'the technique of going to church.'"[16]

Stackhouse is by no means opposed to revival, as biblically conceived. Nor is he committed to the status quo as if it possessed some unique
sanctity. But he does fear that revivalism all too often leads to a worldly obsession with numerical growth, a pragmatic approach to methods of ministry
that run contrary to the biblical text, and a tendency toward theological innovation that threatens to undermine the foundational truths of Christian
proclamation. The result is that "theological pragmatism and relevancy, rather
than fidelity to the gospel, is now the accepted hallmark of the movement:
whatever can be done to avoid decline and stimulate growth."[17]

He proceeds to cite as an example the concept of territorial spirits
and strategic level spiritual warfare found in the teachings of Pentecostal
author C. Peter Wagner. According to what Stackhouse calls "Prayer Warfare"
(his label for Wagner's approach), evangelistic success is suspended on a technique whereby the "strong man" (ruling principality or demon) over a particular area or city is first bound or pulled down. Stackhouse fears, and not
without reason, that this view "has negated, if not entirely overwhelmed, the
traditional emphasis on the finished work of Christ as the victory of God in
the world, and thereby has jettisoned, in the form of gospel preaching, a classical means by which this victory was implemented. In the scheme of Prayer
Warfare, preaching the gospel, and the evangelistic success derived from

gospel preaching, can only take place once the necessary demolition of spiritual forces had occurred."[18]

Aside from the fact that the practical tactics of "Prayer Warfare" lack explicit biblical sanction, Stackhouse believes this approach undermines the sufficiency of Christ's victory by making the proclamation and inherent power of the gospel dependent on a particular methodology of prayer. In this way, the gospel is displaced as the locus of evangelical authority. This leads to the strange and paradoxical situation "of an overrealised eschatological vision, namely revival, resulting in a prayer warfare methodology that understates the gospel's own power to effect conversion. In effect, prayer warfare, with its associations with revival, has contributed to the demise of preaching as an effective means of grace by neglecting the theological grist that has underpinned preaching in the classical sense: namely, the announcement of a victory already secured."[19]

Stackhouse leaves no doubts concerning his view of the church's capitulation to the "numbers game". He sees the obsession with quantitative growth especially in the church planting movement. "When growth replaces qualitative Christian nurture as the rationale of the church, traditional notions of initiation into the gospel are sacrificed on the altar of expediency, and pastoral care of the saints, in the somewhat ambiguous and messy business of real life, is set in opposition, unnecessarily and unbiblically, to the call to evangelise."[20] Again, when "growth" becomes paramount, "issues of spiritual formation are almost entirely subsumed by categories of functionality; theological inquiry replaced by sociological analysis. In the charismatic movement, it has meant the domination of the prophetic-visionary strand over and against the pastoral and the priestly."[21] In sum, what we see is the exaltation of vision over substance.

As stated earlier, Stackhouse refuses to abandon all notion of revival. But he contends, and not without reason, that the current form of revivalism that has beset the charismatic movement has been influenced more by sociologists and statisticians than theologians. So what is the key to genuine renewal? It is in "the formation of a counter-culture religious community [i.e., the local church], rooted in faith and baptism"[22] and forever shaped and energized by the intrinsic power of its gospel message.

Stackhouse is undoubtedly a keen observer of developments within charismatic renewal in the U.K. I sense in reading his book that he has been confronted, as a pastor, with a measure of negative fallout from both excesses in the movement as well as the lack of biblical and theological depth so often characteristic of many who embrace the full range of the Spirit's gifts. Add to this the controversy sparked by the "Toronto Blessing" and one can easily understand the genesis of this book.

I share his concerns. I, too, am bothered by the "faddish" nature of much in charismatic Christianity. But I am not for that reason any less committed to the biblical truth of charismatic experience of the Spirit. This inevitably puts me in an unenviable position. On the one hand, I refuse to settle for anything less than the fullness of the Spirit's life and activity in the church today. I have seen the biblical errors of cessationism and the spiritual bankruptcy of religious life that so often comes with the "quenching" of the Spirit's presence and power. Yet, I am also faced with the shallow, flippant, and presumptuous spirituality of much of "charismania".

Contending for the comprehensive ministry of the Spirit while refusing to sever ties with the classical disciplines and traditions of the church, as rooted in the gospel and written Word, is not an easy task. Let's be honest: it sets one up to get shot at from both sides. This is why I applaud and so deeply appreciate what Stackhouse has attempted to do in this book. This is, if nothing else, a very courageous book. That doesn't mean I think his answers were always on the mark, but at least he's recognized the questions that need to be asked and is willing to venture forth a proposal for where the church needs to go.

Intrinsic or Incidental?

I think it's also important that we distinguish between what is intrinsic to a revivalist mentality and what is only the occasional and unintended effect of it. I've already referred to what Stackhouse perceives as the weariness, anxiety, and even disillusionment that come when the success of revival is forever delayed. "Basic spirituality is subsumed by revival", by which he means, in part, the neglect of traditional practices of discipleship and pastoral care, as rooted in the gospel, due to the ever-expectant focus on impending mass conversions and church growth.

I've witnessed this as well, here in the U.S. But I must also say that many who are committed to fervent intercession for revival are stable and faithful folk, grounded in the Word and not at all inclined to flights of spiritual fancy (I trust it is permissible to say that I include myself among them).

My point is simply that one *need not* fall prey to the onset of "theological amnesia" or the religious despair that occasionally comes with deferred fulfillment. Nor do I think that fear of the latter is sufficient reason to diminish the church's focus or dedication of its resources to continual pursuit, in prayer, of God's eschatological purpose of global harvest (assuming, of course, that the latter has a solid biblical footing).

Thus, I see no reason to conclude that a commitment to a biblically-informed view of revival will invariably lead to pragmatism or a capitulation to worldly standards of success. That some in the charismatic renewal have yielded to the latter is undeniable. But that is no reason to abandon or diminish our embrace of the former. One need only think of the revival theology and praxis of Jonathan Edwards (a non-charismatic, I should add; 1703-58), especially as seen in his treatise *Religious Affections*, to see how it can and should be done.

Conclusion

So, can charismatic "revivalism" survive, perhaps even thrive, alongside and together with the vision of the church outlined in this chapter? I'm hopeful (naïve?) enough to believe it can. There are those who contend there's a fundamental inconsistency between the two, that one cannot embrace both "immediacy" and "sacramentality", both "ecstasy" and "discipline", both "intimacy" and "transcendence". I simply refuse to settle for one over the other (given the fact that all are biblical). I refuse to believe, as do many, that invariably one will swallow up the other or, at best, relegate it to the periphery of church life.

If the divinely ordained marriage of Word and Spirit means anything it is that we must never capitulate to the lie that they cannot dance in tandem, or that something is intrinsic to what they are that invariably leads one to subordinate, or cancel out, the other. I applaud all those who contend that both must be retained and given their full rights in the church. I, for one, refuse to concede that a healthy revivalism that thrives on intercession, intimacy and immediacy cannot co-exist with a classical, sacramental, Word-based ministry. I believe they can. I believe they must.

---

[1]"Paying the Price," by Matthew Green, in *Ministries Today* (July / August 2005), 73.

[2] Ibid.

[3] My use of the term "worship" in this way is not meant to suggest that only corporate singing qualifies as such. Clearly, preaching itself, together with celebration of the sacraments and prayer, are all acts of worship.

[4] Packer, *Truth and Power: The Place of Scripture in the Christian Life* (Wheaton: Harold Shaw Publishers, 1996), 158.

[5] A highly simplistic definition of the *regulative principle* is that only those elements are allowed in corporate worship which find explicit precedent or endorsement in Scripture. Those who advocate the *normative principle* would argue that all is permitted except what is forbidden (either explicitly or by reasonable deduction therefrom).

[6] Perhaps the most extensive, and certainly the most negative, analysis of the "power" theology among charismatics (and in particular, the third-wave theology of John Wimber) is the work by Martyn Percy, *Words, Wonders and Power: Understanding Contemporary Christian Fundamentalism and Revivalism* (London: SPCK, 1996). For a more positive and biblical understanding of "power" in Christian ministry, see "The Empowered Christian Life," J. I. Packer, in *The Kingdom and the Power* (Regal), 207-215; "Should Christians Expect Miracles Today? Objections and Answers from the Bible," Wayne Grudem, in *The Kingdom and the Power* (Regal), 55-110; and especially Deere, *Surprised by the Power of the Spirit* (Zondervan).

[7] Gordon D. Fee, *The First Epistle to the Corinthians* (Grand Rapids, MI: Wm. B. Eerdmans Publishing Co., 1987), 657.

[8] See his book, *The Final Word* (Carlisle: Banner of Truth Trust, 1993).

[9]"The Distinguishing Marks of a Work of the Spirit of God," in *Jonathan Edwards on Revival* (Carlisle: Banner of Truth, 1991), 89. This point is clearly seen in the differing approaches taken to the events that unfolded in both Toronto (1994 -) and Pensacola (1995 -). For an especially critical evaluation of these "revivals", see Hank Hanegraaff, *Counterfeit Revival: Looking for God in All the Wrong Places* (Dallas: Word Publishing, 1997). Michael L. Brown, an active participant in the events associated with the Brownsville Assembly of God in Pensacola, Florida, has written a careful response in *Let No One Deceive You: Confronting the Critics of Revival* (Shippensburg, PA: Revival Press, 1997). See also, Margaret M. Poloma, "The 'Toronto Blessing' in Postmodern Society: Manifestations, Metaphor and Myth," in *The Globalization of Pentecostalism: A Religion Made to Travel*, 363-385, and especially her book, *Main Street Mystics: The Toronto Blessing and Reviving Pentecostalism* (Walnut Creek, CA: Altamira Press, 2003). A balanced assessment can be found in *'Toronto' in Perspective: Papers on the New Charismatic Wave of the mid-1990s*, edited by David Hilborn (Waynesboro, GA: Acute, 2001).

[10] Stackhouse, *The Gospel Driven Church*, 96.

[11] Grant Wacker, "Hand-Clapping in a Gothic Nave: What Pentecostals and mainliners can

learn from each other," in *Christianity Today* Volume 49, No. 3 (March 2005):60.

[12] Ibid., 175.

[13] Ibid., 180.

[14] Ibid., 180-81.

[15] Ibid., 7.

[16] Ibid., 61.

[17] Ibid., 11.

[18] Ibid., 13-14.

[19] Ibid., 15.

[20] Ibid., 28.

[21] Ibid., 29.

[22] Ibid., 33.

Chapter Seven

✾

Exploring the Divide (2)

All Christians, whether cessationist or charismatic, cherish the kingdom of God and acknowledge the crucial role it plays in God's purpose in history. But their perspectives on it do differ in certain respects, especially with regard to the celebrated distinction between the "Already" and the "Not Yet". The distinction relates to the nature and extent to which the kingdom and its blessings are "already" present for our enjoyment, or, conversely, are "not yet" accessible in their full manifestation. Cessationists generally place more emphasis on the latter while charismatics focus on the former.

This has immediate consequences for how each responds both to adversity and blessing in life. For example, cessationists are more likely to acquiesce to what we don't yet have and often suffer from an under-realized eschatology. They are more willing to embrace suffering and strive to understand and yield to its sanctifying purpose. They are far more likely to relegate certain blessings to the future, subsequent to the resurrection and glorification of the body. If not carefully monitored, this can lead to a pessimistic and "defeatist" mentality that, in a sense, "sells God short."

Charismatics, on the other hand, are far more inclined to assume that most of God's gifts are potentially theirs in the present moment. This often breeds a triumphalism that claims, by faith, spiritual privileges believed to be their birthright as the children of God. They have higher expectations (some would say "unwarranted presumption") of divine healing and view such as an opportunity for God to glorify himself. They tend to explain prolonged suffering as due more to demonic oppression or the absence of faith than divine purpose.

I'm encouraged by the fact that this tendency toward an over-realized eschatology has not escaped the notice and critique of other charismatics.[1] Russell Spittler finds similarities between contemporary charismatic spirituality and that of the church in first-century Corinth. He describes this perspective as "a compacted collapse of any linear sequencing of future events into a charismatically enlivened *now*."[2] In essence, it is a failure to take the "long view" on God's purposes, believing that any and all blessings secured by the cross of Christ are designed for our complete enjoyment now.

How Shall We Pray?

This emphasis on the "Already" of the kingdom helps explain why charismatics maintain high expectations of the efficacy of prayer in which there is hardly anything for which they don't make petition. The upside of this is a fervency and perseverance in prayer often absent among cessationist Christians. The latter have slightly lower (perhaps even considerably lower) expectations of prayer, combined with the conviction that some things are off-limits for no other reason than they do not believe that is the sort of thing God regularly does today. If there is an error in charismatic enthusiasm it is that their approach to prayer can occasionally border on presumption. If there is an error in cessationist passivism it is that they are likely to treat prayer as a perfunctory ritual.

This is a good place for a reminder that these observations are of general tendencies and potential dangers. These are not universal and rigid laws. The fact is, there are many charismatics whose approach to prayer is characterized by humility and acknowledgement of the sovereignty of God. Likewise, many cessationists are fervent intercessors whose persistence in prayer reflects the emphasis of both Jesus (Luke 11:5-13) and Paul (Colossians 4:2-4; 1 Thessalonians 5:17).

Still, there are significant differences. Most charismatics anticipate a dialogue when they turn to God in prayer. They expect to hear him speak not only indirectly in Scripture but immediately in the heart. Their prayer meetings are therefore characterized by both exuberant petition and quiet contemplation, the latter ostensibly to make room for God to respond. Cessationist prayer is predominantly monologue, and any claims to having "heard the voice of God" apart from Scripture are regarded with considerable skepticism. I'll have more to say about this in the next two chapters.

Stackhouse believes there is an excessive focus on *intercession* among charismatic revivalists to the exclusion of the broad spectrum of prayer that often appears in other traditions. This overemphasis on intercessory prayer may reflect a static God who "will only yield up his reward to those who pray long enough and loud enough."[3] Stackhouse fears that, where there is an anticipation of revival just around the corner, prayer becomes little more than the means God has established to petition him for the salvation of the unregenerate. Prayer is "stunted when it is driven solely [there's that word again!] by the need to save souls. At this point both evangelism and prayer cease to be organic and integral to the worshipping and praying life of the church and are conceived, instead, as tools for success. Prayer thus becomes a mechanism of evangelistic growth."[4] Stackhouse proposes as a remedy a return to the daily office. He writes:

> "Though the crisis in the contemporary church may seem, ostensibly, to be about its perceived irrelevance, the crisis ought more properly to be identified as one of loss of the church's theological and baptismal identity as a community situated in Christ, 'occasioned by the distance at which the church lives from the source and sources of its faith and life,' namely the scriptures. Hence, the urgency to return to those sources and practices that enable the church to encounter once again the power of those scriptures. The point of the daily office is to root prayer in those same scriptures, and thereby provide the church with a genuinely spiritual and theological model of renewal, rather than one that is merely organizational."[5]

His recommendation has a three-fold focus. First, praying the psalms is essential, in that "what the psalms suggest, by their repeated use in worship and devotion, is a comprehensive training in the grammar of pain – one that resists sentimentality whilst, at the same time, expressing genuine lament. Praying the psalms invites a changed perspective on the question of pain by embracing it as an integral part of biblical spirituality."[6] Second, he suggests the Lord's Prayer as another discipline that enables faith to survive through the instability and many fluctuations of enthusiasm. Lastly, in keeping with his charismatic convictions, Stackhouse endorses the regularity of private prayer in tongues.

My experience has been that those committed to revival have a comparatively healthy view and practice of prayer in all its dimensions. I have had considerable exposure to the overtly charismatic International House of Prayer in Kansas City, Missouri, where a wonderful blend of prayer and worship continue, literally, twenty-four hours a day, seven days a week, three-hundred and sixty-five days a year. As of this moment, there has been no interruption of this pattern for nearly six years!

Although they are certainly given to energetic intercession and a zeal for lost souls, they are not for that reason any less committed to the full range of biblical prayers, whether those in the Psalter or the epistles, that are essential for qualitative growth and Christian development. Granted, contemporary revivalists are typically less Reformed than some of us would prefer, but those who celebrate the sovereignty of God (such as I) would do well to remember that often times "we have not, [precisely] because we ask not" (James 4:3).

Assessing the Supernatural

One would expect that our two groups would have differing views on the nature of miracles and how one ought to respond to claims of supernatural activity. Charismatics accuse cessationists of lacking appreciation for the supernatural and surprising in life, such as power encounters, demonic activity, and divine healing. The latter accuse the former of ignoring the beauty of the natural and routine in life. If the one fails to give God his due for physical healing, the other fails to glorify him for the body's capacity to heal itself. Upon hearing the report of an alleged miracle, cessationists are likely to say, "I'll believe it when I see it." Charismatics, on hearing the same news, are likely to shout: "Praise God!"[7]

Thus, if one group gravitates toward gullibility, the other is vulnerable to skepticism. Likewise, if cessationism is guilty of a functional deism in which a natural explanation for unusual phenomena is too readily accepted, charismatics are guilty of a "super-supernaturalism" that often borders on presumption. This is the term J. I. Packer uses for

> "that way of affirming the supernatural which exaggerates its discontinuity with the natural. Reacting against flat-tire versions of Christianity, which play down the supernatural and so do not expect to see God at work, the super-supernaturalist constantly

expects miracles of all sorts – striking demonstrations of God's presence and power – and he is happiest when he thinks he sees God acting contrary to the nature of things, so confounding common sense. For God to proceed slowly and by natural means is to him a disappointment, almost a betrayal. But his undervaluing of the natural, regular, and ordinary shows him to be romantically immature and weak in his grasp of the realities of creation and providence as basic to God's work of grace."[8]

This theology of the miraculous carries over into their respective approaches to personal evangelism. Cessationists are more inclined to affirm proclamation evangelism, placing their confidence in the capacity of truth to penetrate the heart and bring conviction of sin and faith in Christ. The evangelistic strategy of Billy Graham is a good example of this. Charismatics are more likely to employ some form of power evangelism. They certainly proclaim the gospel and cherish the truth of Christ crucified, but also believe their witness will be more effective if accompanied by a prophetic word, a physical healing, or perhaps a deliverance of the person from demonic bondage. The controversial tactics of Benny Hinn are only one illustration of how some charismatics conceive of power evangelism.

Guidance

When it comes to issues of guidance, both groups would certainly appeal to the Bible. However, charismatics often wait for some form of spiritually imparted revelatory discernment. They are more inclined to see God's leading in circumstantial serendipities than are cessationists. The ways in which God communicated to and provided guidance for Paul in the book of Acts, for example, are viewed as standard fare for believers today. When justifying their reluctance to act, they are often heard to say: "I had a check in my spirit."

Cessationists focus more on practical observation and the long-term consequences of the options before them. They place greater weight on the lessons learned from past experience and would rarely act apart from the counsel of others. Common sense plays an essential role in their decision-making process, whereas charismatics are not hesitant about acting contrary to it if they feel they have a "word" from God. Cessationists are more likely to celebrate the freedom of having any number of equally valid options while charismatics often are fearful of missing or failing to seize God's one, perfect will for their lives. Cessationists put more confidence in objective principles, exegetically derived, whereas charismatics look to subjective promptings, experientially discerned.

Two former students of mine are a good example of differing approaches to guidance. One, whom I'll call "Sally", was approaching her senior year at Wheaton College. She was a quiet and somewhat shy young lady, but fervent in her love for the Lord. She was extremely gifted as a musician and envisioned herself as leading worship in a charismatic church at some point in her future. To this end she prayed passionately and often fasted in seeking confirmation from God. But she neither felt nor heard anything.

I encouraged her as best I could and, in view of her obvious talents, tried to direct her into opportunities for further education and experiences that might serve to open some doors for ministry. But without a "word" from God she felt paralyzed. Upon graduation she moved in with friends, worked at a local coffee shop, and waited. The good news is that she was eventually invited to serve in a Christian ministry that was perfectly suited to her talents. I have no idea, however, what role supernatural factors may or may not have played in assisting her to make that decision.

Another student, "Dave", raised in what one might call "high church Presbyterianism," was no less devoted to Christ and equally fervent about serving God in whatever way he could. But he was torn between following in his father's footsteps and entering the world of business or pursuing ministry by attending theological seminary. "Dave" took every imaginable personality profile test, wrote letters to every friend and family member and former pastor he could think of, seeking their collective wisdom for what he should do. I was aware that he had also consulted with several other faculty members at the college. He certainly prayed, probably no less so than "Sally" did, but without expectations of "hearing" from God apart from what he might discern in Scripture. At no point did he feel as if he should do nothing were God not to "speak" or provide explicit direction.

Eventually "Dave" entered graduate school in pursuit of a Masters degree in business administration. He is now happily working for a company in his former hometown and is actively involved in a local church there. In speaking with him recently he indicated that he was absolutely convinced this was God's will for his life, and I have no reason to doubt it.

Was either "Sally" or "Dave" more biblical than the other in the way they approached decision-making? Or perhaps both of them could have learned something from the other concerning how best to "discern" God's will. I would have been happier had "Sally" been a bit less dependent on receiving a "sign" of some sort before making her decision, and I also encouraged "Dave" to be more open to the possibility that God might speak to him directly as well as through the voice of a friend or cherished counselor. In any case, they are both persuaded they are in the "center" of God's will for their lives.

What's Your Favorite Text?

Yet another obvious difference between the two concerns those portions of Scripture to which they seem to gravitate. Generally speaking, charismatics are far more inclined to appeal to incidents in the Old Testament that they believe reinforce our expectancy for God to act in supernatural ways today. When it comes to the New Testament, cessationists look more readily to the didactic portions of the epistles while charismatics focus on the narrative portions of the gospels. The reason for this is that narratives relate experiences of real people who differ little from you or me, people with whose struggles we can personally identify, people who encountered God in miracle and dream and healing and deliverance and revelation and often dazzling displays of divine power.

Charismatics love narrative because they see in it what they long to experience for themselves. The narrative portions of Scripture demonstrate, rather than merely assert, the reality of God, that he's more than an idea or doctrine to be thought about and argued. He's a real, living active being who meets us in the concrete experiences of life. We *feel* God in narrative, as over against didactic literature where, supposedly (but wrongly) he is known only with the mind via some rational abstraction. Narrative tells the church not only what God did in biblical times but also what one can expect today. Stories bring God into the daily nitty-gritty of life, where he can be seen and heard and felt and enjoyed, rather than simply read about.

Cessationists don't dislike or disregard narrative, but insist that apart from an explicit affirmation by the author that what he *describes* he also *prescribes*, or apart from a corresponding statement in the didactic sections of Scripture, we cannot simply assume that ancient stories are paradigmatic or normative for our lives today.[9] The *principles* that one might discern in how God used to operate are still valid, but not the *power* itself. Doctrine, therefore, always sits in judgment over deed. And without the former explicitly teaching the normativity of the latter, it is both presumptuous and hermeneutically suspect to jump from a biblical story to contemporary expectation.[10]

Miscellaneous Distinctives
(that need not be, but often are, divisive)

When it comes to other theological topics, there is again a noticeable difference of emphasis. For example, whereas not all Arminians are charismatics (think of Norman Geisler and Dave Hunt), most charismatics tend to be Arminian. Or again, while not all cessationists are Calvinists, most Calvinists tend to be cessationist. There are certainly exceptions to this, the present author being one. Let me briefly cite three reasons for this general trend.

In the first place, the cessationist typically (but not always) comes from a denominational tradition that is more explicitly rooted in the Reformed theology of the sixteenth century. Neither Calvin nor Luther were charismatics, as if that even needed to be said, and the traditions they spawned, together with the countless denominational off-shoots, were shaped by confessional statements that did not recognize the on-going validity of the more miraculous spiritual gifts.

The Pentecostal and Charismatic movements, on the other hand, were birthed historically out of the Wesleyan-Holiness tradition, which is typically (if not always) Arminian in terms of soteriology. Likewise, those classical Pentecostal denominations that trace their lineage to the Azusa Street Revival of 1906 had little if any interaction with mainstream Presbyterian or Baptist churches, just to mention two.

Second, charismatics envision themselves as more active in terms of missions, evangelism, and prayer than are their cessationist brethren. This is not altogether accurate, but there is enough truth in it to warrant notice. Thus charismatics are fearful that too great an emphasis on divine sovereignty will undermine the urgency and zeal that are so essential to Christian mission. They believe that the human responsibility to pray and preach and "work out [their] salvation with fear and trembling" (Philippians 2:12) will suffer neglect in a more Calvinistic framework.

Needless to say, or perhaps I do need to say it, this latter point reflects a horrible caricature of Calvinistic theology. These are, after all, reflections of a charismatic *Calvinist*. This is not the place to advance a case for the compatibility of the two, so I simply encourage you to read my article, "Prayer and Evangelism under God's Sovereignty" in which I contend for the consistency between divine sovereignty and an active and energetic commitment to both prayer and evangelism.[11]

That said, it would be unwise to ignore what are undeniable tendencies in both camps. If some charismatics appear to place excessive confidence in what humans can do, rendering God at least partially contingent, some cessationists can be so assured of God's ultimate triumph that they slip into an unbiblical fatalism.

The third reason has already been briefly noted. Let me say again that I do not believe there is anything theologically intrinsic to the Calvinistic emphasis on divine sovereignty that requires a cessationist view of spiritual gifts. Neither is there a necessary connection between the Arminian emphasis on free will and a belief in the contemporary validity of charismatic manifestations. But the fact remains that those who embrace a Reformed view of the Christian faith tend to place a comparatively greater emphasis on the centrality of the mind over the affections and are thus less inclined to acknowledge the validity of subjective experiences or so-called "power encounters" or to pursue either of them as an essential element of one's relationship with God.

Yet another slight distinction between the two pertains to their attitude toward tradition. If some cessationists tend to deify tradition, and show great hesitancy in deviating from it, charismatics have been known to demonize it and care little for the past unless it has immediate relevance for the future. Church "history" for many charismatics extends back only as far as their own birthday! Some cessationists, on the other hand, are so entrenched in "tradition" that, to use the words of J. I. Packer, their "grooves have become graves."

One other distinctive between the two camps relates to the person and earthly ministry of Jesus. Cessationists tend to highlight the deity of Christ, and generally attribute his miracles to the expression of his divine nature, whereas charismatics describe Jesus more in terms of his humanity and insist that he performed his miracles as a man in conscious dependence on the activity of the Spirit working through him.

The reason for this isn't hard to discern. Charismatics are quick to look to the earthly life of Jesus as a paradigm for ministry today.[12] The miracles he performed, the healings he effected, the demons he drove out are not primarily proofs of his divinity but manifestations of the operation of the Holy Spirit in and through the man, Jesus of Nazareth. Charismatics certainly don't deny the deity of Christ. They are as vocal in their resistance to theological liberalism as are cessationists. But their focus is more on the reality of his human nature and the remarkable things that God accomplished through him.

Thus they point to Jesus as being both "full of the Holy Spirit" and "led by the Spirit" (Luke 4:1) as he entered the wilderness to face the temptation of the enemy. Following his defeat of the devil there, Jesus "returned [to Galilee] in the power of the Spirit" (Luke 4:14) who had "anointed" (Luke 4:18) him for ministry and proclamation of the good news (see also Matthew 12:28; Luke 5:17; 10:21). On the day of his resurrection, Jesus' first act was to breathe on the disciples and "impart" to them the same Spirit who had empowered him for ministry (John 20:21-23).

Cessationists don't deny these texts, but would argue that the power of Christ was the immediate effect of his divine nature. Indeed, the tangible manifestations of the former could be looked upon as undeniable evidence of the latter. Cessationists affirm the miraculous ministry of Jesus and see in it proof of his messianic identity. Healings and exorcisms, for example, do not so much constitute the essence of the kingdom that we, today, may expect to emulate, but serve rather as evidence of its breaking into human history. For the cessationist, then, Jesus is typically viewed as the *God*-man, with the divine nature serving as the center of his earthly consciousness and personality. Charismatics are more inclined to speak of the *man* Christ Jesus, who was also mysteriously God.

On the one hand, I side with the charismatic perspective on this point. Yet there is truth in both views and thus no reason why they cannot and should not be embraced. This dual emphasis is no grounds for division. Indeed, this mystery of the two natures, human and divine, in one person is at the heart of the historic faith of the church. We cannot afford to minimize either one lest we distort the reality of the Incarnation. How the dual nature and singular personhood of Jesus Christ can be intelligently affirmed is for another book. But neither charismatics nor cessationists can afford to ignore the other.[13]

Worship Wars

Aside from the distinction between Word and Spirit, perhaps nothing more readily sets apart our two groups than that of worship. Here, above all else, we stand in need of an approach characterized by *both/and* rather than *either/or*.

What both groups share in common is their conviction that worship must be theocentric: it is concerned with glorifying God. Where they differ is on the ways and means. Cessationists believe God is most glorified when biblical truths about him are accurately and passionately proclaimed in song, liturgy, and recitation of Scripture. The focus of worship is to *understand* God and to represent him faithfully in corporate declaration. Worship is thus primarily didactic and theological and their greatest fear is emotionalism.

Charismatics, on the other hand, believe God is most glorified not only when he is accurately portrayed in song but when he is experienced in personal encounter. Charismatic worship does not downplay understanding God but insists that he is truly honored when he is *enjoyed*. Worship is thus emotional and relational in nature and their greatest fear is intellectualism.

Admittedly this is perhaps a bit too tidy. Cessationists would no doubt agree that God is to be enjoyed, but they see this as primarily a cognitive experience. Charismatics contend for a more holistic enjoyment. God is not merely to be grasped with the mind but felt in the depths of one's soul. The mind is expanded but the affections are also stirred (and the body may well move!).

Perhaps the best way to illustrate this difference is the way both groups think of God's *presence* in times of corporate praise. Cessationists view God's presence as a theological assumption to be extolled while charismatics think of it as a tangible reality to be felt. Hymns of the former stress divine transcendence. Songs of the latter stress divine immanence. Cessationists tend to fear excessive familiarity with God. They "know that God's will cannot be confined, let alone reduced, to a calculus of human reckoning and desire."[14] Charismatics tend to fear relational distance. They want nothing to do with an impersonal religion that relegates God to a remote and deistic heaven. Their longing is for the "nearness and now-ness" of God.

The spiritual atmosphere cessationists cultivate is characterized more by fear and reverence when compared to the charismatic desire for joy and love. Again, the former prizes form, the latter freedom. A cessationist service is somewhat controlled, both in terms of what is regarded as acceptable physical posture and the length of time devoted to corporate singing. Charismatic worship is emotionally free and physically expressive, with the characteristic lifting of hands and dancing. And whereas cessationists more often sing *about* God, charismatics prefer to sing *to* him.

There is a humble solemnity in most cessationist services versus the exuberant celebration among charismatics. This invariably elicits criticism from both sides. The cessationist is offended by what appears to be an overly casual, if not presumptuous, approach to God. Is not our God a consuming fire, holy and righteous? The charismatic sees in cessationist worship an excessively formal, if not lifeless, approach to God, if they dare approach him at all. And without denying that God is holy, the charismatic is emboldened by what he believes is God's own passionate longing for relational intimacy.

Stackhouse is quick to acknowledge the benefits of contemporary worship and its focus on both "immediacy" and "intimacy" with God. He does not believe, as apparently some within the charismatic movement do, that "contemporaneity" and "theological substance" are irreconcilable. He argues that, in the right context of worship, "spiritual encounter of an ecstatic nature should be positively encouraged."[15]

But he also fears that, if left unchecked and not tethered to biblical truth, contemporary worship will come to be valued only for the interest it can generate or experience it can induce. In other words, worship becomes an instrument for the effects it produces rather than a celebration of God as he is in himself. In such cases "worship takes on an authority of its own so that only in and through the experience of worship, and the way we perform in worship, can grace be appropriated; hence, the pressure to make something happen. Worship as spiritual formation is sidelined in favour of worship as effect."[16]

I have to concede that I have encountered this mentality in charismatic churches. One can often sense that the worship leader is working hard at eliciting from the congregation a certain response, a height of emotion or some physical posture that would indicate they are "fully engaged". Merely to bear witness in song and prayer to the splendor of God seems not enough. A service was "successful" only if "breakthrough" was achieved or singing reached a certain decibel level or tears were shed in sufficient quantity. There's nothing intrinsically wrong with any of these responses. In fact, some cessationists, regrettably, are meticulous in their efforts to ensure that such reactions never occur! There is a carefully orchestrated "glass ceiling" on what is permissible during worship. On the other hand, charismatics need to be careful lest they conclude that God was not honored simply because certain manifest effects were absent.

Stackhouse focuses particularly on the belief in some charismatic circles that revival is itself dependent on what happens in the moment of worship. He cites the popular song "Lord You Have My Heart" in which, he argues, "there is an implicit belief that drawing near to God in worship will bring down the glory of God, and presumably the revival. This is not a celebration of the glory that already inheres within the gospel of Christ, but a further glory, encapsulating all the hopes of a revived land, that can only be uncovered by intensity: the community of feeling that charismatic spirituality has often been identified with."[17]

I'm only partly in agreement with Stackhouse here. Yes, we should celebrate the glory that "inheres within" the gospel and see that glory and power as the foundation for life and growth and mission. But this doesn't preclude the need for fresh impartations or anointings of power for present ministry. Clearly, we are touching here on the delicate tension, but not contradiction, between the "already" of our conversion and reception of the Spirit and the "not yet" of what God offers and invites us to receive.

And let's not too quickly dismiss the importance of "intensity", if by that one means both the individual and collective depth of hunger, desperation, and longing for God to act in ways that will bring honor to his name. Perhaps it is going too far to say that revival is suspended on intensity, but the Scriptures do encourage persistence and struggle and passion and concentrated, single-minded, focus as important elements in the heart's pursuit and search for God (I have in mind the principle underlying such texts as Psalm 63:1-8; 84:1-12; 91:14-15; Jeremiah 29:12-13; 33:3; Luke 11:5-13; just to mention a few).

Stackhouse takes direct aim at Matt Redman's song, "Lord, Let Your Glory Fall," "in which the numinous experience of the priests in the temple in 1 Kings 8 is retold. The tempo of the song reflects the fairly buoyant and upbeat mood that is the hallmark of charismatic musicianship; but what is problematic with this lyricism is the repeated discontentedness of the worshipper with the status quo and an inadequate understanding of the factualities of revelation. In the retelling of the drama, and in the expression of desire for more (again, an entirely legitimate desire [a concession I'm glad to see Stackhouse make!]), the song, nevertheless, inhabits a peculiarly pre-

Christian hermeneutic that forestalls on the fulfillment of the promise of glory in the coming of Christ and the Spirit."[18]

I think Stackhouse is both right and wrong in this critique. He's right in pointing out that the "glory" that "fell" at the dedication of Solomon's temple was an adumbration or foreshadowing of the "glory" that has come in the person of Christ and the descent of the Spirit at Pentecost. I myself hesitate to sing those words for the simple fact that I don't believe "glory" will come to the church, in any literal or tangible sense, apart from that which is already ours by means of the indwelling Christ. The "glory" that hovered over the mercy seat in the Holy of Holies has now taken up residence in the individual believer and in the body of Christ, or the church, corporately. Such "glory", in its visible and concrete Old Testament manifestations, will not again be seen and should not again be expected until it appears in the person of our returning Lord at the close of history (see Titus 2:13 where the blessed hope is identified as "the appearing of the glory of our great God and Savior Jesus Christ").

So, yes, from a purely redemptive-historical point of view, the lyrics fail to take note of the way that Old Testament episode found its consummate fulfillment in the incarnation of Christ and the events associated with the day of Pentecost. My point is simply that the "glory" that appeared then, in Solomon's day, now resides in its fullness in the heart of every believer.

On the other hand, I want to defend Redman's intent. Surely his point is that today we long less for the literal and visible coming of such glory and more for its practical and often life-changing operation. This is similar to our simultaneous affirmation of God's omnipresence and our praying for him to "come" or "draw near" in his "manifest" presence. Or again, Christ already lives in and abides with every Christian, but we pray for him to "dwell" in our hearts "through faith" (Ephesians 3:17). Other examples could be cited in which an accomplished theological truth may as yet be "released" into our experience in transforming power. I suspect this is what Redman had in mind and I concur with him.[19]

[Were it not for the fact that Stackhouse is a charismatic, this would be a perfect illustration of the differences between our two groups. I can hear the charismatic protest: "This sort of theological nit-picking is precisely what I dislike most about cessationists. I'm trying to love God and engage with his heart in a tender moment of intimate worship and all you want to do is exegete the song! For heaven's sake, ease up and enjoy God's presence."

The cessationist is quick to respond: "See, that's just what I mean. You charismatics don't care what you sing as long as it makes you feel good. If you continue in your indifference toward theological accuracy you could well end up worshiping a false god. Don't forget, we're supposed to worship in both 'spirit *and* truth'!"]

Immediacy vs. Mediacy

Related to the above is the difference one often sees in the way the sacraments are understood. There is certainly no uniform approach to the ordinances of the church among those who are cessationists, but they tend to place more emphasis on the sacramental nature of life than do charismatics. This is due in no small part to the emphasis on "immediacy" among charismatics, as over against the recognition of "instrumentality" among cessationists. The Roman Catholic scholar Yves Congar cites protestant theologian Gerard Delteil:

> "The charismatic form of expression seems to be linked to a theology of immediacy – an immediacy of the Word grasped via the text, an immediacy of God's presence grasped through experience, an immediacy of relationship expressed by speaking in tongues and an immediacy that by-passes history.'"[20]

As a rule, but not without exceptions, cessationists are more open to the possibility that the physical can be a medium or perhaps even an embodiment of the spiritual. They have a greater appreciation for religious symbolism and are more likely to highlight both baptism and the eucharist in their corporate worship than are charismatics. This is due in large part to an incipient gnosticism that permeates much of the charismatic world. Charismatic theology in general is often characterized by a dualism between spirit and body as well as heaven and earth, in such a way that the beauty of creation and the "physicality" of God's redemptive purposes are diminished.[21]

Wacker again makes the point that for mainliners, or cessationists, sacramentalism extends beyond the elements of the Lord's Table. Other material objects, such as "stained glass in the nave, [and] carved wood in the chancel – become sites for the intersection of the supernatural and the natural. Mainliners know that Christians experience God with their senses too."[22]

Some are surprised that a charismatic Baptist such as Stackhouse would emphasize the sacraments of the church. But he clearly believes that "the loss of the concept of mediation, inherent in a sacramental understanding of religion, . . . is central to the diminution of Christian identity" so evident in much of the charismatic tradition.[23]

Stackhouse attributes much of this to the fact that it is the musician, rather than pastors and theologians, who set the agenda for worship in today's church. Thus the hallmark of worship today is that it is "immediate, intimate and most definitely non-sacramental (indeed immediacy and non-sacramentality are two ways of saying the same thing)."[24] The result has been a diminishing of transcendence. The loss of the theological notion of mediation means that God is all too near. Thus, what is encouraged is an "ecstatic" rather than "incarnational" view of religion which can, at times, undermine the genuinely human and material dimension of Christian spirituality.

I'm a bit torn at this point. My love for "immediacy" in contemporary worship was initially stirred by the lifeless formalism of more traditional approaches. I longed for God to be "near". I was done with any form of Christian "deism" that relegated God to a distant and uninvolved transcendence. Yet, I also can appreciate Stackhouse's point. But why must we choose between worship that is "ecstatic" and "incarnational"? Why must we choose between a God who is immanent and transcendent? Is it not possible to formulate a theology and praxis of worship that honors both the intimacy of God's nearness as well as the awe and reverence of his holy otherness? Personally speaking, I simply refuse to settle for anything less.

The strongest element in Stackhouse's call for a retrieval of the sacramental dimension is found in its ability to sustain focus on the centrality of the gospel of what God has done in and through Jesus Christ and the indwelling Spirit. And it does this primarily through evoking "remembrance" of God's movement toward us in Christ. Indeed, "this is the basis of all missiological activity by the church, because it is only out of the church's awareness of the gospel's power to initiate and sustain its own inner life that it can go forth into the world confident of the efficacy of its message."[25]

Stackhouse acknowledges that "according to certain preconceptions, the language of remembrance is inert, dead language that stultifies spiritual growth, in contrast to the vital and pressing language of revival. However, as [Gordon] Fee points out, *anamnesis* [remembrance] is not the recalling of past events for the sake of nostalgia; rather, in the light of the resurrection, it is the recalling into the present the very real and substantial events of death and resurrection, in order that they might be celebrated, enjoyed, even participated in."[26] In sum,

> "The deployment of the sacrament of the word, baptism and eucharist, are not the church being overly academic – nor overly liturgical, for that matter – but the church being itself: the church attending to what it has done historically to keep alive truly gospel speech. After all, it is Paul who tells us that the Lord's Supper proclaims 'the death of the Lord until he comes'. And by retaining this sacrament of grace, the church challenges the reduction of the gospel to method or experience. It is a summons not only to adhere to but also participate in the facticity of the death and resurrection of Christ, initiated by baptism and sustained by communion, with the notion of remembrance central to both."[27]

An additional word of clarification is in order concerning the nature of sacramental theology. Contrary to much Protestant opinion, the sacraments are not barriers between God and man, but bridges. They are not designed to keep God at arm's length or to inhibit our intimacy with him. The very purpose of a sacrament is to mediate the sanctifying, life-changing, powerful presence of divine grace to the heart of the believer. Sacraments are not substitutes for the person of Christ, but the divinely-ordained means by which our Lord makes himself and his love and his sin-killing power available to the redeemed.

We should never think of the sacraments, whether the Eucharist, baptism, the preached Word or whatever, as if they stood between us and God to keep the two apart. Precisely the opposite is the case! God ordained them that he might draw near and make himself known and bring into present experience the reality and joy of that intimacy with Jesus Christ that his cross was designed to secure. I applaud Stackhouse's efforts to make this point and join him in calling back the evangelical world to a biblical appreciation for the classical "means of grace".

Angels

One final distinction is the way in which both groups view the role of the angelic realm in human experience. This is essentially an extension of their respective views on whether and to what extent we should expect supernatural manifestations in the course of daily life. Cessationists believe in the existence of angels and demons, but are reluctant to account for inexplicable phenomena, much less routine occurrences, by appealing to angelic activity or demonic attack. They are somewhat skeptical of reports of angelic manifestations and thus do not live with the expectation of angelic encounters in daily experience.

For charismatics, on the other hand, angels and demons are a functional reality of every-day life. They feel little, if any, hesitation in attributing unusual phenomena as well as scandalous sin to the presence and power of either angelic or demonic entities. It should come as no surprise, therefore, that whereas cessationists generally deny that Christians can be demonized, charismatics affirm it and regard deliverance ministry as an essential, indeed routine, component of the church's responsibility.

Have charismatics gone too far at times in defaulting to angelic intervention to explain otherwise inexplicable phenomena? Yes. Have cessationists gone too far in ignoring the potential for angelic activity commensurate with what we see in the experience of both Old and New Testament believers? Yes. Is it possible to affirm the reality of angelic manifestations without falling prey to sensationalism and hype? Yes. Is it possible to question some claims to an angelic presence without being accused of deism or skepticism? I hope so.

Unity?

What does all this bode for unity? Again, our two groups take what appear to be decidedly different approaches. Cessationists tend to draw the boundaries of orthodoxy more narrowly, insisting that theological agreement on a wide range of issues is essential for meaningful cooperative engagement. Charismatics, on the other hand, draw them more broadly and look to a shared experience of the Spirit and a devotion to Jesus as sufficient grounds for unified action. If the danger in the former is arrogant exclusivism, in the latter it is naïve sentimentalism.

It must be noted, however, that contrary to widespread opinion many classical Pentecostals have shunned traditional ecumenical efforts on grounds that they are lacking an adequate theological base. For example, at a recent conference on the campus of Notre Dame University (October 7-9,

2001), Pentecostal scholar and Fuller Seminary professor Cecil Robeck made the following observation:

> "Pentecostals are not convinced that current ecumenical structures are the best means of demonstrating this visible unity. . . . They are not convinced that these organizations have given adequate attention to the doctrinal basis for membership in these organizations. In short, they wonder just how many of those who hold membership in these ecumenical organizations are genuinely Christian. . . . They believe that many of these churches have given up on evangelistic and missionary efforts in which the proclamation of the Gospel is made in clear and uncertain terms, and that it has been *replaced* by efforts in social justice. Both are essential. . . . Pentecostals will continue to reject out of hand . . . all calls to embrace theologically pluralistic or inter-religious agendas that exclude evangelization, and all demands that they adopt what they believe to be the relativistic standards of special interest groups and lobbies, for the sake of ecumenical agreement."[28]

I didn't begin this study with the expectation that either cessationists or charismatics would lay aside their convictions and openly embrace the other. I do hope, however, that some of the animosity, mistrust, and misrepresentation of which both are guilty would diminish. As difficult as it may be for some charismatics to accept, their cessationist brethren really do love God and have no desire to minimize the power of the Holy Spirit. And the latter need to recognize that most charismatics are more passionate about the glory of God and the authority of Scripture than they are about the gifts of tongues and prophecy.

Above all else, both groups are united by something far greater than anything that may otherwise divide them: the centrality and exclusivity of Jesus Christ and their common devotion to the glory of his name and the expansion of his kingdom. My prayer is that as our understanding of each other increases, suspicion and disdain will decrease. Perhaps as they do, our love and appreciation for the other will deepen and our commitment to mutual affirmation and support will grow.

Some might suggest that it is commendable for a person to embrace the strengths of both sides while repudiating their respective weaknesses. But actually to live and minister in the reality of that convergence must eventually lead them into theological schizophrenia. I've been walking in that convergence and serving the kingdom on its basis for some eighteen years now and I've never felt more sane (although I suppose others might take exception)! On those occasions when I tend to gravitate to one side to the exclusion of the other, I remind myself that the man who wrote Romans 9 also said, "I thank God I speak in tongues more than you all" (1 Corinthians 14:18).

Summarizing Stackhouse

Since I have used Ian Stackhouse and his book as a foil in these two chapters, it may prove helpful to briefly summarize his thesis, one from which both cessationists and charismatics can learn much.

He certainly does not advocate reversing the positive strides that have come with charismatic renewal. He simply believes that genuine spiritual progress can only be attained as we remain connected to and build on the classical tradition, rather than abandon it. The path into the future is through the past. I agree with him that the enemy of the church is not primarily structural or cultural, whether in the form of postmodernity or secularization, but in "a churchmanship that refuses to deploy its doctrinal, theological and sacramental resources for the fight."[29] In other words, "the nature of the crisis is theological amnesia concerning the dogmatic core of historic and evangelical Christianity, to which the answer . . . is the recovery of the classical practices of the church as a way of reconnecting with the gospel."[30]

Stackhouse summarizes his proposal in this way, one with which I am sure most cessationists would agree:

> "A return to classical ministry and the wider tradition is part of the overall progress of renewal spirituality: for renewal is best realised when we attend to those things – preaching, sacraments, prayer and pastoral care – that reconnect the church to the original gospel of what God has done in and through Christ. The church is most likely to be renewed not by the promise of programmatic change, or by some new wave of charismatic phenomena, though these will have their place, but by attending to those practices that are not so much guarantors of growth, but the given

means by which God promises to sustain the faith of the church. . . . Specifically, our hypothesis is that in the trajectory of renewal the continued process of innovation requires a complementary process of retrieval: a return to the wider catholicity of the tradition, coupled to a Pentecostal and Reformed theology, as a way forward."[31]

Some of you, I suspect, especially those who are charismatic, are fearful that if what Stackhouse and I are recommending is embraced the church will suffer loss of personal intimacy, freedom in worship, emotional vulnerability, spiritual power, expectation of the miraculous and other charismatic dynamics for the sake of which you left the traditional evangelical church in the first place. I, too, have no desire for a careless return to the former ways of empty ritual and intellectual arrogance. But that is certainly not what Stackhouse proposes. His call is for the biblically grounded integration of both Word (and all it entails in terms of disciplined life and theological integrity) and Spirit (and all it entails in terms of spiritual vibrancy and supernatural activity). Dare we even attempt to do otherwise? I think not.

---

[1] See, for example, the recent work of Simon Chan, *Pentecostal Theology and the Christian Spiritual Tradition* (Sheffield: Sheffield Academic Press, 2000), especially the chapter, "Pentecostal Asceticism" (73-96).

[2]"Corinthian Spirituality: How a Flawed Anthropology Imperils Authentic Christian Experience," in *Pentecostal Currents in American Protestantism*, 12.

[3] Stackhouse, *The Gospel Driven Church*, 197.

[4] Ibid., 198-99.

[5] Ibid., 202-03.

[6] Ibid., 207.

[7] This is not to suggest that charismatics are incapable of self-examination. Some of those involved in or at least sympathetic to the charismatic movement who have written critical, but constructive, analyses include Tom Smail, Andrew Walker, and Nigel Wright, *The Love of Power or the Power of Love: A Careful Assessment of the Problems Within the Charismatic and Word-of-Faith Movements* (Minneapolis: Bethany House Publishers, 1994), Michael L. Brown, *Whatever Happened to the Power of God* (Shippensburg: Destiny Image, 1991), and J. Lee Grady, *What*

Happened to the Fire? Rekindling the Blaze of Charismatic Renewal (Grand Rapids: Chosen Books, 1994).

[8] *Keep in Step with the Spirit*, 193-94.

[9] For a defense of this principle by a continuationist, no less, see Gordon D. Fee and Douglas Stuart, *How to Read the Bible for All Its Worth* (Grand Rapids: Academie Books, 1982), 87-102. Fee, a well-known Pentecostal scholar, wrote this chapter.

[10] For an attempt to justify the appeal to narrative as a source for normative experience and doctrine, see the insightful study of William W. Menzies and Robert P. Menzies, *Spirit and Power: Foundations of Pentecostal Experience* (Grand Rapids: Zondervan, 2000).

[11] The article is found in the book, *Still Sovereign*, edited by Thomas R. Schreiner and Bruce A. Ware (Grand Rapids: Baker Book House, 2000), 307-23.

[12] One notable charismatic exception to this is Keith Warrington, as seen in his book *Jesus the Healer: Paradigm or Unique Phenomenon?* (Carlisle: Paternoster Press, 2000).

[13] In this regard I especially recommend Gerald Hawthorne's ground-breaking work, *The Presence and the Power: The Significance of the Holy Spirit in the life and ministry of Jesus* (Dallas: Word Publishing, 1991).

[14] Wacker, "Hand-Clapping in a Gothic Nave," 61.

[15] Stackhouse, *The Gospel Driven Church*, 45.

[16] Ibid., 48.

[17] Ibid., 53.

[18] Ibid.

[19] Stackhouse concludes his chapter on worship with this provocative statement: "The loose structure [of charismatic worship] is performed in the name of informality, relevance and immediacy, and is close to the centre of charismatic ideology; it is expressive – we ought to remember – of an understandable mistrust of ritual and form. But the irony is that the loss of distinctive liturgical space, transcending ordinary time, means in fact that no time is sacred. Immediacy and accessibility could mean, paradoxically, worship that is escapist and, strangely, irrelevant. Devoid of all theological ritual, alternative worship may be no real alternative at all, but a mimicking of the culture, and theologically insufficient to sustain Christian faith" (66).

[20] "The Renewal in the Spirit: Promises and Questions," in *I Believe in the Holy Spirit*, translated by David Smith (New York: Crossroad, 1997), 165.

[21] There are certainly exceptions to this general rule. One of the first to address the issue was the Anglican John Gunstone in his work, *Pentecost Comes to Church: Sacraments and Spiritual Gifts* (London: Darton, Longman, and Todd, 1994). I should also mention the charismatic renewal among Presbyterian, Anglican (see especially Stephen Hunt, "The Anglican Wimberites," *Pneuma* 17.1 (Spring 1995):105-118; and Mark J. Cartledge, "A New *Via Media*: Charismatics and the Church of England in the Twenty-First Century," *Anvil* 17.4 (2000):271-283) and Catholic believers (see the writings of Francis MacNutt and Ralph Martin). In his presidential address to the Society for Pentecostal Studies, John Christopher Thomas spoke of reappropriating the sacraments into Pentecostal ecclesiology (see his "Pentecostal Theology in the Twenty-First Century," *Pneuma* 20.1 [Spring 1998], 3-19). One should also consult the web site of the recently (1992) formed Charismatic Episcopal Church (www.iccec.org), where this statement of purpose is found: "The Charismatic Episcopal Church exists to make visible the Kingdom of God to the nations of the world; to bring the rich sacramental and liturgical life of the early church to searching evangelicals and charismatics; to carry the power of Pentecost to our brothers and sisters in the historic churches; and finally, to provide a home for all Christians who seek a liturgical-sacramental, evangelical, charismatic church and a foundation for their lives and gifts of ministry."

[22] Wacker, "Hand-Clapping in a Gothic Nave," 60.

[23] Stackhouse, *The Gospel Driven Church*, 125.

[24] Ibid., 127.

[25] Ibid., 135.

[26] Ibid., 137.

[27] Ibid., 149.

[28] Cited by Thomas C. Oden in "Faith & Order, Act II," *Touchstone* (March 2002), 54.

[29] Stackhouse, *The Gospel Driven Church*, 234.

[30] Ibid., 275.

[31] Ibid., 77-8.

PART THREE

He is There and
He's Still not Silent

Chapter Eight

God Still Speaks!

"Why is it that when we speak to God we call it prayer, but when God speaks to us we call it schizophrenia?" (Lily Tomlin).

That's not just a good joke, it's a good question. All Christians say they pray. All Christians claim they speak to God, at least every once in a while. But many of these same people would regard as mentally deluded someone who had the audacity to claim that God actually spoke back to them! It's a strange irony, indeed, that talking to God is regarded as the height of spirituality, whereas God talking to us is viewed as grounds for psychiatric intervention.

One of my favorite movies is *Field of Dreams*, starring Kevin Costner as Ray Kinsella, an Iowa farmer who claims to have heard a voice, saying: "If you build it, he will come." Based on his interpretation of its meaning, Costner constructs a baseball diamond in the middle of his lucrative corn crop, threatening to plunge his family into bankruptcy and incurring the ridicule of everyone in the community. If that were not enough, he then experiences numerous "visitations" from famous baseball players, long since dead. After reading in chapters 1-4 of my spiritual journey you may be tempted to conclude that I am as seriously disturbed as Costner's character. After all, most of our psychiatric hospitals are filled with people who are adamant about having heard such voices and seen similar visions.

My daughter recently gave me the special edition DVD of that film as a Christmas present. I couldn't help but laugh when I viewed the deleted scenes, a standard element in most DVD's. For whatever reason the director chose not to include the scene in which Costner visits a local physician to determine if he's truly sane. After placing a weird contraption on Costner's head the "doctor" peers into his ear with a small flashlight, ostensibly to determine if the light will come out the other side! I also appreciated the scene in which his wife, played by Amy Madigan, tries to "reassure" her husband with the promise: "I'm going to visit you once a month . . . wherever they put you!"

O.K., just one more. Costner's wife, "Annie," is working in their garden when he approaches her with more news of what's been happening in his corn field. "Annie, I just saw a vision," he announces. This, over and above, of course, the numerous times he had heard the "voice". Somewhat bemusedly she walks away declaring, "Well, they're just going to have to burn you at the stake if this keeps up!"

So, I understand your fears. There are people who haven't heard voices, but claim to, that *need* to be institutionalized. Most of us in the western world have been conditioned to respond with a healthy skepticism when someone insists they heard a voice other than those we hear in ordinary conversation with ordinary people. But if you are a Christian who believes in the God of the Bible, the idea of communication from the heavenly realm should not be quite the shock to you that it is to unbelievers.

Fear and Skepticism

Why are so many evangelical Christians opposed to or skeptical of the suggestion that God still speaks? Whenever I speak about this subject in mainstream Protestant churches, some cringe in fear while others get angrily defensive. Having spoken with many of them about this, I've concluded that the primary reason for their reaction is their belief that if God were to speak outside the Scriptures or were to bestow the gift of prophecy to the church it would undermine both the finality and sufficiency of the Bible, God's written Word.

Cessationists insist that prophecy in the New Testament is the infallible report of a divinely inspired revelation, no different in quality from Old Testament prophecy and therefore equal to the Bible itself in authority. Prophecy, they argue, consists of the very words of God himself. Prophecy, therefore, is infallible and binding on the theological and moral convictions of all Christians.

If such prophecy were still being given, the finality of the Word of God would be seriously threatened. If such prophecy were still being given, or if God were to speak to his people through other means, on what grounds could one insist that the biblical canon is closed? Would we not be forced to open the canon and begin inserting new verses in new chapters in new books bearing the names of contemporary "prophets"?[1]

The situation is complicated by those ill-informed extremists who "prophesy" based on what they claim was the voice of God. Few have forgotten (although I wish they would!) the California pastor who in the mid-90s "prophesied" (on national TV, no less) that on June 9th a catastrophe of cosmic proportions would strike our land. June 9th came and went, leaving in its wake not only a discredited pastor but also an indelible reproach on anything that dares call itself "prophetic".

Furthermore, cessationists believe that if people begin to act and believe in response to their claim of having "heard God" or having received a prophetic utterance, their reliance on the sufficiency of the Bible for all of life would be undermined. It would result in people living their lives and often justifying bizarre (or at least unwise) behavior based on subjective impressions rather than on the objective and infallible written Word of God. People will neglect or ignore the counsel of Scripture because of something "God told" them. Worse still, they'll be prone to control and manipulate others on the "authority" of some divinely revealed directive.

One must admit that this is indeed a potential problem. In fact, it's more than potential. I have known a number of people who were inclined to neglect Scripture as the source of truth and direction because they valued the "present-tense" voice of God above his "past-tense" voice. Jonathan Edwards (1703-58), during the revival known as The First Great Awakening, was forced to deal with the claims of people to having heard God speak outside of the Bible. He found it to be a uniquely problematic issue. Listen to his description:

> "And one erroneous principle, than which scarce any has proved more mischievous to the present glorious work [his way of referring to the revival], is a notion that 'tis God's manner now in these days to guide his saints, at least some that are more eminent, by inspiration, or immediate revelation; and to make known to 'em what shall come to pass hereafter, or what it is his will that

they should do, by impressions that he by his Spirit makes upon their minds, either with or without texts of Scripture; whereby something is made known to them, that is not taught in the Scripture as the words lie in the Bible."[2]

Edwards proceeded to identify no fewer than five negative consequences of this. Given my profound appreciation for Edwards, we would do well to listen and respond carefully to his concerns.

Satanic Deception?

First, he argues that "by such a notion the Devil has a great door opened for him; and if once this opinion should come to be fully yielded to and established in the church of God, Satan would have opportunity thereby to set up himself as the guide and oracle of God's people, and to have his word regarded as their infallible rule, and so to lead 'em where he would, and to introduce what he pleased."[3] Evidently Edwards believed that it was virtually impossible, or at least extremely difficult, to discern the voice of God and distinguish it from the voice of Satan. I'll have more to say on this below.

I would like to make one other comment on this first point in response to Edwards. He undoubtedly believed, as do all cessationists, that in the first century a.d., prior to the closing of the biblical canon, God spoke to his people through dreams, visions, words of knowledge, and other forms of prophetic revelation. So why wouldn't his objection apply no less to *that* day and age than he believes it does to his own (and ours)? In other words, if the mere existence of extra-biblical revelation gives Satan the "opportunity . . . to set up himself as the guide and oracle of God's people," then that would have been as great a problem to the churches in first-century Corinth and Thessalonica and Colossae, for example, as it was to the eighteenth-century church in Northampton, Massachusetts, or is to the twenty-first church in Kansas City or Chicago or Paris. And if that alleged "problem" was, in God's mind, *insufficient* reason to withhold such extra-biblical revelation then, why should it be any different in Edwards' day or our own?

Evidently the early first-century church did quite well in discerning God's will and ways when extra-biblical revelation was prevalent. Why cannot we today do equally as well? In fact, I suggest we can do even better, insofar as we have the final authoritative canon of Scripture by which to assess and judge all claims of prophetic revelation. In other words, if Edwards' argument is valid, it proves too much: it would weigh against the existence of extra biblical revelation *at any and all times*, including the apostolic era, something Edwards would by no means countenance.

This potential threat of Satanic deception of the saints that extrabiblical revelatory guidance would allegedly create is nowhere explicitly mentioned in the New Testament. If this were as big a problem as Edwards wants us to believe, it is stunning that no warnings or guidelines or instructions were given by the apostles to alert people in the first century. Certainly there are numerous descriptions of Satan's activity among unbelievers, blinding and hardening and deceiving them concerning the person of Jesus. There are also warnings about demonic temptations aimed at believers, but nowhere do the New Testament authors question the validity of extra-biblical revelation or the spiritual gift of prophecy because of some Satanic capacity to "guide" and "lead" us contrary to the will of God. In other words, if there is a potential for Satan to dupe and deceive believers, it is nowhere related to the presence of extra-biblical or subjective revelatory activity of the Spirit.

One passage of Scripture that may shed light on the issue is 1 John 4:1-6, a text on which Edwards had much to say in addressing the issue of revival in his day. He found in this passage several criteria by which to judge the source and validity of the various physical and emotional "manifestations" during the First Great Awakening. But it also speaks to the issue of discerning between the work of God and that of the enemy. In fact, I believe this passage demonstrates that Edwards' resistance to prophetic gifts based on a fear of Satanic deception is unfounded, assuming, of course, that the believer avails himself of the resources God has provided. Let's look at it more closely.

> "Beloved, do not believe every spirit, but test the spirits to see whether they are from God, for many false prophets have gone out into the world. By this you know the spirit of God: every spirit that confesses that Jesus Christ has come in the flesh is from God, and every spirit that does not confess Jesus is not from God. This is the spirit of the antichrist, which you heard was coming and now is in the world already" (1 John 4:1-3).

The background to this passage is the abundance of supernatural activity and phenomena in the early church: tongues, healings, prophecies, deliverance, etc. John's readers were apparently given to the *uncritical acceptance* of anything supernatural. It remains for the apostle to inform them that *the supernatural is not always divine!* The emphasis here is not so much on the character of the spirit, whether it be false or genuine, but on its origin, whether it be divine or diabolical. John is clearly concerned with the "two spirits" which inspire contrary confessions of the Lord Jesus Christ.

This text tells us that the primary distinguishing feature of the enemy is denial of the incarnation of Christ and reassures us that we need not fall prey to his deception. But it also speaks of the confidence we have for victory over the efforts of Satan to mislead and distort. In other words, we have a solid basis on which to know the difference between the spirit of antichrist and the Spirit of God. The confession of Jesus as Christ incarnate is the means by which to determine the origin of a "spirit", whether it be of God or the Devil.

All believers, says John, have the responsibility to test the spirits to determine their origin (4:1). "Unbelief," notes John Stott, "can be as much a mark of spiritual maturity as belief."[4] In other words, Christians must resist the temptation to be naïve and gullible about supernatural and miraculous phenomena. The fact is, "many false prophets" have gone out into the world. Neither Christian faith nor love is to function indiscriminately. It is the duty of us all to judge, weigh, assess, evaluate, and to exercise our discernment.

John's point is that the doctrine of the incarnation is the standard and test of truth and falsehood (4:2-3). The *origin* of the inspiring spirit may be discerned by the teaching of the prophet through whom it speaks; specifically, what he says concerning the incarnation. The ESV translates v. 2 - "every spirit that confesses that Jesus Christ has come in the flesh is from God." The issue is the object or content of the verb "to confess" (a word that refers to a profession of faith in and allegiance to). This is not merely confession of certain propositions about a person, but the confession of a Person, of whom certain propositions are true. The phrase may be taken in any of three ways.

The object of the confession may be the entire phrase "Jesus Christ has come in the flesh"; i.e., the confession needed is of the *fact* of the incarnation as a historical event. Or, it may be "Jesus Christ *as* come in the flesh"; i.e., one must confess that the person called Jesus Christ is such a one who came in the flesh. Finally, the object of the confession may be "Jesus" as "Christ come in the flesh"; i.e., the confession is that the man Jesus of Nazareth is himself the incarnate Christ or Son.

The false prophets asserted that Jesus was merely a man upon whom the "Christ" (a heavenly emanation) came at his baptism and from whom he left before the crucifixion. Thus the heresy consisted of a denial of the permanent assumption of human nature by the eternal Son of God, the second person of the Trinity. The point John makes is this: Jesus of Nazareth is the "Christ" or "Eternal Son of God" incarnate. The divine person, the Son, has permanently assumed and taken to himself human flesh. Jesus Christ then is not a mere man upon whom divinity descended but is himself the God-man, one person with two natures, one human and one divine. Hence the supreme heresy is to deny the incarnation and deity of Jesus Christ.

John gives two negative signs of "not being of God". In 1 John 3:10 the one who does not practice righteousness is "not of God" and in 4:3 the one who does not confess Jesus is "not of God". Furthermore, such a one is not merely "not of God", he is, positively speaking, "*of the devil*" (3:10) and "*of antichrist*" (4:3). The "of" suggests both allegiance and ownership, hence "belonging to", as well as the idea of "spiritual dependence."

> "Little children, you are from God and have overcome them, for he who is in you is greater than he who is in the world. They are from the world; therefore they speak from the world, and the world listens to them. We are from God. Whoever knows God listens to us; whoever is not from God does not listen to us. By this we know the Spirit of truth and the spirit of error" (1 John 4:4-6).

Here we see that Christians are assured of a theological victory over false prophets and heretics. They have not succeeded in deceiving you. You know the truth and have rejected their lies. Why? How? Because "he who is in you is greater than he who is in the world"! Having contrasted Christians ("you") with the heretics ("them"), he now compares the spiritual forces who are *in* the respective antagonists. Yes, Satan is great, but God is greater! Yes, Satan is powerful, but God is infinitely more powerful!

The "He" who is in the Christian is either God the Father (1 John 3:20; 4:12-13), God the Son (1 John 2:14; 3:24), or God the Holy Spirit (1 John 2:20,27), or the Triune God in the fullness of his divine presence. John does not say "greater are *you*" but "greater is *He*". It isn't you, but *God in you* that brings the assurance of victory. I. Howard Marshall explains:

> "Other people may be taken in by the false teachers who deny Christ, but John does not believe that his 'children' will do so. They have their source in God (cf. 3:10), and consequently they have the inner power of the truth to enable them to withstand error. In this sense they can be said to have 'overcome' the uphold-ers of false teaching. This probably does not mean that they have physically driven them out of the church; rather they have proved victorious over the temptation to accept false doctrine. *False belief is as much a sin as unrighteous behavior or lack of love* [emphasis mine]. Victory over it, however, is not due to any innate strength of believers, but rather to the fact that the One who lives in them is greater, i.e., more powerful, than the one at work in the world. God is mightier than the evil one."[5]

Some may argue that I have misapplied this passage, that the only thing of which John assures us is the ability to know if someone is true or false based on their confession or denial of the Incarnation. This is far and away different, for example, from being able to discern whether an "impres-sion" directing us to take some specific action is of God or the enemy. That is true, but if we can confidently know when a "spirit" is or is not of the truth by noting where it stands on the doctrine of the incarnation, can we not also apply other biblical standards to judge the origin of any purported "voice" or "impression"? I think the answer must be Yes.

John continues by arguing that the response of the audience to the respective messages reveals their true character and is yet another criterion by which to know the spirit of truth and the spirit of error (4:5-6). At first glance, these verses sound like the height of arrogance. John says that *if you know God you will listen to what I say!* If you don't listen to what I say and receive my teaching then you are in bondage to the spirit of error. No ordi-nary individual Christian could ever make such a bold claim. But John is here speaking *as an apostle with the full authority and inspiration of Christ behind his words*. Stott explains:

> "He is carrying a stage further the argument of the first three verses. There the test of doctrine was whether it acknowledged the

divine-human person of Jesus Christ; here the test is whether it is accepted by Christians and rejected by non-Christians. There is a certain affinity between God's Word and God's people. Jesus had taught that His sheep hear His voice (Jn. 10:4,5,8,16,26,27), that everyone who is of the truth listens to His witness to the truth (Jn. 18:37), and that 'he who is of God hears the words of God' (Jn. 8:47). In the same way John asserts that since 'we are of God (6) and 'ye are of God' (4), you listen to us. There is a correspondence between message and hearers. The Spirit who is in you (4) enables you to discern His own voice speaking through us (2). So you can recognize God's Word because God's people listen to it, just as you can recognize God's people because they listen to God's Word."[6]

So, my reason for citing this text in First John was simply to emphasize that so long as we avail ourselves of the truth of apostolic teaching we can be confident that Satan will neither dupe nor deceive us. This isn't to say we are utterly invulnerable or beyond the potential to be misled. Our capacity for yielding to the truth of the Word is often compromised by fleshly self-indulgence. But we need not be spiritually paralyzed or resort to a denial of God's present tense voice for fear that such will expose us to the destructive influence of the Enemy, for "greater is He who is in you than he who is in the world."

Edwards' concerns are echoed in the writings of several contemporary cessationists such as Richard Gaffin. I earlier responded to Gaffin's objections in a book devoted to addressing the validity of spiritual gifts today (see below where I mention the book, *Are Miraculous Gifts for Today? Four Views*). Here is a summation of what I said.

Gaffin [and Edwards preceding him] objects to the possibility of post-canonical revelation on the grounds that we would be "bound to attend and submit to" it no less than to Scripture. Aside from the fact that this wrongly presupposes that contemporary prophecy yields infallible, Scripture-quality words from God, the problem is one Gaffin himself must face. For were not the Thessalonian Christians, for example, "bound to attend and submit to" (lit., "hold fast"; 1 Thessalonians 5:21) the prophetic words they received, no less than to the Scripture in which this very instruction is found? Evidently Paul did not fear that their response to the spoken, prophetic word would undermine the ultimate authority or sufficiency of the written revelation (Scripture) that he was in process of sending them. The point is this: non-canonical revelation was not inconsistent with the authority of Scripture then, so why should it be now? This is especially true if contemporary prophecy does not necessarily yield infallible words of God.

Someone might ask, "But how should we in the twenty-first century, in a closed-canonical world, respond to non-canonical revelation?" The answer is, "In the same way Christians responded to it in their first-century, open-canonical world, namely, by evaluating it in light of Scripture" (which was emerging, and therefore partial, for them, but is complete for us). Such revelation would carry for us today the same authority it carried then for them. Furthermore, as noted earlier, we are in a much better position today than the early church, for we have the final form of the canon by which to evaluate claims to prophetic revelation. If they were capable of assessing prophetic revelation then (and Paul believed they were; witness his instruction in 1 Corinthians 14:29ff. and 1 Thessalonians 5:19-22 to do precisely that), how much more are we today! If anything, contemporary claims of prophetic revelation should be easier to evaluate and respond to than such claims in the first century.

Therefore, if non-canonical revelation was not a threat to the ultimate authority of Scripture in its emerging form, why would it be a threat to Scripture in the latter's final form? If first-century Christians were obligated to believe and obey Scripture in the open-canonical period, simultaneous with and in the presence of non-canonical prophetic revelation, why would non-canonical revelation in the closed-canonical period of church history pose any more of a threat?

Gaffin argues that contemporary prophecy cannot, in fact, be evaluated by Scripture because of its purported specificity. But this is no more a problem for us today than it would have been for Christians in the first century. Did not *they* evaluate prophetic revelation in spite of the latter's specificity and individuality? If they were obedient to Paul's instruction they certainly did (1 Corinthians 14:29; 1 Thessalonians 5:21-22). Why, then, can't we? And are we not, in fact, better equipped than they to do so insofar as we, unlike them, hold in hand the final form of canonical revelation whereby to make that assessment?

Gaffin [and Edwards] believes that to admit the possibility of revelation beyond Scripture unavoidably implies a certain insufficiency in Scripture that needs to be compensated for. But one must ask, "What is

Scripture sufficient *for*?" Certainly it is sufficient to tell us every theological truth and ethical principle necessary to a life of godliness. Yet Gaffin himself concedes that God reveals himself to individuals in a variety of personal, highly intimate ways. But why would he need to, if Scripture is as exhaustively sufficient as Gaffin elsewhere insists? That God should find it important and helpful to reveal himself to his children in personal and intimate ways bears witness to the fact that the sufficiency of the Bible is not meant to suggest that we need no longer hear from our Heavenly Father or receive particular guidance in areas on which the Bible is silent.

Scripture never claims to supply us with all possible information necessary to make every conceivable decision. Scripture may tell us to preach the gospel to all people, but it does not tell a new missionary in 2005 that God desires his service in Albania rather than Australia. The potential for God speaking beyond Scripture, whether for guidance, exhortation, encouragement, or conviction of sin, poses no threat to the sufficiency that Scripture claims for itself.

Neglect of Scripture?

Edwards was also convinced that admitting the existence of extra-biblical revelation would soon "bring the Bible into neglect and contempt. Late experience in some instances has shown that the tendency of this notion is to cause persons to esteem the Bible as a book that is in a great measure useless."[7] But again, the Bible itself nowhere warns us that extra-biblical revelatory activity will lead to the neglect of the written Word. That a few fanatical folk who are probably already inclined to ignore the clear teaching and authority of Scripture fall into error on this point is no argument that we should deny what the Bible itself says about the on-going voice of the Spirit beyond the close of the canon.

Incorrigible?

A third objection raised by Edwards is that "as long as a person has a notion that he is guided by immediate direction from heaven, it makes him incorrigible and impregnable in all his misconduct: for what signifies it for poor blind worms of the dust to go to argue with a man, and endeavor to convince him and correct him, that is guided by the immediate counsels and commands of the great Jehovah?"[8] Again, however much a problem this may have been in Edwards' day or is in ours, it is no justification for dismissing the teaching of the New Testament. People who are determined to follow sinful ways will do it irrespective of what the Bible says. Whether or not one believes in post-canonical revelation is ultimately irrelevant.

I might also add that people who embrace Edwards' view can also do the same thing with the written Word. I have witnessed countless instances where someone dogmatically and inflexibly held to a particular interpretation of a text (as baseless as it might be) to justify a decision or to rationalize unwise behavior. These people were convinced they "were guided by immediate counsels and commands of the great Jehovah" as set forth in his *written* Word. The only way to address this kind of abuse is the same way we should address those who appeal to God's voice to rationalize unwise and errant behavior: careful and more extensive and deliberate analysis of the meaning and significance of the biblical text.

Failed Prophecies?

Edwards also pointed to numerous instances of failed prophecies. He was surprised that "such multiplied, plain instances of the failing of such supposed revelations in the event don't open everyone's eyes. I have seen so many instances of the failing of such impressions, that would almost furnish an [sic] history."[9] Two points should be made here.

First, we've misunderstood the nature of New Testament prophecy if we think of it as primarily predictive in nature. The purpose of the gift is less foretelling the future than forth-telling the heart of God for a particular person. If people, as was perhaps the case in Edwards' day, focus on foretelling or predicting future events, they will invariably go astray.

Second, yes, there are instances, often many, of 'the failing of such impressions.'" But Edwards' response comes perilously close to what Paul himself warned against in 1 Thessalonians 5:19-22. For a variety of reasons, one of which was assuredly the "failure" of some to accurately foretell the future, people in Thessalonica were on the verge of "despising" prophetic utterances. Paul's counsel is to resist the temptation to do so, otherwise one will be in danger of "quenching the Holy Spirit". I have elsewhere addressed how we are to respond to the claim of prophetic insight, and I encourage you to read my comments.[10] My point here is simply that the proper, biblical response to the abuse of prophecy is not to reject it or despise it or discard it or forbid it but to judge it, to weigh it, to evaluate all such claims and then follow the apostle's advice: "hold fast what is good, abstain from every form of evil" (1 Thessalonians 5:21-22).

Discontent?

In Edwards' fifth and final point he makes this plea:

> "And why can't we be contented with the divine oracles, that holy, pure Word of God, that we have in such abundance and such clearness, now since the canon of Scripture is completed? Why should we desire to have anything added to them by impulses from above? Why should not we rest in that standing rule that God has given to his church, which the Apostle teaches us is surer than a voice from heaven? And why should we desire to make the Scripture speak more to us than it does?"[11]

Believing in extra-biblical revelatory activity of the Spirit is not because of lack of contentment with Scripture. In fact, it is precisely because of what Scripture itself teaches concerning the activity of the Spirit that leads us to embrace so-called "impulses from above". I personally believe in the on-going revelatory activity of the Spirit precisely because I am unreservedly "contented" with the absolute truthfulness of everything Scripture says. I also contend that Edwards' objection is based on a false notion of what constitutes the "sufficiency" of Scripture (see above and my comments in response to Gaffin).

These may still strike some of you as rather formidable arguments against the idea I'm advocating in this book that God does indeed speak today. But as much as I admire Edwards, on this point I think he is in error. It isn't my purpose now to address in detail such arguments (although some may think that is precisely what I just did!). I only raised the objections as Edwards voiced them so that we would be aware of the opposition that often comes against the contemporary validity of revelatory gifts of the Spirit.

I do want to point out, however, that one thing characterizes all of Edwards' arguments: not one of them is biblical! That is to say, none of his points is derived from any explicit statement in Scripture. They are all based on supposed practical negative consequences or the fanatical behavior of people who from the beginning obviously had a deficient view of biblical authority and a low esteem for the canonical Word.

Before I leave this subject, a few other things may be said in response to the cessationist claim. First of all, careful study reveals that prophecy in the New Testament, unlike prophecy in the Old Testament, is not equal to Scripture in authority, but contains a mixture of infallible divine revelation with fallible human interpretation and application, and thus must be judged or evaluated in the light of the Bible. This is not the place for a detailed explanation of this view. If you desire such, I encourage you to read my chapter in the book *Are Miraculous Gifts for Today? Four Views*, ed. by Wayne Grudem (Grand Rapids: Zondervan, 1996) as well as Wayne Grudem's excellent book, *The Gift of Prophecy in the New Testament and Today* (Westchester: Crossway Books, 1988). I have also addressed some of Edwards' concerns in my book, *The Beginner's Guide to Spiritual Gifts* (Regal Books, 2002; see especially the chapter titled, "Who Said God Said?").

Second, we must continue to affirm that the Bible and the Bible alone is God's absolutely authoritative revelation to which all subjective impressions, prophetic insights and utterances must conform. The first assertion in my doctrinal statement for Enjoying God Ministries is unequivocal on this point: "We believe that only the sixty-six books of the Bible are the inspired, and therefore inerrant, Word of God. It is the final authority for all we believe and how we are to live." This is more than an abstract affirmation; it is a practical guideline that controls all we believe, do, and say.

Third, we should avoid prefacing our prophetic utterances with "Thus saith the Lord," a declaration which implies infallibility and morally obligatory revelation. The fact is, the Lord may well be speaking through the utterance. But that is something that is better not to assert on the front end but to determine after the fact, that is, after the "word" has been biblically evaluated.

Fourth, we must be biblically wise and extremely cautious in appealing to God's "voice" or using prophecy as a means for one person giving specific guidance to another person in the decision-making process (I address this at length in *The Beginner's Guide to Spiritual Gifts*).

And finally, as I said above, we need to be more precise about what we mean by the *sufficiency* of Scripture. What is the Bible sufficient *for*? I believe it is sufficient and perfectly adequate to provide us with every doctrine and ethical principle necessary for us to believe and behave as we should. But the doctrine of the sufficiency of the Bible is not meant to suggest that we don't need to hear from God or receive particular guidance in areas on which the Bible is silent. The close of the biblical canon marks the point at which the general principles of God's universal will are complete. All the doctrines, as well as all ethical principles, essential for the life of God's people have been revealed. Nothing further will be said by God to extend or expand or contradict them. The Bible establishes the theological and ethical boundaries of what God will ever say.

But guidance and revelation and wisdom by which we gain the knowledge of how to apply these principles and truths in the practical details and decisions of life are ongoing. When we listen to God we do not expect him to say anything doctrinally or ethically new. But we do expect him to speak to the situation in which we find ourselves with wisdom and direction and insight and encouragement in *living out* the truths he has *written in*.

The Centrality of Scripture

I know what some of you are thinking. "How can Sam so vigorously contend for the gift of prophecy and still say he believes in the centrality of Scripture?" Aside from the fact that if it weren't for the centrality of Scripture I wouldn't believe for a moment in the validity of prophecy, the answer to your question is an easy one.

Nothing I have written in this book should be taken as an indication that I have a low regard for Scripture or that I no longer value it as supreme in its divinely ordained role to provide guidance, counsel, truth, and stability for the Christian. A close look at an important Pauline text will help us work through this point.

In 2 Timothy 2:7, Paul provides his spiritual son with a crucial word of counsel: "Think over what I say, for the Lord will give you understanding in everything." This remarkable passage speaks both to the charismatic who may be inclined to unduly exalt extra-biblical revelation and to the cessationist who may be inclined to diminish it.

What I have to say, in light of what Paul said, may prove painful for both groups, but it is my charismatic friends whom I particularly have in mind. I want to address what I perceive to be the primary reason why some charismatics, particularly preachers and teachers, have neglected the written word of God. I'm tempted to call it *intellectual sloth,* but I'll settle for the less inflammatory term, *illuminism.*

Look carefully at Paul's words and note three things. First, the *command* "think over what I say" is a reference to Paul's prior instruction and exhortations to Timothy mentioned in 2 Timothy 1:13 ("Follow the pattern of the sound words that you have heard from me") and 2:1-2 ("You then, my child, be strengthened by the grace that is in Christ Jesus, and what you have heard from me in the presence of many witnesses entrust to faithful men who will be able to teach others also"). Second, there is a *promise* that "the Lord will give you understanding in everything". And third, we must not overlook the *relationship* between the command and the promise as indicated by the word "for".

A number of you reading this may feel a tension between the command to "think" and the promise of "illumination". The latter is so much easier, less demanding, and seemingly more "spiritual" than the former. Thus many of you use the promise as an excuse to ignore the command. People say: "If God is going to give me understanding in everything, I don't need to think. I only need to sit quietly in the prayer room or on a hillside in the cool of the day and wait until the Spirit illumines my heart or speaks prophetically to me." The result is all too often "insight" and "comprehension" that has nothing to do with Scripture and is often contradictory to it.

On any number of occasions in charismatic conferences or churches I have visited, I've heard the following: "God showed me something powerful the other day", only to discover that what God allegedly showed this person is not only absent from the Word but in explicit conflict with it. Why is this such a common phenomenon? I briefly answered this above, but let me expand on it a bit.

There's no way to avoid the fact that such an approach is easier. It purportedly provides the preacher or teacher with a shortcut to "truth" that eliminates the need for long hours of research and study and careful reflection on the text of Scripture. Related to this is the tendency toward anti-intellectualism in charismatic circles which accounts, at least in part, why those in that tradition are less inclined to attend seminary or to devote themselves to the study of Greek and Hebrew. There are certainly exceptions to this, as I noted in an earlier chapter. But the potential for an "immediate word from heaven" does not always make for a life dedicated to the written Word.

Also, as indicated, it seems more spiritual. "Wow, God spoke to you and told you what the truth is!" We easily fall prey to the notion that some-one who regularly hears from God is, for that reason, more loved of God or more highly favored or "filled" and "anointed" with the Spirit than the aver-age believer who patiently slugs it out in Scripture, line upon line.

Finally, and perhaps most important of all, we fail to note the sig-nificant causal relationship ("for") between the two elements in Paul's exhor-tation. Paul's point is that we are to think, study, and dig deeply into the Word "because" (or, "for") God will give understanding. In other words, illumina-tion is the fruit of investigation. The former doesn't preclude need of the lat-ter. The latter is the pathway to the former. Should we pray for divine illu-mination? Of course! Should we expect God to speak? Absolutely. But only as and after we have "thought" about what the text says.

The Spirit's ministry of illumination does not replace the human work of meditation on God's Word. Illumination comes through meditation. We can't afford to presume that the promise of divine light and understand-ing is given to everyone: "it is made to those who *think*."[12] Praying and think-ing are not two mutually exclusive options. The person who only thinks and does not pray is as bad and dangerous and unbalanced as the person who only prays and never thinks. Yes, God has promised to speak to us, to illu-mine our minds and spirits, to disclose and reveal the secrets of his heart and ways, but he promises to do this through and in response to our diligent devotion to studying and understanding the text.

I recently heard from a young man who described the leadership of his church as having adopted the position that what they need isn't informa-tion, but revelation. May I suggest that what we need is revelation about the information! We desperately need the Spirit to speak about the Word already spoken.

We should also take note of the delicate balance here between the sovereignty of God and human responsibility. Clearly Paul expected Timothy to exercise his cognitive powers, to apply himself to the things that Paul had spoken by inspiration of the Spirit, with complete confidence that in and through his obedience to that task God the Holy Spirit will speak and enlighten and convict and reveal his heart to us.

Cessationists are not exempt from criticism. Some are known for thinking that thinking precludes the need for God to speak. The inscrip-turated word is the only one that we should ever expect to receive. Some have virtually deified their minds. They have such a high opinion of their opinions that the voice of God needn't be heard. But Paul's point is that the purpose of thinking is to provide us with a framework within which the Spirit can speak understanding and bring additional insight into the text.

The Power of the Word

God has invested the biblical text with the power to change human lives and transform the experience of the church. If for no other reason we must think about, meditate upon, and study the Word.

For example, the Word of God is the means or instrument by which the Holy Spirit regenerates the human heart. That is to say, *the proclamation or communication of the Word is the catalyst for the inception of spiritual life*. The apostle Peter makes this clear in his first epistle: "Since you have been born again, not of perishable seed but of imperishable, through the living and abiding word of God; . . . And this word is the good news that was preached to you" (1 Peter 1:23,25; see also Romans 1:16-17; 10:14-15; 1 Corinthians 1:18-25). Observe that this "word" which brings life is a "*preached*" word!

The Word of God is the spring from which the waters of faith arise. Paul says in Romans 10:17 that "faith comes from hearing" and that hearing comes "by the word of Christ." Skepticism and doubt and anxious unbelief are suffocating the people of God. We desperately need faith and renewed confidence in every promise and purpose of God. But faith doesn't happen "willy-nilly" or appear miraculously out of thin air like manna from heaven. Faith comes only if and when we hear the word of Christ.

It is from or through the Scriptures that the Spirit imparts perseverance and encouragement. This is Paul's point in Romans 15:4, "For whatever was written in earlier times was written for our instruction, that through *perseverance and the encouragement of the Scriptures* we might have hope." So often we want to jump the chasm between our current discouragement and the promise of hope. What we fail to realize is that God has constructed a bridge, not a catapult, for his people. There is no easy way to be thrust across the valley of despair onto the mountain top of perseverance. It only comes if we are prepared to walk on the bridge of God's written and revealed Word. The fruit of the vine, in this case perseverance and encouragement, is ours only by laboring in the vineyard of God's inspired Word. There simply is no supernatural shortcut to endurance. We need a disciplined, systematic diet of the Word if we are going to fight successfully to persevere and not quit.

In a similar vein, Paul declares that it is from or through the Scriptures that joy and peace arise. He prays in Romans 15:13 that God would "fill you with all joy and peace *in believing*, so that by the power of the Holy Spirit you may abound in hope." We could render this any number of ways, all of which make the same point. It is only "as" you believe or "because" you believe or "in connection with" believing that these affections become yours. However we may choose to translate Paul's words, the point is that God will most assuredly *not* fill you abundantly with these affections if you *don't* believe.

Both joy and peace are therefore the fruit of *believing*, which in turn yields hope. But believe "what"? Belief is confidence placed in the truth of what God has revealed to us in Scripture about who he is and our relationship to him through Jesus. It is a Spirit-induced knowledge and delight in the person of God as revealed in Jesus, a confident assurance of the promises of God, and a joyful reliance on the power of God to grant us all that is necessary for life and godliness.

This is not some ethereal belief that lacks boundaries and substance. The consistent witness of Scripture is that our belief must fix itself in the foundational truths of divine revelation. We believe all and only what God has revealed to us in his Word. We earlier saw in Romans 10:17 and 15:4 that the Word of God is the effectual source of both faith and perseverance. As I said, these virtues don't fall like manna from heaven. They spring up from the soil of Scripture!

So, once again, how do these affections become ours? As with Paul, so too with us, it must begin with prayer, a heartfelt and persistent cry to God that the Holy Spirit would stir them up within, that he would kindle a flame of fascination and delight and satisfaction in God that no sin can rival. But this will avail on if we set our hearts and minds to explore deeply the revelation of God and all he is for us in Jesus as set forth in Scripture.

What this means is that "the fight for joy is the fight to see and believe Christ as more to be desired than the promises of sin. . . . We look to the Word, we ponder, and we plead with God that the eyes of our hearts would be opened to see the superior glory and joy."[13] And Paul's prayer here in v. 13 makes it clear that in this fight we are utterly dependent on the Spirit to make the promises of God more desirable to us than the promises of sin.

The problem is that people want joy, peace, and faith without believing, or at least without the hard work that true believing requires. They expect it as their "spiritual birthright". They pray for it. They are angry with God when it doesn't happen. But the Spirit, to a large extent, restricts his faith-awakening, joy-imparting, peace-producing ministry to the Christ-centered Word. This is what Jonathan Edwards had in mind when he spoke of "*laying ourselves in the way of allurement,*" i.e., taking steps to posture our lives in that place where the Spirit is most likely to energize faith: Scripture, the sacraments, worship, prayer, etc.

The Word of God also accounts for the on-going operation of the miraculous in the body of Christ. We read in Galatians 3:5, "Does he then, who provides you with the Spirit and works miracles among you, do it by the works of the Law, or by hearing with faith?" Let me make three observations about what Paul says here, each of which builds on the other:

First, it is God who continually and generously supplies you with the Spirit. Although you have already received the Spirit, there is a sense in which there is yet more! Second, this fresh supply of the Spirit finds expression in miracles. Third, and most important, at least for our purposes, the instrument God uses is the faith that we experience *upon hearing the Word of God!* When we hear the Word of God (in preaching and teaching and private study), our thoughts and hearts become God-centered; our focus is on his glory and thus our faith in his greatness expands and our confidence in his ability to work miracles deepens, all of which is the soil in which the seeds of the supernatural are sown. *Apart from the principles and truths of biblical texts, there will be little, long-lasting, Christ-exalting faith; and apart from such faith there can be no (or at best, few) miracles.*

It is the Word of God, expounded and explained and applied, that yields the fruit of sanctification and holiness in daily life. Consider the following, taking careful note of the italicized words.

> "And for this reason we also constantly thank God that when you received from us the word of God's message, you accepted it not as the word of men, but for what it really is, the word of God, *which also performs its work in you who believe*" (1 Thessalonians 2:13).

> "In pointing out these things to the brethren, you will be a good servant of Christ Jesus, *constantly nourished on the words of the faith and of the sound doctrine* which you have been following" (1 Timothy 4:6).

"Like newborn babes, long for the pure milk of the word, that *by it you may grow in respect to salvation*" (1 Peter 2:2).

"For the word of God is living and active and sharper than any two-edged sword, and piercing as far as the division of soul and spirit, of both joints and marrow, and able to judge the thoughts and intentions of the heart" (Hebrews 4:12).

The power of the Word of God is perhaps nowhere better seen than in Psalm 19. There we are told that "the law of the Lord is perfect, restoring the soul" (v. 7a). It renews, refreshes, and brings the soul back where it belongs. Moreover, "the testimony of the Lord is sure, making wise the simple" (v. 7b). In saying the Word is "sure" the psalmist means it is true in principle and verifiable in life's situations. It makes the simple "wise," i.e., the Bible takes the undiscerning and naïve and gullible person and makes him/her wise.

Yogi Berra is quoted as saying, "When I came to a fork in the road, I took it." If only it were so easy! But as John Piper reminds us, "Every fork in the road does not have a biblical arrow."[14] We need *wisdom* for decision-making. It comes from Scripture. The man or woman who is immersed in the Word is equipped to choose wisely where no explicit direction is found.

As if that were not enough, "the precepts of the Lord are right, rejoicing the heart" (v. 8a). In saying that his precepts are right or never wrong, we find the assurance that they always can be counted on to provide truth and accuracy. If your heart needs joy, and whose doesn't, dive into God's word. Immerse yourself in its refreshing, sin-killing, joy-energizing power.

"The commandment of the Lord is pure, enlightening the eyes" (v. 8b). As "pure" or "radiant" (NIV) the word of God is devoid of sin or malice or corrupting influence. From this it derives its capacity to bring understanding so that we can see how to live, what to do, and how to think.

It comes as no surprise, then, that the Word of God is what brings us satisfaction and joy and delight, so that we will not be enticed and tempted by the passing pleasures of sin. The psalmist thus concludes that,

"they (i.e., the laws, precepts, commandments of God's Word) are more desirable than gold, yes, than much fine gold; sweeter also than honey and the drippings of the honeycomb. Moreover, by them Thy servant is warned; in keeping them there is great reward" (vv. 10-11).

This same emphasis is found scattered throughout Psalm 119. Consider, for example, the following brief sampling, and ask yourself if such vivid and passionate language accurately describes your attitude toward the glory and power of God's Word:

"In the way of your testimonies *I delight as much as in all riches*" (v. 14).

"*I will delight* in your statutes" (v. 16).

"*My soul is consumed with longing* for your rules at all times" (v. 20).

"Your testimonies are my *delight*" (v. 24).

"Behold, *I long* for your precepts" (v. 40).

"for I find my *delight* in your commandments, *which I love*" (v. 47).

"The law of your mouth is *better to me than thousands of gold and silver pieces*" (v. 72).

"*Oh how I love your law!*" (v. 97).

"How *sweet* are your words to my taste, *sweeter than honey to my mouth!*" (v. 103).

"Your testimonies are my heritage forever, for they are *the joy of my heart*" (v. 111).

"Therefore *I love your commandments above gold, above fine gold*" (v. 127).

"*I rejoice* at your word like one who finds great spoil" (v. 162).

"My soul keeps your testimonies; *I love them exceedingly*" (v. 167).

Finally, and perhaps most important of all, the written and preached Word is the means by which the glory of God is revealed and imparted to those who listen with faith. This we see in 2 Corinthians. 4:3-6. There Paul declares that

"even if our gospel is veiled, it is veiled only to those who are perishing. In their case the god of this world has blinded the minds of the unbelievers, to keep them from seeing the light of the gospel of the glory of Christ, who is the image of God. For what we proclaim is not ourselves, but Jesus Christ as Lord, with ourselves as your servants for Jesus' sake. For God, who said, 'Let light shine out of darkness,' has shone in our hearts to give the light of the knowledge of the glory of God in the face of Jesus Christ."

Paul himself literally saw the glory of God revealed in the literal face of Jesus when he was encountered on the Damascus road. That which Paul saw, he now sets forth by means of "the truth" (v. 2) of the gospel addressed to the ears of his hearers (i.e., to the Corinthians, to you and me). When we by grace respond in faith, light from the glorified Christ shines into our darkened hearts (v. 6).

Don't miss this: *the glory of God is present in the proclamation of the gospel (4:4-6)!* This is why Paul is so appalled at the "peddling" (2:17) and "adulterating" (4:2) of the gospel by his opponents in Corinth. This is not a matter of mere words or a routine speech or a competitive attempt to appear more powerful or persuasive or verbally impressive than the other guy. The proclamation of the truth of the gospel is not entertainment. It is not a platform for a preacher to enhance his reputation or pad his pocketbook or impress people with his eloquence.

A preacher or teacher must never open the Scriptures flippantly or casually, as if setting forth the truths of the gospel were no different from any other form of communication. The same applies anytime anyone shares the gospel with a passing stranger in a restaurant or distributes a tract to a friend. Just think of it: when you speak or write or share the message of the cross, *"the light of the knowledge of the glory of God as revealed in the face of Jesus"* (v. 6) is shining forth. What an awesome calling we have! What an exquisite treasure we carry (4:7)!

---

[1] One of the primary difficulties with this view is that it requires us to believe, for example, that the anonymous disciples of Acts 19:1-7 and the four daughters of Philip in Acts 21:9, together with countless Christians in the churches at Thessalonica, Rome, Galatia, Ephesus, and Corinth, just to mention a few, all prophesied inspired and infallible revelatory words that contributed to the foundation of the church universal. If the spiritual gift of prophecy functioned as cessationists contend, would Paul have encouraged all Christians to zealously desire and pursue it, as we read in 1 Corinthians 14:1 and 39? I think not.

[2] Jonathan Edwards, *The Great Awakening*, edited by C. C. Goen (New Haven: Yale University Press, 1972), 432.

[3] Ibid., 432.

[4] John R. W. Stott, *The Epistles of John: An Introduction and Commentary* (Grand Rapids: Eerdmans, 1976), 153.

[5] I. Howard Marshall, *The Epistles of John* (Grand Rapids: Eerdmans, 1978), 208.

[6] Stott, *The Epistles of John*, 158.

[7] Edwards, *The Great Awakening*, 432.

[8] Ibid., 432-33.

[9] Ibid., 433.

[10] Sam Storms, *The Beginner's Guide to Spiritual Gifts* (Ventura: Regal Books, 2002), 105-118.

[11] Edwards, *The Great Awakening*, 434.

[12] John Piper, *Brothers, We are Not Professionals: A Plea to Pastors for Radical Ministry* (Nashville: Broadman & Holman Publishers, 2002), 79.

[13] Ibid., 105.

[14] John Piper, *Desiring God: Meditations of a Christian Hedonist* (Sisters, OR: Multnomah Publishers, 2003), 150.

Chapter Nine

✤

But Is Anybody Listening?

The God of the Bible is a speaking God. The whole of Scripture, from the Garden of Eden to the New Heavens and New Earth, is a record of God speaking in human history to his people. He spoke to Adam and Eve, to Noah, to Enoch, as well as to Abraham, Moses, Samuel, Solomon, and a seemingly endless list of men and women in the Old Testament.

God's voice was heard frequently in the New Testament as well. In the book of Acts alone we find God speaking on the day of Pentecost, to Philip (Acts 8), to Paul (Acts 9), to Peter and Cornelius (Acts 10), to prophets in Antioch (Acts 13), to disciples of John the Baptist (Acts 19), to the four unmarried daughters of Philip (Acts 21), just to mention a few.

I assume you agree with me that that the principal way God speaks to us is through the written word of the Bible. This is the primary revelation of God's voice. This is the repository of his infallible and always authoritative will. The Holy Spirit enlightens and convicts and persuades us concerning its meaning and application to our lives. This was the point I labored to make from 2 Timothy 2:7 in the previous chapter. No alleged revelation, no purported voice, no insight or impression from God will *ever* conflict with the revelation of Scripture. If it does, it isn't God speaking.

But there are several other ways in which God communicates with his people. For example, God has spoken audibly on several occasions and, I believe, may still do so today (although quite rarely). Among those who heard the audible voice of God are Abraham (Genesis 22:1-2,10-12), Moses (Exodus 3:3-6), the nation Israel (Deuteronomy 5:22-24), Samuel (1 Samuel 3:1-10), Elijah (1 Kings 19:11-13), John the Baptist (at the baptism of Jesus in Matthew 3:16-17), Peter, James, and John (Matthew 17:5-6; cf. 2 Peter 1:17-18), the general public (John 12:27-30), Paul (Acts 9:3-7; 23:11), Peter (Acts 10:9-16), and John (Revelation 1:9-12).

God also speaks to us through angelic messengers, as he did to Joshua (Joshua 5:13-15), Samson's parents (Judges 13), Isaiah (Isaiah 6:6-13), Daniel (Daniel 9:20-27), Zacharias (Luke 1), Mary (Luke 1), Philip (Acts 8:26), Peter (Acts 5:19-20), and others (see esp. Hebrews 13:1). God also communicates through dreams (Genesis 20:3; 37; Daniel 2,4,7; Matthew 1,2; Acts 2,10) and visions (e.g., Numbers 12:6; Daniel 10:1-9; Acts 2:17; 9:10-12; 10:1-6; 10:9-16; 16:9-10; 18:9-10; 22:17-18), and even through creation itself (Psalms 19, 104; Romans 1:18ff.).

My Calvinistic friends would happily acknowledge that God spoke often and in a variety of ways until the death of the last apostle. But most of them insist that with the close of the biblical canon, God's voice has fallen silent. Whatever he needs to say, he has already said. Whatever we need to hear, we can find in the words of the inspired biblical text. If it can legitimately be said that God speaks today it is only in the sense that his voice is alive and fresh and always relevant in the words of Holy Scripture. I addressed this issue in the previous chapter, so I won't revisit it now, other than to say that this is the primary point of contention that perpetuates the divisions between evangelical cessationists and evangelical charismatics.

Gracious Incursions into our Souls

In this chapter I want us to consider whether God, today, might also speak directly into the heart or mind or spirit of his people through what Dallas Willard calls "gracious incursions into our souls."[1] I want to suggest that God puts words, phrases, sentences, images and the like into our minds, *stamped with the indelible print of his voice*. Although undeniably subjective and occasionally slippery, "impressions" are a valid means of divine communication in our heart.

In spite of the inescapable "subjectivity" of impressions, I believe we may justifiably expect that when God wants to tell us something, he will not be unduly obtuse. His purpose isn't to mislead or confuse but to guide us clearly and carefully. Whether through thoughts or perceptions that we intuitively recognize could only come from him, he makes his heart known. When God communicates he does so with specific information, often times in propositional utterances.

People in biblical times were not left to wonder about "hunches" or "impulses" or "feelings". If God's voice is occasionally "vague" it is to awaken us from slumber or perhaps alert us to our presumptuous attitude, or perhaps challenge us to press into his heart ever more intensely. I agree with Willard who said, "It is to be expected . . . that *if* there is something He would have us know, He will be both able and willing and will in fact plainly communicate it to us, if we are but open and prepared by our experience to hear and obey."[2] Even in the case of visions, dreams, and trances, there is *verbal* communication. God "guides not as we might guide a child by the hand or a horse by the reins, but through the instructions he speaks – instructions that we hear and then act upon."[3]

What kinds of things does God say?

Most of the directives of the Holy Spirit are practical, suggesting what to do, where to go, and with whom to speak. They are *not* ethical principles. The rules and regulations that bind our conscience and carry absolute and universal moral authority for the Christian are provided only in Scripture. Whereas the Spirit will often lead us in the daily application of biblical principles or how to wisely navigate the confusing waters of human relationships, he will *not* dictate new laws of right and wrong. Rather they are words that concern the "here and now" of people and their actions; often divine directives concerning ways in which God's people are to fulfill the mandate to preach the gospel to all nations (what might be called "divine appointments").

In my own case the voice of God has pierced my heart with power when I was in need of conviction concerning sin that I could not, or would not, see. I will never forget one occasion when we were still living in Ardmore, Oklahoma. Ann and I were not communicating well with each other and *it was all my fault* (seriously). But I couldn't see it. I rationalized my behavior, saying to myself: "I'm not disobeying Scripture. There's nothing intrinsically wrong with what I'm doing."

Suddenly, and without warning, there erupted in my brain this simple question: "But does it honor her?" Like a bolt from the blue, the Spirit had spoken. My mind immediately turned to Peter's counsel in 1 Peter 3:7 that husbands live with their wives in an understanding way and "honor" them as fellow-heirs of the grace of life. No one had to convince me that God had spoken. I never argued with myself about the authenticity or origin of this word. The clarity of conviction overwhelmed and subdued any potential protest.

Permit me to share another incident. I won't go into detail other than to say that I had allowed my selfish aspirations for promotion and recognition to cloud my passion for Jesus. I was oblivious to it until one unforgettable night. As I lay awake, pondering the source of my self-imposed misery, suddenly, and again without warning, the Spirit employed the lyrics of a song I had been repeatedly playing in the tape deck (these were pre-CD days!) of my car. Like a laser beam of merciful conviction, my mind was set alight with the words: "My own ambition, quenching first love's flame." Ouch! There was no use contending with God. His word pierced and wounded my soul, and then just as quickly healed it (but only after I repented!).

Who Will Hear?

Whereas what I said in Part One of this study may sound remarkable, it is important to remember that one doesn't have to *be* remarkable to hear God's voice. God doesn't speak merely to alleged superstars or supersaints. He speaks to ordinary believers who are exceptional only by virtue of their insatiable hunger for him. So, to what *kind* of people does God speak?

A quick glance at the book of Acts reveals that he speaks not only to apostles but to average Christians like Ananias (Acts 9), to deacons like Stephen (Acts 6-7) and Phillip (Acts 8), to unsaved Gentiles like Cornelius (Acts 10), to unnamed believers in congregations like the one in Antioch (Acts 13), to Phillip's four unmarried daughters (Acts 21), and to elders at the church in Jerusalem (Acts 15), just to mention a few examples.

This may well be the biggest and most formidable obstacle to Christian people hearing the voice of God today. They labor under the stifling misconception that there are certain individuals of high calling and superior intellect or perhaps greater moral achievement whom God, because of their accomplishments, favors with the capacity to hear him more readily. If nothing else, often one encounters the view that only ordained clergymen hear God's voice, as if God is more inclined to speak to those with a clerical collar or a diploma hanging on the wall. In light of this, let me mention a few foundational principles on how to hear God's voice.

How to Hear

First of all, *it is doubtful you will hear God's voice if you don't believe he is speaking.* Many do not hear God, not because he isn't speaking, but because of their worldview. Our worldview, that is to say, our presuppositions and theological assumptions about the nature of reality, largely determines what we experience, what we allow ourselves to see, hear, understand, even what we are willing to acknowledge as **real**. So, when I talk about worldviews I don't mean "looking at" but "looking through". In other words, your world view isn't so much *what* you see but *how* you see.

If your spiritual worldview rules out the likelihood of God speaking today outside the Bible, you will, in all probability, dismiss his voice as something or someone other than God. Your instinctive reaction will be to write it off as your own imagination or, worse still, Satan. And sometimes that may well be true. How to know the difference between God and other voices is something I'll take up later on. Here my point is simply that if you are skeptical about God's speaking, you will always be inclined to reject the authenticity of what you think is his voice. That is why it's so important to embrace a biblical worldview in which at the very heart of reality is a God who communicates regularly with his people.

Second, *God is more inclined to speak when he knows he is being heard. That is to say, God speaks primarily to those who are willing to listen.* This principle is based on a truth found repeatedly in Scripture, namely, that the hungry are those who get filled; the thirsty are those who receive drink; those who seek, find; those who pursue, obtain (see Jeremiah 29:13; Matthew 5:6; Psalm 25:4-5; Isaiah 30:18-19; 40:31; Joshua 5:14).

I believe God would say to us: "If you are content to live without hearing my voice, you will." In other words, if you are O.K. with a life of silence, God will, in all likelihood, leave you to it. This isn't an issue of God loving one of his children more than others. But the fact remains that God has suspended certain blessings on the persistent pursuit and persevering prayers of his children. If we do not have, it is often times simply because we do not ask (James 4:2).

Third, *hearing God's voice is less dependent on your abilities than on your affections.* What I mean is that God is far more concerned with the depth of your commitment than he is with the diplomas on your wall. Earnest desire, not educational achievement, is of greatest value to him. This isn't to belittle the mind or to suggest that ignorance is a virtue. It simply means that

God doesn't suspend his communication with us on how many books we've either read or written!

His question to us is: "Are you willing?" not "Are you able?" Or again, God is quick to speak to those who are quick to obey. Most of us are inclined to protest: "But *who am I* that God should speak to *me*? I've never accomplished much for the kingdom. My gifts are few and my talents unimpressive."

We assume that God speaks only to special people, unique people, extraordinarily endowed people, people with spectacular gifts, people with ecclesiastical authority, people with power and prestige and influence. We tend to think being *human* debars us from hearing God: we are too frail, too fragile, too fickle, too sinful, too weak. We don't have beauty or position; we can't speak well in public; our education is minimal, and therefore God wouldn't speak to us. Nothing could be farther from the truth.

In fact, numerous individuals in the Bible to whom God spoke appealed to their inadequacy and unworthiness. Moses (Exodus 4:10-14; 3:11) insisted that he was a poor communicator and was hardly the sort of person God would want to represent him before Pharaoh, and Gideon (Judges 6:14-17) argued that he was the least among all those in the least of all the tribes of Israel.

The issue, then, is not your native talents or eloquence or education. The only thing that ultimately matters is whether or not your heart is inclined to say yes to what God asks you to do. "So if you find yourself in the position of the one who can honestly say, 'God has never spoken to me,' then you might ask: 'Why *should* God speak to *me*? What am I doing in life that would make His speaking to me a reasonable thing for Him to do?'"[4] As Willard goes on to say,

> "Perhaps we do not hear the voice [of God] because we don't expect to hear it. But perhaps we don't expect it because we know that we fully intend to run our lives on our own and never seriously considered anything else. The voice of God would therefore be an unwelcome intrusion into our plans. By contrast, we expect the great ones in The Way of Christ to hear that voice just because we see their lives wholly given up to doing what God wants."[5]

I think Willard's point is that the question, "How do I hear the voice of God?" needs to be replaced by the question, "What would I *do* if I heard it?" Are you truly open to the extent to which the voice of God might disturb your plans? Are you prepared to follow the Father's faintest whisper, no matter where it leads? If not, it's unlikely you will ever hear it.

Finally, and most important of all, *the humble hear* (see Psalm 25:9; Isaiah 57:15; 66:1-2; James 4:6; 1 Peter 5:5-6; and especially Numbers 12:1ff.) Why is humility or meekness so appealing to God and so conducive to hearing him speak? Because humility is simply another way of describing preference for or submission to God's will. The proud want *their* way. The humble want *God's* way. The proud will exploit God's voice for their own glory, to exalt themselves in the eyes of others. The humble use it for God's glory. The proud man is so full of himself that there is little room for God. He is so enamored with what others say *about* him that he can't hear what God says *to* him.

Look with me at what has to be one of the most intriguing and important texts in all of Scripture.

> "For thus says the high and exalted One who lives forever, whose name is Holy, 'I dwell in a high and holy place, and also with the contrite and lowly of spirit in order to revive the spirit of the lowly and to revive the heart of the contrite" (Isaiah 57:15).

Why is it intriguing? Because it is simultaneously one of the most encouraging verses and one of the most terrifying. This verse is good news to some and terrifying to others. Here is why.

Who is this God of whom Isaiah speaks? What is he like? He is exalted! Transcendent! Eternal! Holy! Where does he live? In a high and holy place. But he also lives with the contrite and lowly of spirit, in other words, with the humble. The humble heart is God's home. He dwells with, blesses, speaks to, heals, encourages, upholds, and grants power to the humble of heart. That is why this is one of the most encouraging verses in all of Scripture.

But it is also one of the most terrifying verses in all of Scripture. For if God dwells with the humble, he departs from the proud. If God draws near to the lowly in spirit, he withdraws from the haughty and arrogant. If he blesses those who go low, his disfavor rests on those who lift themselves up. God will have nothing to do with proud, self-reliant, self-sufficient, self-promoting, self-congratulatory, self-aggrandizing men and women. If he is present and intimate with the humble, he is absent from the proud. "God opposes the proud, but gives grace to the humble" (James 4:6; 1 Peter 5:5). Try to envision your most powerful enemies, the most aggressive opposition you've faced, the most imposing obstacles you've had to confront . . . they are nothing in comparison with the infinite energy and power of God! You do **not** want God to be in opposition to you.

If that isn't clear enough, listen to the wisdom of Solomon in Proverbs 16:5 – "Everyone who is proud in heart is an abomination to the Lord; assuredly he will not be unpunished." We have no greater enemy than pride. It is the mortal enemy of our souls. It will deafen our ears to the voice of God. It will harden our hearts to his loving presence. If we coddle it, toy with it, nourish it, it will eat us alive. It is the mortal enemy of all that God promises to us in his word. The sure and certain way to go down in God's eyes is to go up in your own.

What is Pride?

A warning like that is only effective if we know what to look for. So let me briefly say a word about the characteristics of pride.

First of all, the proud person is a theological know-it-all who can't be taught. He's simply not open to instruction from others. His "show" of interest in what is said by others is just that, a show, a public performance. If he offers an interested response it is often patronizing at best. He or she is unteachable and uncorrectable. The proud heart says, "I've arrived. I've already been where these other people are only now beginning to go. I'm here to show them how it's done. They're mere babes. I'm an adult."

Pride also shows itself in a quickness to judge and to speak cynically of the sins and shortcomings of others, often with levity or flippancy. The humble Christian will either be silent about the sins of others or speak of them with grief, pity, and a "There, but for the grace of God, go I."

The prideful person is obsessed with comparisons, always measuring himself/herself against others. The proud person finds his identity in relation to someone he thinks of as lesser (which encompasses just about everyone). The humble person finds his identity in relation to someone he knows is greater: Jesus!

Pride invariably leads to inflexibility. After all, if you consider yourself an expert and others as mere rookies, what need is there for you to change? The humble person is pliable and flexible, except where sin or duty are in view.

Pride leads to separatism: "If I'm a notch above these others, fellow-shipping with them will only drag me down. They are beneath my dignity and unworthy of my time." The truly humble person cherishes unity.

The proud person is self-defensive, especially when it is suggested he might be proud! When persecuted or crossed or slandered or attacked, the proud person is angrily defensive of his actions and largely oblivious to all personal failures.

Perhaps the worst thing about pride is how easily it comes to the human soul. Humility, on the other hand, is hard to find. It isn't lurking around the corner, waiting to pounce on you unawares. It probably won't be found in your office or school, and it's often in short supply even in the church. Don't bother checking out the self-help section at Barnes & Noble or tuning in to a TV talk show. You won't find it.

The world, flesh, and the devil have conspired to conceal humility from us and to mock it should it ever appear. Nothing is more contrary to our natural instincts than humility. Humility doesn't come naturally. It isn't produced in us like the liver secretes bile or the way eyes produce tears or the top of our heads sprout hair. Our hearts do not and will not produce humility except insofar as Jesus Christ is supreme in every aspect of our lives. *Only to the degree that the supremacy of Jesus Christ is our pre-eminent value and his glory our all-consuming pursuit will humility ever find its proper place in our souls.* Humility doesn't bubble up from deep within. It's not like breathing or blinking our eyes or sneezing. Humility is as contrary to our nature as goodness is to the devil or evil is to God.

Again, the point of this brief excursus on pride is simply to say with as great clarity and forcefulness as possible: *the humble hear God.*

How to Know It Is God

One question on everyone's mind when this sort of thing happens is, "How can I be sure that it's God I'm hearing and not my own imagination run wild? How can I know the difference between the voice of the Shepherd and the voice of Satan?"

Before I answer that question there is one caution that should be issued. It would be easy, but wrongheaded, for people to walk away with what might be called the "Message-a-Minute" view of divine guidance. "On this view God is either telling you what to do at every turn of the road, or He is willing and available to tell you if you only would ask Him."[6] God does not want you to be afraid or hesitant to use your mind and common sense. It is dangerous to demand supernatural intervention when God has already provided you with sufficient wisdom and understanding, together with his written word, to make a decision. We must also be careful not to think that guidance by these latter means is sub-spiritual or reserved only for those believers whose faith is weak or whose maturity is second-rate.

So what, then, are we to do when we *think* God has chosen to speak in a more overt and supernatural way? Are there principles that will help us discern the voice of the Lord? Yes.

There are several key indicators we need to be aware of. We are not to swallow gullibly everything that purports to be the word of the Lord, but must always test and evaluate prophetic utterances, even as the Scriptures instruct us to do (cf. 1 Corinthians 14:29; 1 Thessalonians 5:19-21). Let me briefly mention six indicators or tests that will help us distinguish the voice of God from that of Satan or your flesh.

What Saith the Scriptures?

First of all, anything God says outside of Scripture will always conform with what he has already said inside of Scripture. The voice of God within your heart will never, ever lead you to diminish the authority of Scripture or speak in such a way as to lead you to disregard its teachings. "The Holy Spirit will not invent things," observes Klaus Bockmuehl; "his teaching will always be identical in substance with the teaching of Jesus. This is an important clue for determining all inspiration and revelation that is truly of the Spirit. It will always be true to, and compatible with, Christ's own teaching in Scripture."[7] As far as Jesus was concerned, "It is written" brought an immediate end to every argument. No one could appeal to overturn the verdict of scripture for that would be to appeal against the judgment of God himself. Certainly, if it was good enough for Jesus, it ought to be good enough for us!

We need to think more clearly about the way Scripture functions in judging purported revelatory words. If a man claims that he has "heard" God approve of his extra-marital affair, one need only cite the seventh commandment, "You shall not commit adultery" (Exodus 20:14). A friend of mine related to me an incident in which an acquaintance of his believed God was directing him to leave his church and become an active member of The Way International, a sect that explicitly denied the deity of Jesus Christ. Again, this sort of alleged "divine guidance" is readily exposed by a quick and decisive appeal to the overwhelming biblical witness to the deity of our Lord. But neither of these examples (or those similar to them) is meant to suggest that in the *absence* of an explicit biblical text addressing your situation you should immediately conclude that you have truly heard the voice of God.

One must also consider the ethical and theological principles of Scripture that are often times less than explicit. There may not be a specific text that directly addresses your circumstances but there may well be applicable, though unexpressed, truths apart from which the passage would otherwise make no sense. One thinks of the many issues in bio-medical ethics today that appear to have little, if any, background in the biblical text. I know of no text that explicitly addresses such thorny matters as stem cell research or *in vitro* fertilization or even certain cases of so-called euthanasia. But that does not mean the Bible provides no guidance at all concerning the moral status of these practices. The meaning of the image of God in man, the inception and value of human life, and other such concepts are indirectly addressed or implicitly assumed, from which valid and morally binding obligations can be legitimately deduced.

We should also search Scripture for patterns in the way God deals with his people, as well as either the presence or absence of historical precedents to aid us in determining if what we think God may have spoken is consistent with how he has interacted with men and women in past days. A person may believe that God has prophetically confirmed a career choice only to discover from a deeper study of the written word that it would be inconsistent with a particular divine attribute. In other words, the God who is revealed in Scripture simply is not the sort of God who would lead a person into a particular vocation, even though that vocation may be unknown to the biblical author because entirely unique to the twenty-first century.

My point here is simply that the Scriptures are far more capable of providing the standards, principles, and guidelines essential for judging the validity of purported revelatory words than most people imagine. I suspect that a basic familiarity with the book of Proverbs alone would go a long way in providing the necessary practical insight to determine if one has truly heard the voice of God.

What I'm proposing may well require a more intense, in-depth analysis of the biblical text than that to which many believers are accustomed. Perhaps the common fear that prophetic revelation is dangerous reflects how pervasive biblical and theological illiteracy has become in the contemporary church. I'm not saying that the reality of extra-biblical revelation poses no challenge, but neither should we reject it out of hand simply because some fear that it would cast us adrift on the sea of subjectivity, helplessly beholden to whatever self-proclaimed prophets declare is the word of the Lord. I have far too much confidence in the depth and clarity of biblical revelation and the wide-ranging scope of its wisdom to give up so easily.

The Will to do God's Will

A second guideline in hearing God's voice is obedience. In John 7:16-17 we read that "Jesus answered them, [saying], 'My teaching is not Mine but his who sent Me. If anyone's will is to do God's will, he will know whether the teaching is from God, or whether I am speaking on my own authority'" (John 7:16-17). The point is that when our lives are attuned to the purposes of God, when our wills are committed and submissive to his will, the Holy Spirit produces in our hearts a sensitivity to his voice. We will feel an intuitive revulsion against anything opposed to him or that does not proceed from him. In other words, *doing leads to knowing*. This is why Jesus could hear the Father so well, for as He said, "I always do the things that are pleasing to Him" (John 8:29).

The more by the grace of God we obey the will of God, the more the nature of God is formed in our souls. And, thus, the more like God we become the more in sync will our hearts be to his voice. Like is attracted to like. To the degree that we are at moral and spiritual odds with God we are less likely to discern the "sound" of his voice. But when the impulse of our will harmonizes with his, or when the passions of our soul are aligned with the passions of his, our capacity to hear him will increase and the potential for deception diminishes.

That Sounds Familiar

Thirdly, experience is a helpful, though not infallible, indicator. When one first hears God's voice he/she may not recognize it. But after repeated experience, through trial and error, we come to discern the familiar way in which God speaks. God's voice is *self-authenticating*. When you hear it, it has the "feel" of God. There is a serene authority to his voice. God's voice bears within itself the marks of its divine origin.

A fourth indicator of whether or not it is God speaking is the quality of what is said. We respond to the voice of another person by taking note of its quality, whether it be high or low, its tone, style, speed, accent, spirit (passionate or cold, empathetic or stiff, frightening or reassuring), etc. The quality or spirit or tone of God's voice will be unmistakably characterized by peacefulness, confidence, and joy. It will be reassuring, filled with love and goodness. God's voice does not threaten or intimidate. He promises and persuades and woos. God doesn't drive us; he leads. God's voice doesn't tear down with critical words that bite and belittle and destroy. He speaks as a tender father who loves and cherishes and protects and heals. In other words, God never speaks out of character! What he says is always a perfect reflection of who he is.

This is another reason why the study and memorization of Scripture must be foundational to a life of intimacy with God. As our knowledge of God and his ways deepens, so does our ability to know if he's the one talking! I've been married thirty-three years to Ann and I feel I know her pretty well. There are things I'm convinced she would never say. There are requests of me she'll never make. There are patterns in her voice I instinctively recognize. Since she and I are both human, we aren't beyond making mistakes about each other. But the likelihood of my intuitively knowing her heart and desires and passions far exceeds what I might know of an enemy or complete stranger.

This is also one way by which we can differentiate between *conviction* that comes from the Holy Spirit and *condemnation* that comes from the Enemy. The former is usually definite and highlights the specific sin or issue that must be addressed. The Lord will tell you exactly what you've done. Satan's condemnation, on the other hand, is typically indefinite and vague and fuzzy. You feel guilty but can't identify any specific sin that accounts for it. There is a sense of dread that descends on your soul, but you can't put your finger on why.

Furthermore, conviction by the Spirit is generally recognizable. It will typically be something you have failed to confess, usually from the immediate past, that you know has not been dealt with. Condemnation, on the other hand, is elusive. If you can pinpoint it, it often turns out to be something for which you long ago received forgiveness. Lastly, conviction by the Spirit is attended with a definite solution and the assurance of mercy. God never convicts us without providing hope by directing our hearts to the finality and sufficiency of the cross. When we obey, we experience relief from the pain and guilt. With condemnation comes despair. If a solution is offered, it is usually irrational and unscriptural. The pain in our soul only intensifies.

I once heard someone say that God's voice will alert you to your depravity without belittling or destroying your dignity. Satan's voice, on the other hand, will insist that because of your depravity you have no dignity.

The Community of Faith

The fifth aide in discerning God's voice is the principle of community. What do the wise and mature men and women in your church say regarding what you think you've heard? People who are seasoned veterans of the Christian life as well as knowledgeable in the Scriptures should always be consulted. I'm not suggesting they are infallible or that you need always take their advice. But older and more experienced believers who themselves have struggled to develop spiritual discernment are an indispensable resource that only the arrogant and foolish will ignore.

Recently I received a phone call from a close friend who was faced with a pastoral crisis of sorts. One of the men in his home group believed he had heard God tell him that a young girl in the church was going to die of cancer. His immediate response should have been to take this "word" to the Elders of the church and process with them in prayer whether this was genuinely a "word of knowledge" or an unfounded fear that owed its origin to something other than God. Instead, he impetuously called the young girl, even by-passing her mother and father, and warned her of what he was certain was to come. As you can well imagine, it was a disastrous and emotionally devastating decision.

It's precisely events such as this that reinforce in the minds of many cessationists that they are right about rejecting claims to God speaking beyond the written text. But again, abuse is no excuse for disuse. Abuse should lead to correction, not prohibition. What we should learn from such unfortunate occurrences is the importance of "processing prophecy" through the community of faith. There is spiritual safety in numbers and the collective wisdom of the body of Christ.

The Fruit of the Spirit

Sixth, and finally, what are the consequences of what you have heard? What is the moral harvest it has produced? Does it arouse humility or pride? Does it provoke sacrifice or selfishness? Does it stimulate gratitude or presumption? Does it increase love for Jesus or breed indifference? Does it turn you from self to God or from God to self? In sum, test every voice by the tendency it has to produce and prolong the fruit of the Spirit in your life.

This is actually one of the helpful ways in which we discern true prophecy from false. Paul says in 1 Corinthians 14:3 that "the one who prophesies speaks to people for their upbuilding and encouragement and consolation." If what someone passes off as "prophecy" consistently tears down and discourages and disregards the welfare of the one for whom it is allegedly intended, you are well within your rights to question whether the purported "revelation" came from God.

Perhaps these criteria for discerning the voice of God are not enough for you. Perhaps you regard the issue as too subjective and slippery. Your tendency is to say: "When I am *absolutely certain* that it is God speaking to me, then I will listen." But you cannot make infallibility a condition for listening to God. If you do, you will never hear him. Communication is unavoidably fallible, especially when one of the parties involved is weak and sinful. Even the infallibility of the speaker (God) does not guarantee the infallibility of the hearer (us).

Three Suggestions

If hearing God speak continues to be a struggle for you, don't give up. Hear first the voice of God in Scripture and heed its counsel. Then do three things.

First of all, *be silent*. Perhaps one of the reasons you don't hear God speak is that you yourself never stop talking! By "silence", however, I don't mean utter passivity. Rather, sit quietly and meditate on the word of God. God's advice to Joshua was that he "meditate on it [the written Law] day and night, so that you may be careful to do according to all that is written in it; for then you will make your way prosperous, and then you will have success" (Joshua 1:8).

As the psalmist said, "I will ponder all your work, and meditate on your mighty deeds" (Psalm 77:12; cf. Psalm 119:97-100). And again, "I remember the days of old; I meditate on all that you have done; I ponder the work of your hands" (Psalm 143:5).

A second word of advice is: *be patient.* "Our soul waits for the Lord; he is our help and our shield" (Psalm 33:20). Yet again the psalmist exhorts himself, saying, "For God alone, O my soul, wait in silence, for my hope is from him" (Psalm 62:5; cf. Isaiah 40:31).

Finally, *be confident.* After all, it is not a stingy, mute taskmaster to whom you cry, whose voice you long to hear. It is your Heavenly Father who delights in doing good things for his people. After exhorting his followers to persevere in prayer (Luke 11:5-10), Jesus drives home his point with an illustration bolstered by infallible logic: "What father among you, if his son asks for a fish, will instead of a fish give him a serpent; or if he asks for an egg, will give him a scorpion? If you then, who are evil, know how to give good gifts to your children, how much more will the heavenly Father give the Holy Spirit to those who ask him!" (Luke 11:11-13).

Some Cautions[8]

Let me conclude with a few words of caution regarding how prophecy is *not* to be used.

First of all, avoid using prophecy to establish doctrines or practices that lack explicit biblical support. The Bible is the final and all-sufficient treasury of every doctrine or theological truth that God will ever give. Neither should we expect new ethical principles through prophetic ministry. What is right and what is wrong has been finally and forever settled in the written Word of God.

Second, don't appeal to prophecy to set behavioral standards on secondary issues. Be wary of those who claim to know whether or not it is "God's will" that Christians attend movies or drink wine or play pool or engage in other activities not explicitly commanded or prohibited in Scripture.

Third, avoid using prophecy to disclose negative or excessively critical information in public. Remember that, according to 1 Corinthians 14:3, prophecy is designed to encourage, edify and console people in the church. It is not its purpose to humiliate or embarrass them.

Fourth, be careful before you yield governmental authority in the church to those who have the gift of prophecy. By all means listen to them! Seek their counsel and insight. But at the same time remember that church leadership is the responsibility of the Elders. The New Testament doesn't say "Be subject to the prophets" but rather "Be subject to the Elders" (1 Peter 5:5; Hebrews 13:17). Paul didn't go from city to city to ordain or appoint prophets, but Elders (Acts 14:23; 20:17; 1 Timothy 5:17; 1 Pt. 5:2; Titus 1:5). Whereas it's good that some Elders/Pastors are prophetically gifted, that alone does not qualify them for office. Elders are to be "able to *teach* " (1 Timothy 3:2), not necessarily able to prophesy.

Fifth, be cautious about excessive dependence on prophetic words for making routine, daily decisions in life.[9] There are certainly exceptions to this "rule", as Paul's words in Galatians 6:1-2 would indicate (cf. also his movements in Acts 16). Typically, though, Paul emphasizes the importance of "reckoning" with the circumstances of whatever situation one is facing. Consider the needs of people, the principles of Scripture, and seek the counsel of those who have a track record of wisdom (see Philippians 2:25; 1 Corinthians 6:5).

Concerning his travel plans, Paul writes, "And if it is fitting for me to go also, they will go with me" (1 Corinthians 16:4). Here Paul will make his decision based on a sober evaluation of what is *fitting* or *advisable* in view of the circumstances and what he feels would please God. Of course, nothing he says rules out the possibility that prophetic insight could play a role. In other texts Paul appeals to "knowledge," "discernment," and "spiritual wisdom and understanding" (Philippians 1:9-10a; Colossians 1:9) as essential in the decision-making process. Certainly, revelatory insight from the Lord can be crucial in such deliberation, but God does not want us to be paralyzed in its absence.

Finally, resist the pressure to prophesy in the absence of a divine revelation. Prophetically gifted people are under constant pressure to produce on demand. "I need a word from God, and I need it now," is not an uncommon thing heard by those in prophetic ministry. At all costs, resist the temptation to speak when God is silent. Some of the most severe denunciations and warnings of judgment are reserved for those who claim to speak for God, but don't (see Ezekiel 13:1-9; Jeremiah 23:25-32).

Zealous for Prophecy

I've often been asked, "What should be done when people begin to grow in their zeal for spiritual gifts like prophecy? What should be said when people are increasingly hungry for the manifestation of the Spirit's power? What should our response be when Christians display a persistent and intense desire for the supernatural work of the Spirit in their lives and in the life of the church?"

If you listen closely, you will detect behind that question a measure of fear. There is concern that people who yearn for the ministry and power of the Spirit are turning soft on doctrine or may be inclined to neglect spiritual disciplines, or perhaps they long for the miraculous as an excuse for ignoring Bible study and evangelism and prayer.

How do you think the apostle Paul would respond to such a question, especially if the people who have this desire for spiritual gifts have already shown themselves to be somewhat immature? I want us to think about this in the light of what Paul said to the Christians in Corinth. To a body of believers given to excess and immaturity, Paul said: "Pursue love, and earnestly desire the spiritual gifts, especially that you may prophesy."

So let me now respond to this concern that perhaps many of you have by articulating three principles and then asking one question.

First, *we must begin by saying without hesitation that character always takes precedence over gifting.* This isn't to diminish the importance of the Spirit's gifts. It is simply to point out that the fruit of the Spirit is pre-eminent. Gifts are not the goal, but rather the means by which we attain the goal of a transformed heart and a Christ-like life. The problem in Corinth, and in many churches today, is that people were exercising the Spirit's gifts in the absence of character. But *power is not necessarily a measure of piety* (cf. 1 Corinthians 13:1ff.).

Failure to remember this first principle results in a tendency to exempt gifted people from ordinary responsibilities and biblical obligations or to hold them to a different (often lower) standard of accountability. The mistake, often a fatal one, is thinking that anyone so extraordinarily gifted must be unusually close to God, invulnerable to temptation, so full of the Spirit as to be beyond the power of the flesh.

But we would do well to remember the experience of the apostle Paul himself. He experienced what may well have been the greatest "power encounter" in the history of the church. In 2 Corinthians 12 he describes his translation into the third heaven where he heard and saw things that he was forbidden to disclose. It's hard to imagine a more stunning and breathtaking revelatory experience than that. Yet, immediately on his "return" he felt pride and self-importance and elitism rising in his soul. Far from eradicating sin from his heart, it served only to stir it up. I would have expected Paul to return from this remarkable spiritual journey free from sin, perfect in spirit, devoid of wicked motives or self-serving intentions.

Far from it! Paul immediately felt the sting of self-promotion. Perhaps he thought: "Well, I must be a pretty special sort of guy for this to have happened to me. I don't know of anyone else who's had an experience remotely like mine. Sure, Peter saw a vision (Acts 10) and others have been used to heal the sick. But I was the one to whom God chose to reveal ineffable secrets of the unseen world. I guess that makes me one of a kind. And rightly so, if I do say so myself!"

Power did not automatically yield purity. Should it have? Perhaps. Well, maybe not automatically, but Paul's response to his heavenly transport ought to have humbled him and awakened his heart to the immeasurable glory and incomparable majesty of God. If nothing else, he might have reacted as Isaiah did upon seeing the Lord of glory enthroned and praised by adoring seraphim (Isaiah 6:1ff.). But for whatever reason, in Paul's case it was pride and self-elation, not humility or repentance, that gripped his soul.

The point, again, is simply that supernatural power and heavenly encounters of a revelatory sort are not guarantees of growth or maturity or spirituality.

This is not meant for a moment to suggest that power and revelatory encounters are bad or not to be desired. Let us never forget that Paul also spoke in 2 Timothy 3:5 of people who had "the appearance of godliness" but denied its "power". Power without purity leads to fanaticism. But purity without power often leads to Pharisaism.

The second principle comes in the form of counsel: *To those who are eagerly hungry and zealous for the power of the Holy Spirit and his gifts, I say: Good! God bless you!*

In addition to the command in 1 Corinthians 14:1, we read in v. 5 that Paul wants all "to prophesy". In 14:12 he acknowledges that the Corinthians "are eager for manifestations of the Spirit" and encourages them to strive to excel in building up the church. The argument of chapter 14 would indicate that this is his way of encouraging the pursuit of prophecy, given its capacity to edify others in the body (14:3,4,5). Again in 14:12 and 14:39 Paul explicitly commands the Corinthians to desire and pursue the gift of prophecy.

The verb translated "earnestly desire" (ESV) means to have a strong affection for, to ardently yearn, to zealously long for. Or to use modern lingo, "I want you to want it really bad!" So, do you? This is not an option! This is not an issue of personality, as if some are more inclined than others to experience this kind of spiritual phenomenon. This is not an issue of "It's for that church but not this one. After all, we've got our mission statement and they've got theirs. If that's what God is calling them to pursue, fine, but we have a different divine mandate."

No. All churches, no matter how different they may be, have an identical mandate when it comes to obeying Scripture. No one is exempt or special or unique in such a way that they can justify disobedience to God's Word. This is not a suggestion or mere advice or wise counsel. This is a divine command, a mandate from God himself. If you and I are not earnestly desiring spiritual gifts, especially prophecy, we are disobedient.

This is not an issue for prayer. You do not respond to this passage by saying, "Well, ok, I'll pray about it." No. *You don't pray about whether or not you are going to obey God.* God is not giving us a choice. He's giving us a command. The only choice you have is whether or not you are going to obey.

Can you imagine the reaction if we responded to other commands in Scripture the way many respond to 1 Corinthians 14:1? "I don't feel led to flee fornication. I think that's meant for other Christians but I don't sense that's my calling." Or "The prohibition against adultery just isn't compatible with where I am in God right now," or "Being a generous giver to the needy is a wonderful calling for some churches, but we're just not into that sort of thing at this stage of our growth as a church."

I confess that I'm somewhat baffled by Paul's advice. I could understand this exhortation if it were given to a church with undeniable maturity, a church like that in Thessalonica or Philippi or Ephesus. *To a church with great character and in need of power, this exhortation makes sense. But Corinth was a church with great power and little character!*

This counsel of Paul's strikes us as odd, unwise, if not downright dangerous. To the very people guilty of abusing spiritual gifts, Paul says be eager for more! Is he not simply pouring gasoline on a raging fire? If a man is drowning you don't throw him a life jacket filled with lead. You don't say to a struggling alcoholic, "Hey buddy, have a drink!"

What this reveals is that suppression of spiritual zeal is never the answer. Too much power is never the problem, but too little maturity is. I know of no place in Scripture where the absence of spiritual power is portrayed as a good thing. Observe what Paul does not say: "Settle down Corinthians. Cool it! Put on the brakes! Ease up on this supernatural stuff. Forget about spiritual gifts. Don't you realize that spiritual gifts are what got you into trouble in the first place?"

The reason he doesn't say that is because spiritual gifts were not the cause of their troubles: immaturity and carnality were. Let us never forget that spiritual gifts were God's idea. He thought them up. He gave them to the church. They are his ordained means for edifying the body and consoling the weak and encouraging those in despair. Spiritual gifts were formed and shaped by God. They operate in his power (1 Corinthians 12:6b) and manifest his Spirit (12:7). If spiritual gifts are the problem, then there's no one to blame but God.

This brings me to my third principle. *The solution to the abuse of spiritual gifts is not disuse, but proper use.* Paul does not recommend that the Corinthians abandon spiritual gifts or de-emphasize spiritual power. He simply gives them guidelines on how these powerful manifestations of the Spirit are to be properly exercised in the body of Christ to the edification of God's people.

The policy we implement in our churches today often turns out to be far removed from that of Paul. Here is what often happens. There are basically three stages to it.

First, *we see something being done badly* in the church. We note someone abusing a gift, perhaps using it to manipulate another person. Or perhaps an individual is wounded by the misguided zeal of another Christian. Then, second, *we feel rising up within our souls an emotional prejudice* against what was done. We feel revulsion in our hearts, we take up an offence and feel our souls recoiling, so to speak, withdrawing, if you will, from anything that remotely looks like what we have just witnessed. Finally, *we either resolve in our hearts never to get involved in anything like that again or we pass a rule in the church forbidding that it ever be allowed.* Prohibition is always easier than regulation. It is always easier to legislate against something than it is to repair it and make it useful for the people of God.

A Painful Question

Those are my three principles. And now for my question: "How much of your Christian life is shaped by your revulsion at the ugly things you

213

see in the church? How much of what you allow yourself to do or to believe is governed by the abuses you have seen, rather than by the Scripture that you read? Are you motivated largely by your disdain for the ugliness of what others have done or by the beauty of what Christ has commanded?"

I was shocked when I finally discovered how much of what I believed and pursued and desired and prayed for was determined more by my reaction against the ugly things I saw in other people than by the beautiful things I see in God's Word.

Listening to the Text

Let's look more closely at 1 Corinthians 14:1-5. I have three observations.

First, some have pointed out, correctly, that the exhortation to "earnestly desire" spiritual gifts (1 Corinthians 12:31; 14:1) is in the plural. But they conclude from this, incorrectly, that Paul's command is therefore directed not to individual believers but to the corporate church. They argue that this is grounds for rejecting the idea that Christians should seek any spiritual gift.

But of course the verb is plural, as are virtually all Paul's commands in letters other than those addressed to individuals (such as Philemon, Titus, and Timothy). Paul is writing to *everyone* in the church at Corinth, each of whom is responsible for individually responding to an exhortation that has validity for the entire church. In other words, what is the corporate church if not a collection of *individuals* on *each* of whom the obligation falls? The plural of this exhortation simply indicates that *all* believers in Corinth are to heed the apostolic admonition. It is a duty *common* to everyone. That includes us as well.

I can well imagine someone in Corinth (or today) responding to this attempt to evade Paul's obvious intent by saying: "How can we as a church pursue spiritual gifts if none of us as individuals is allowed to?"

Second, Paul is not denouncing the gift of tongues. It was the apostle himself who said, "I thank God I speak in tongues more than you all" (v. 18; cf. v. 5). What he is contrasting in vv. 1-5 isn't prophecy and tongues, but prophecy and *uninterpreted* tongues in the corporate meeting of the church. As he makes clear in v. 5, if there is interpretation, tongues can function in the same way prophecy does.

Third, prophecy has been given to us by God so that we might be built up, encouraged, and consoled (v. 3). Do you need edification, encouragement, and consolation? Who doesn't? That's what prophecy was designed by God to accomplish. No wonder Paul commands us to earnestly desire that we might prophesy. Not to dazzle people. Not for sensationalism. Not to draw attention to ourselves, but to display the love of God for his people, to confirm his presence and power in our lives, and to show his providential care.

So what will you do with this divine command? To obey or not to obey, that is the question.

---

[1] Dallas Willard, *In Search of Guidance* (Ventura: Regal Books, 1984), 19. A more recent and somewhat revised version of this book is available from InterVarsity under the title, *Hearing God: Developing a Conversational Relationship with God* (Downers Grove: IVP, 1999).

[2] Willard, *In Search of Guidance*, 219.

[3] Klaus Bockmuehl, *Listening to the God who Speaks* (Colorado Springs: Helmers and Howard, 1990), 83.

[4] Willard, *In Search of Guidance*, 81.

[5] Ibid., 83.

[6] Ibid., 62.

[7] Bockmuehl, *Listening to the God who Speaks*, 65.

[8] This material is taken largely from my book, *The Beginner's Guide to Spiritual Gifts*, 101-02.

[9] These thoughts are largely dependent on the insights of John Piper, taken from his sermon on Romans 12:1-2, "Why the Gift of Prophecy is Not the Usual Way of Knowing God's Will," April 1, 1990 (available at www.desiringgod.org).

Chapter Ten

Peter and a Puritan on Passion
and Principle

I'm certain the apostles Peter and Paul, as well as John, Luke and other New Testament authors, were aware of the categories that are the focus of this book. They spoke explicitly of the mind and our obligation to bring every thought captive to Christ (2 Corinthians 10:5; 1 Peter 1:13). They never hesitated to rebuke those who would diminish the importance of truth as foundational to Christian life and ministry (Romans 16:17-18; 1 Peter 1:22-2:3; 2 Peter 1:3-11. They were no less adamant concerning the role of the Spirit (1 Corinthians 12-14; 1 Peter 4:10-11). Nothing would have struck them as more absurd than the suggestion that anything significant could be accomplished for the sake of Christ apart from the power of the Holy Spirit. A life devoid of either truth or affection was hardly one worth living.

In this chapter I want to look at one text from Peter's first epistle which speaks directly to the essential relation between mind and affection, between principle and passion. Although he undoubtedly faced this divorce in one form or another in the first century, I doubt he, or Paul, could ever have anticipated the breadth of the divide that has emerged in the twenty-first.

To help us with our examination of Peter's perspective, I'm going to employ the insights of Jonathan Edwards as found in his famous treatise *Religious Affections*.[1] Although Edwards was a cessationist, his observations on the role of the affections in Christian experience are profound and, in my opinion, far exceed anything I've read by any charismatic author, past or present. So, permit me to interweave his observations with my own as we undertake this study.

Joy Inexpressible

"Though you have not seen him, you love him.
Though you do not now see him, you believe in him
and rejoice with joy that is inexpressible and filled with glory"

(1 Peter 1:8)

Peter envisions the pinnacle of Christian living as a dynamic interplay between solid, substantive belief in all that God is for us in Jesus and a joy and affection for Jesus that quite simply exceed the capacity of the human mind to grasp and the human tongue to utter. Not all the collective brilliance of the human race can conceive or articulate the heights of joy and love that are available to the believing heart.

Not all Christians are happy with that sort of language. In theory they may nod their heads, but when it comes to their own religious experience, affections such as Peter describes are either dismissed as undignified and indecent or as incompatible with a faith that is rigorously intellectual. Some fear that people who *feel passionately* do so as an *excuse* for not *thinking profoundly*. These people are often secretly terrified of their feelings. They view their passions and affections as an alien element in their psychological makeup, a dangerous and threatening intrusion rather than a divinely ordained feature of what it means to be created in the image of God.

Such folk concede that we may not be able to escape or entirely suppress our affections, but we should be leery of them. They have the potential to submerge our souls in the murky waters of fanaticism and subjectivity and must therefore be monitored with great care and concern. It's not surprising that there is great suspicion toward anything that might arouse or evoke our affections or lead to their public and overt expression.

Spiritual Affections

You may not be able to define the word "obscenity", but I suspect you know it when you see it! That's true of our affections as well. It's difficult to think of a good definition, but we know them when we *feel* them! Some would never use the word "affection" except perhaps to describe romantic feelings that pass between a man and a woman. But this is not the sense in which Edwards employs it.

Affections are more than ideas or thoughts or intellectual notions in our heads. They are lively and vigorous passions, for example, of either delight, love, joy, and hope, on the one hand, or displeasure, hatred, grief, or despair, on the other. When we evaluate our response to someone or something in life, we use such terms as sorrow, happiness, revulsion, attraction, bitterness, anger, peace, fear, and delight. All these are what Edwards called *affections*.

Whatever the mind or understanding perceives, the inclination either is pleased with and approves or opposes and disapproves. Certainly there are varying degrees of both delight and disgust. Some ideas or objects elicit intense disdain, while others stir deep and heartfelt joy. Still other things that our minds grasp have comparatively little impact on us. Whereas we are rarely if ever left utterly indifferent to them, our souls are not greatly stirred. There are countless occasions in the course of human existence when we make choices, when our wills are exercised in the pursuit of some option to the exclusion of another. But only those acts of will that are vibrant and sensible and vigorous deserve the name "affections".

These affections almost invariably have an impact on our bodies. Edwards argued that because of the way God created us as holistic beings "there never is any case whatsoever, any lively and vigorous exercise of the will or inclination of the soul, without some effect upon the body, in some alteration of the motion of its fluids, and especially of the animal spirits. And on the other hand, from the same laws of the union of soul and body, the constitution of the body, and the motion of its fluids, may promote the exercise of the affections."[2]

It's important to remember, however, that the mind, not the body, is the seat and source of spiritual affections. Only the soul or immaterial element is capable of thinking and understanding and thus of loving or hating, or experiencing joy or sorrow over what is known. The many physiological sensations we experience, the rush of blood, rapid breathing, goose bumps, chills down the spine, an increased heartbeat, etc., are but effects of affections and are not to be identified with them. Thus a disembodied spirit, now in heaven with Christ, is as capable of love and hatred, joy or sorrow, hope or fear, or other affections, as those of us who remain in the body. The holy angels, as well as God himself, are filled with righteous and intense spiritual affections, yet they do not have a physical body or blood or adrenaline or hormones or literal eyes, ears, and noses.

So how do "affections" differ from "emotions" or "feelings"? Certainly there is what may rightly be called an emotional dimension to affections. Affections, after all, are sensible and intense longings or aversions of the will. Perhaps it would be best to say that whereas affections are not less than emotions, they are surely more. Emotions can often be no more than physiologically heightened states of either euphoria or fear that are unrelated to what the mind perceives as true.

Affections, on the other hand, are always the fruit or effect of what the mind understands and knows. The will or inclination is moved either toward or away from something that is perceived by the mind. An emotion or mere feeling, on the other hand, can rise or fall independently of and unrelated to anything in the mind. One can experience an emotion or feeling without it properly being an affection, but one can rarely if ever experience an affection without it being emotional and involving intense feelings that awaken and move and stir the body.

Affections and Christian Living

So the more important questions is: "What role, if any, do the affections play in the Christian life?"

Although it may not be immediately evident, I believe Peter is telling us that, far from being secondary or sub-Christian, *the very essence of Christianity is the enjoyment of sanctified affections*. Let me say it again with even greater emphasis. What characterizes the Christian life in its purest and most concentrated form is the enjoyment of sanctified or holy affections.

One can easily point to numerous texts of Scripture that seem to portray the essence of our relationship with God as more than merely mental or intellectual. Our affections or emotions are absolutely crucial. For example, we are often commanded to experience *joy* (Psalms 37:4; 97:12; 33:1; 149:2; Matthew 5:12; Philippians 3:1; 4:4; 1 Thessalonians 5:16). We read of the critical importance of *fear* and *awe* of God (Jeremiah 17:7; Psalms 31:24; 33:18; Psalms 146:5; 147:11; Romans 8:24; 1 Thessalonians 5:8; Hebrews 6:19; 1 Peter 1:3), together with *hope* (that confident expectation and yearning for the future consummation of all that God has promised; see Psalms 31:24; 33:18; 146:5; Jeremiah 17:17; etc.), *hatred* (Proverbs 8:13; Psalms 97:10; 101:2-3;119:104; etc.), *holy desire* (Isaiah 26:8-9; Psalms 27:4; 42:1-2; 63:1-2; 84:1-2; etc.), and *sorrow* and *mourning* (Matthew 5:4; Psalms 34:18; 51:17). I could also list numerous texts that speak of *gratitude, compassion, mercy, zeal* and the like, each of which is a passion, an emotional energy that characterizes our relationship both to God and his people.

People of Passion

A brief look at a few key figures in Scripture also reveals how much of their relationship to God was wrapped up in passion and affection. Consider David, King of Israel and prolific psalmist. I think most Christians turn instinctively to David's poetry for devotional meditation or during times of depression because of the honesty of his desperation for God and the intensity of his spiritual appetite. As Edwards notes,

> "Those holy songs of his . . . are nothing else but the expressions and breathings of devout and holy affections, such as humble and fervent love to God, admiration of his glorious perfections and wonderful works, earnest desires, thirstings and pantings of soul after God, delight and joy in God, a sweet and melting gratitude to God for his great goodness, holy exultation and triumph of soul in the favor, sufficiency and faithfulness of God, his love to, and delight in the saints, . . . his great delight in the Word and ordinances of God, his grief for his own and others' sins, and his fervent zeal for God, and against the enemies of God and his church."[4]

Another example would be the apostle Paul. Although you may not think of Paul as an emotional or passionate person, there is hardly an epistle he wrote that does not drip with feelings and earnest longings of soul and spirit. Edwards contends that Paul was "inflamed, actuated and entirely swallowed up, by a most ardent love to his glorious Lord, esteeming all things as loss, for the excellency of the knowledge of him, and esteeming them but dung that he might win him. He represents himself, as overpowered by this holy affection, and as it were compelled by it to go forward in his service, through all difficulties and sufferings (2 Corinthians 5:14-15)."[5]

Paul's letters are filled with references to his overflowing affection for the church (2 Corinthians 12:19; Philippians 4:1; 2 Timothy 1:2; and especially 1 Thessalonians 2:7-8). He speaks of his "bowels of love" (Philippians 1:8; Philemon 12,20) for them, of his pity and mercy (Philippians 2:1), of his anguish of heart and the tears he shed for their welfare (2 Corinthians 2:4), of his continual grief for the lost (Romans 9:2), and of his enlarged heart (2 Corinthians 6:11). Countless texts could be cited in which Paul portrays his life as filled with godly passions and desires.

Surely Jesus himself was a passionate man greatly moved in heart and spirit with holy affection. He was not ashamed or hesitant to pray with "loud crying and tears" (Hebrews 5:7). The gospel writers speak of him as experiencing amazement, sorrow and grief (Mark 3:5), zeal (John 2:17), weeping (Luke 19:41-42), earnest desire (Luke 22:15), pity and compassion (Matthew 15:32; 18:34), anger (John 2:13-19), love (John 15:9), and joy (John 15:11).

In Luke 10:21 Jesus is said to have "rejoiced in the Holy Spirit" as he was praying to the Father. He himself said in John 15:11 and 17:13 that one of the principal aims in his earthly mission was to perfect the joy of his followers. Thus our joy is the joy of Jesus in us!

Other examples could be cited, but one in particular comes to mind. Think for a moment of heaven itself. The essence of life in heaven, says Edwards, "consists very much in affection. There is doubtless true religion in heaven, and true religion in its utmost purity and perfection. But according to the Scripture representation of the heavenly state, the religion of heaven consists chiefly in holy and mighty love and joy, and the expression of these in most fervent and exalted praises."[6]

One simply cannot understand and appreciate the great things of God without being moved with passion and zeal and joy and delight and fervor. The reason, notes Edwards, why people are not affected by such "infinitely great, important, glorious, and wonderful things, as they often hear and read of in the Word of God, is undoubtedly because they are blind; if they were not so, it would be impossible, and utterly inconsistent with human nature, that their hearts should be otherwise than strongly impressed and greatly moved by such things."[7]

Quintessential Christianity

Having made my point, let's return to what Peter says in our passage. He contends that *love for Jesus* and *joy in Jesus* are nothing less than the pinnacle of Christian living. I can anticipate your objection: "Hold on! I'll concede that our affections are important. But how can you say that the enjoyment of sanctified affections is the essence and pinnacle of the Christian life? Isn't that going a bit far?" I don't think so. Look with me again at what Peter says.

The recipients of this epistle were enduring excruciating persecution, oppression, and affliction. One need only glance at 1 Peter 1:6; 2:20-21; 3:17; and especially 4:12-18 to see this is true. He makes it clear here in chapter one that our ability to rejoice simultaneously with the anguish of trials and troubles is based on two things.

Peter first reminds his readers of the *duration* of trials and suffering. He says in v. 6 that they are "for a little while." In other words, they are temporary, not eternal. Trials and pain will pass. No matter how bad it gets here on earth (and yes, it can get incredibly bad), one day it will give way to the glory and pleasure of heaven (see 2 Corinthians 4:16-18). Knowing the duration of trials and suffering gives us strength to endure without taking offense at God.

He then points, secondly, to the *design* of trials. In v. 7 he says that suffering works to purify our faith. His point is that God never wastes pain. The trials and tribulations of this life serve to sanctify us and to conform us to the image of Jesus himself. 1 Peter 1:7 thus reminds me of two verses in Psalm 119.

> "Before I was afflicted I went astray, but now I keep Thy word" (119:67).
> "It is good for me that I was afflicted, that I may learn Thy statutes" (119:71).

Such experiences have a unique capacity to highlight the differences between what is true and sincere in the heart of a person as over against what is false and hypocritical. They cause the "genuine beauty and amiableness" of true spirituality to appear more clearly. Indeed, "true virtue never appears so lovely, as when it is most oppressed." Trials and pains "tend to refine [our faith], and deliver it from those mixtures of that which is false, which encumber and impede it; that nothing may be left but that which is true."[7]

A close look at v. 7 indicates that Peter wants us to envision the parallels between the effect of fire on gold and that of trials on faith. His point is that just as fire burns away the dross and alloy from gold, leaving it pure and solid, so also the flames of trials and tests and oppression burn away the dross of our faith. Hypocrisy and superficiality and self-confidence and pride do not easily survive the flames of persecution and tribulation (see Psalm 66:10; Malachi 3:3; Isaiah 48:10).

If we follow the logic of Peter's thought in vv. 6-7 we discover that v. 8 describes what is left of Christian faith that has passed through the furnace of afflictions. In other words, v. 8 is Peter's portrayal of the end product of persecution and pain. This is Christian experience in its purest and most pristine form. This is quintessential faith, first-rate faith, faith that is as free as it can be, this side of heaven, of sinful additives and preservatives! Peter has no illusions of perfection, but he does envision a relationship with Jesus absent the peripheral elements. This, says Peter, is the very essence of authentic Christianity.

Let me illustrate what Peter means. Formulate a mental picture of a solid block of granite, untouched by human hands. When a master sculptor approaches such an object, he takes hammer and chisel and, in effect, begins to chip away everything that doesn't look like a human. He cuts, hammers, and pounds away until the finished product stands before us in all its glory. In a sense, that's what God does with us through our trials and oppressive circumstances. He uses them like a spiritual hammer and chisel to chip away from our lives everything that doesn't look like Jesus! The result is what Peter describes in 1 Peter 1:8.

Or consider the athlete who fails to maintain a strict training regimen. He becomes a couch-potato, eating and drinking and refusing to exercise. Over time his muscles suffer from atrophy. He gains excessive weight. His reflexes aren't as sharp as they used to be and his lung capacity is greatly reduced. When he runs (if he ever gets off the couch), his legs feel heavy and lifeless. Then he recommits himself to a rigorous exercise program. Over the next few weeks he burns away body fat and strengthens his muscles. His endurance level increases and he returns to his former shape. The result is a finely honed body, ready for competition. The physical effect of exercise on his body is analogous to the spiritual effect of trials on our faith.

So what am I saying? Simply that 1 Peter 1:8 portrays for us what Christian faith looks like when refined and shaped and purified by the fire of hardship and tribulation. Here is Christian faith in its preeminent expression. And of what does it consist, but *love for Jesus* and *joy in Jesus.*

When Peter talks about love for Jesus he means unashamed, extravagant affection for the Son of God. Though we do not see Jesus with our physical eyes (at least I never have!), we still love him. One need not see Jesus in the flesh, so to speak, to experience unbridled passion for him. The first and greatest commandment is that we are to love the Lord with all our heart, soul, mind, strength, and will. That is what Peter has in mind here.

When King David spoke of this kind of passion for God he compared it to the plight of a thirsty deer, alone and desperate in the desert. Even as the deer pants after the water brooks, so our souls long for the Son of God (Psalm 42:1-2; cf. 63:1). To love the Son of God, to experience passion for Jesus, is to yearn from the depths of one's being for his presence and his smiling approval. To love him with the energy of our whole soul is to settle for nothing less than his will and his ways.

Peter also speaks of joy in Jesus. The end-product of a faith that has been purged and purified is joy inexpressible and full of glory. This isn't to say that joy is absent prior to the onset of trials. We are responsible to "rejoice always" (1 Thessalonians 5:16), before, during, and after hardship. Peter's point is simply that the quality and sincerity and fervency of joy are both refined and intensified by trials. Thus far from being secondary or something to suppress and avoid, joy is described here as that which characterizes Christian experience in its highest and most sanctified form. Two things in particular are said about joy in Jesus.

First, Peter describes it as being *inexpressible* or *unutterable*. This is a joy so profound that it is beyond mere words. It is ineffable, all-consuming, overwhelming, speechless joy! This joy defies all human efforts at understanding or explanation. The words have not yet been created that would do justice to the depths of this kind of joy. The human tongue has not yet been found that can articulate the heights to which this kind of joy elevates us. You'll never know this kind of joy until you can't find words to describe it. This is joy that declares, "I will not be confined to the dimensions of your mind or reduced to the definitions in your dictionary."

But Peter also describes this joy as *full of glory* or *glorified.* This word evokes images of God's glory in the Old Testament, that bright, shining radiance of his presence. This, then, is a joy shot through and through with the resplendent majesty of the beauty of God's being. It is not fleshly joy, or worldly joy, or the joy that comes from earthly achievements or money or fame. It is a joy that has been baptized, as it were, in the glory of God himself. "In rejoicing with this joy," says Edwards, "their minds were filled, as it were, with a glorious brightness, and their natures exalted and perfected: it was a most worthy, noble rejoicing, that did not corrupt and debase the mind, as many carnal joys do; but did greatly beautify and dignify it: it was a prelibation of the joy of heaven, that raised their minds to a degree of heavenly blessedness."[8]

Where is the Mind?

But in the midst of his focus on our affections we must not miss Peter's reference to the mind and the critical role of knowledge ("you *believe* in him," v. 8b). Neither love for Jesus nor joy in him exists in an intellectual vacuum. Peter is careful to point out that our inability to "see" Jesus is not a hindrance either to our love for him or our confident belief in who he is and what he has accomplished.

But even more explicit is the connection between faith and joy. Peter appears to suggest that the joy in Jesus which transcends human speech is itself the fruit of our faith in him. How could it be otherwise? One cannot meaningfully rejoice in a person of whom one knows nothing! Our knowledge of the incarnate Christ and his redemptive work is the foundation of our faith in him to be true to his covenant commitment. And faith or belief in the integrity of his person, the saving power of his atoning death, and the literal reality of his life-giving resurrection is the soil in which the flower of inexpressible joy blooms.

Love that is not tethered to the revelation of the one true God easily becomes idolatry, and joy that is not deeply rooted in the historical realities of what Christ has accomplished is little more than infatuation. When trials ensue (as vv. 6-7 indicate they most assuredly will) such fleeting feelings, divorced as they are from truth, will collapse, a mere subjective vapor of little value in sustaining the human soul.

The joy that Peter portrays as the quintessence of Christian experience is one that erupts from the volcanic depths of knowledge of the truth. This is joy that energizes and empowers the human heart to withstand any and all trials. This is the joy that elevates the human soul to heights of confident celebration, a delight that no pain or tribulation or shattered dream can diminish. It is that glorious work of the Spirit in my heart that empowers me to say:

A sudden tsunami may sweep away my house and family, but my "life is hidden with Christ in God" (Colossians 3:3)!

A terrorist may separate my head from my body, but nothing can separate me "from the love of God in Christ Jesus" my Lord (Romans 8:39)!

An incurable disease may ravage my body, but God causes "all things" to "work together for good for those who are called according to his purpose" (Romans 8:28)!

An unfaithful spouse may walk out, never to return, but God has promised, "I will never leave you nor forsake you" (Hebrews 13:5)!

Affectionless Spirituality?

What we've seen thus far is that the sort of religion or spirituality that pleases God is one that consists largely in "vigorous and lively actings of the inclination and will of the soul, or the fervent exercises of the heart"[9] (see Romans 12:11; Deuteronomy 6:4-5; 10:12; 30:6).

Spirituality is actually of little benefit to anyone, least of all to ourselves, if not characterized by lively and powerful affections. Nothing is so antithetical to true religion as lukewarmness. God is displeased with weak, dull, and lifeless inclinations. Consider those many biblical texts where our relationship to God is compared to "running, wrestling or agonizing for a great prize or crown, and fighting with strong enemies that seek our lives, and warring as those that by violence take a city or kingdom."[10]

Not only are affections the essence of true spirituality, they are also the spring or source of virtually all our actions. There is hardly any human activity or pursuit that is not driven or to some degree influenced by either love or hatred, desire, hope, fear, etc. If we should eliminate from the world all love and hatred and hope and fear and anger and zeal and desire, that is to say, all affections of the soul, the world would lie motionless and dead. Whether it be covetousness or greed or ambition or sensuality or any such worldly experience, apart from such affections energizing this activity mankind would be passive and uninvolved.

Consider for a moment why it is that so many hear the Word of God and respond so pathetically. They hear of the glorious perfections of God, his almighty power and boundless wisdom, his majesty and holiness, his goodness and mercy; they hear of the unspeakable love of God and of the great things that Christ has done and suffered; they hear of the beauty of heaven and the misery of hell, and yet they "remain as they were before, with no sensible alteration on them, either in heart or practice, because they are not affected with what they hear; and ever will be so till they are affected. I am bold to assert, that there never was any considerable change wrought in the mind or conversation of any one person, by anything of a religious nature, that ever he read, heard or saw, that had not his affections moved."[11] Only as people are affected by the great truths of Christianity are they moved to love God and seek him and plead with him in prayer and brought low in humility and repentance. Simply put, affections are the spring and source of virtually all significant spiritual endeavors.

So much is it the case, notes Edwards, that true spirituality consists in affections that one may say "that without holy affection there is no true religion: and no light in the understanding is good, which don't [sic] produce holy affection in the heart; no habit or principle in the heart is good, which has no such exercise; and no external fruit is good, which don't [sic] proceed from such exercises."[12]

There is a lot of "religion" in the world, rituals, rites, gestures, beliefs, acts of moral virtue, charity, as well as organizations and institutions and traditions designed to perpetuate and promote it, ostensibly to the glory of God. But without holy affections, all such activities and the effort to advertise them are nothing but wind. Those who would insist on the intellect of man or the doctrinal accuracy of his thoughts as the pinnacle of religious expression need to consider that no idea or attitude or theory or doctrine is of value that does not inflame the heart and stir the affections in love and joy and fear of God. Those who would argue that moral obedience is the essence of religion fail to see that such behavior is only good to the degree that it springs from and finds its source in the holy affections of the heart as they are described in Scripture.

Yet another proof of this is the Scriptural portrayal of "hardness of heart" as the essence of sin and moral rebellion (see Mark 3:5; Romans 2:5; Ezekiel 3:7; Psalm 95:7-10; 2 Chronicles 36:13; Isaiah 63:17; etc.). "Now by a hard heart," notes Edwards, "is plainly meant an unaffected heart, or a heart not easy to be moved with virtuous affections, like a stone, insensible, stupid, unmoved and hard to be impressed. Hence the hard heart is called a stony heart, and is opposed to a heart of flesh, that has feeling, and is sensibly touched and moved."[13]

Scripture is also clear that a tender heart is the one that is easily and readily impressed by what ought to affect it. For example, God commends Josiah because his heart was tender, by which he surely meant that his heart was "easily moved with religious and pious affection"[14] (see 2 Kings 22:19).

The Fear of Fanaticism

The reaction of many to this argument is to some extent understandable. They point to those who in a season of revival or renewal allowed their zeal and affections to lead them into error. Others experienced high affections but produced little fruit and even appeared to have "returned like the dog to his vomit" (2 Peter 2:22). That critics would then dismiss affection altogether as having little if anything to do with true spirituality is simply an example of moving from one extreme to another. It is as much an error to focus on high affections without regard to their source or nature as it is to dismiss affections entirely as unimportant to the reality of true religion. Satan is happy with either error. He would as much have us fall into a lifeless formality as he would that we were stirred and energized by affections unrelated to truth.

We must never forget that whereas there is more to true spirituality or religion than affections,

> "yet true religion consists so much in the affections, that there can be no true religion without them. He who has no religious affection, is in a state of spiritual death, and is wholly destitute of the powerful, quickening, saving influences of the Spirit of God upon his heart. As there is no true religion where there is nothing else but affection, so there is no true religion where there is no religious affection. As on the one hand, there must be light in the understanding, as well as an affected fervent heart; where there is heat without light, there can be nothing divine or heavenly in that heart; so on the other hand, where there is a kind of light without heat, a head stored with notions and speculations, with a cold and

unaffected heart, there can be nothing divine in that light, that knowledge is no true spiritual knowledge of divine things. If the great things of religion are rightly understood, they will affect the heart. The reason why men are not affected by such infinitely great, important, glorious, and wonderful things, as they often hear and read of, in the Word of God, is undoubtedly because they are blind; if they were not so, it would be impossible, and utterly inconsistent with human nature, that their hearts should be otherwise than strongly impressed, and greatly moved by such things."[15]

The fact that a person has much affection doesn't prove he is truly spiritual. But if that individual has *no* affection it most assuredly proves he has no true religion. "The right way, is not to reject all affections, nor to approve all; but to distinguish between affections, approving some, and rejecting others; separating between the wheat and the chaff, the gold and the dross, the precious and the vile."[16]

If our thesis is correct, and true spirituality lies in the experience, enjoyment and expression of holy affections, it is to our shame that we are no more affected with the great truths of Scripture than we are. This is especially the case when we consider how profoundly moved and affected people are by worldly things that have little if anything to do with God and the revelation of himself in the face of Jesus Christ. And yet how common it is among people that their affections are far more engaged in worldly affairs than with the revelation of God in Jesus. Edwards' words are an especially relevant indictment of our society and deserve a close and repentant reading:

"In things which concern men's worldly interest, their outward delights, their honor and reputation, and their natural relations, they have their desires eager, their appetites vehement, their love warm and affectionate, their zeal ardent; in these things their hearts are tender and sensible, easily moved, deeply impressed, much concerned, very sensibly affected, and greatly engaged; much depressed with grief at worldly losses, and highly raised with joy at worldly successes and prosperity. But how insensible and unmoved are most men, about the great things of another world! How dull are their affections! How heavy and hard their hearts in these matters! Here their love is cold, their desires languid, their zeal low, and their gratitude small. How they can sit and hear of the infinite height, and depth, and length, and breadth of the love of God in Christ Jesus, of his giving his infinitely dear Son, to be offered up a sacrifice for the sins of men, and of the unparalleled love of the innocent, and holy, and tender Lamb of God, manifested in his dying agonies, his bloody sweat, his loud and bitter cries, and bleeding heart, and all this for enemies, to redeem them from deserved, eternal burnings, and to bring to unspeakable and everlasting joy and glory; and yet be cold, and heavy, insensible, and regardless! Where are the exercises of our affections proper, if not here? What is it that does more require them? And what can be a fit occasion of their lively and vigorous exercise, if not such a one as this? Can anything be set in our view, greater and more important? Anything more wonderful and surprising? Or more nearly concerning our interest? Can we suppose the wise Creator implanted such principles in the human nature as the affections, to be of use to us, and to be exercised on certain proper occasions, but to lie still on such an occasion as this? Can any Christian who believes the truth of these things, entertain such thoughts?"[17]

If ever there were occasion for the exercise of human affection it would be in regard to those things or objects that are most worthy of our energy and joy and delight.

"But is there anything which Christians can find in heaven or earth, so worthy to be the objects of their admiration and love, their earnest and longing desires, their hope, and their rejoicing, and their fervent zeal, as those things that are held forth to us in the gospel of Jesus Christ? In which not only are things declared most worthy to affect us, but they are exhibited in the most affecting manner. The glory and beauty of the blessed Jehovah, which is most worthy in itself, to be the object of our admiration and love, is there exhibited in the most affecting manner that can be conceived of, as it appears, shining in all its luster, in the face of an incarnate, infinitely loving, meek, compassionate, dying

Redeemer. All the virtues of the Lamb of God, his humility, patience, meekness, submission, obedience, love and compassion, are exhibited to our view, in a manner the most tending to move our affections, of any that can be imagined; as they all had their greatest trial, and their highest exercise, and so their brightest manifestation, when he was in the most affecting circumstances; even when he was under his last sufferings, those unutterable and unparalleled sufferings he endured, from his tender love and pity to us. There also the hateful nature of our sins is manifested in the most affecting manner possible, as we see the dreadful effects of them, in that our Redeemer, who undertook to answer for us, suffered for them. And there we have the most affecting manifestation of God's hatred of sin, and his wrath and justice in punishing it; as we see his justice in the strictness and inflexibleness of it; and his wrath in its terribleness, in so dreadfully punishing our sins, in one who was infinitely dear to him, and loving to us. So has God disposed things, in the affair of our redemption, and in his glorious dispensations, revealed to us in the gospel, as though everything were purposely contrived in such a manner, as to have the greatest possible tendency to reach our hearts in the most tender part, and move our affections most sensibly and strongly. How great cause have we therefore to be humbled to the dust, that we are no more affected!"[18]

Affections and Public Worship

That holy affections are the essence of true spirituality can also be seen from what God has commanded concerning our public worship. Edwards argues that virtually all external expressions of worship "can be of no further use, than as they have some tendency to affect our own hearts, or the hearts of others."[19]

Consider, for example, the singing of praises to God, which seem "to be appointed wholly to excite and express religious affections. No other reason can be assigned, why we should express ourselves to God in verse, rather than in prose, and do it with music, but only, that such is our nature and frame, that these things have a tendency to move our affections."[20]

Some actually orchestrate worship in such a way that the affections of the heart are reined in and, in some cases, even suppressed. People often fear the external manifestation of internal zeal and love and desire and joy. Though they sing, they do so in a way that the end in view is the mere articulation of words and declaration of truths. But if that were what God intended, why did he not ordain that we recite, in prose, biblical truths about him? Why sing? It can't be simply for the aesthetic value of music or because of the pleasure it brings, for that would be to turn worship manward, as if we are now the focus rather than God. We sing because God has created not only our minds but also our hearts and souls, indeed our bodies as well, in such a way that music elicits and intensifies holy affections for God and facilitates their lively and vigorous expression.

The same may be said of how God operates on our souls in the preaching of his Word. Books and commentaries and the like provide us with "good doctrinal or speculative understanding of the things of the Word of God, yet they have not an equal tendency to impress them on men's hearts and affections."[21] So, with a view to *affecting* sinners and not merely *informing* them, God has appointed that his Word be applied in a particularly lively way through preaching.

Therefore, when we think of how public worship should be constructed and what methods should be employed in the praise of God and the edification of his people, "such means are to be desired, as have much of a tendency to move the affections. Such books, and such a way of preaching the Word, and administration of ordinances, and such a way of worshiping God in prayer, and singing praises, is much to be desired, as has a tendency deeply to affect the hearts of those who attend these means."[22]

When people object that certain styles of public worship seem especially chosen for their capacity to awaken and intensify and express the affections of the heart, they should be told that such is precisely the God-ordained purpose of worship. What they fear, namely, the heightening and deepening of the heart's desire and love for God, and the expansion and increase of the soul's delight and joy in God, what they typically call "emotionalism" or even "manipulation", is the very goal of worship itself. For God is most glorified in his people when their hearts are most satisfied (i.e., when they are most "affected" with joy) in him.

Edwards was not so naïve to suggest that the mere presence of intense and heartfelt affections was proof that a person was the object of God's saving grace. In fact, he devotes the remainder of *Religious Affections* to distinguishing between affections that are genuine and God-given and those that are not. I can only recommend with the greatest sincerity that you devote yourself to studying Edwards on this most important point.

A Rose by any other Name

Envision for a moment that you are not reading my words but listening to me speak in an auditorium. Suddenly I pull from beneath the podium a rose of incomparable beauty. I hold it high for all to see. One can hear gasps of amazement coming from the audience.

This is a rose of almost indescribable brilliance. Its color is bright and radiant and almost blinding. No less impressive is its fragrance. The aroma fills the auditorium (I know it's only one rose, but it's only an illustration!). My desire is that you experience this rose up close and personal, so I invite you to the platform to take a closer look, a closer smell.

To display it for all to see and smell, I glue the rose to the platform on which I'm standing. Perhaps a little duct tape is also employed to secure it firmly to the floor. Then, one by one, each of you passes by. Some will only look, stunned by the radiant color of this unusual flower. Others bend over and experience its enchanting aroma. A few even dare to touch it and speak of its soft and pliable petals.

I then announce that the rose will remain where it is overnight and that all may return tomorrow to experience its beauty yet again. The next day all return and once more make their way to the front of the auditorium. But something's different. The color isn't quite what it was the day before. The rose has slightly wilted and leans to one side. I then announce that the rose will be available yet again tomorrow and encourage all to return.

By the third day, something horrible has happened. The formerly brilliant color has turned a dull and dreary brown. The formerly soft petals have become brittle and fall to the floor when touched. The smell has turned putrid, far from its former fragrance. It doesn't take much to account for the changes. The rose was glued to a lifeless wooden platform. Without the nutrients derived from good soil, apart from the light of the sun, absent the water and care of a meticulous gardener, the rose is doomed to wither and fade.

Hear me well. Just as certain as that rose will turn brown and brittle and lose its allure, so too will our souls if they are not deeply and securely rooted in the soil of Holy Scripture. We may flourish for a season, perhaps even impress people with the color of our spirituality and the fragrance of our good deeds and the tenderness of our love for others. But in the absence of a continual supply of truth and knowledge and devotion to cultivating a mind aflame with the revelation of who God is in Christ, we will become like a wilted rose.

Affections such as joy and love and hope and peace are essential to true Christian living, the sort of living that honors and glorifies and exalts Jesus. But they cannot long survive if severed from the rich soil of truth and doctrine and ever-expanding understanding in the mind of the splendor and majesty of God.

Conclusion

Charles Spurgeon would never have been accused of fanaticism or emotionalism. Yet he understood the critical importance and incomparable delight of enjoying God. Although he was addressing the church of the 19th century, his reflections on Psalm 32 have special relevance for us today:

> "Our happiness should be demonstrative; . . . men whisper their praises decorously where a hearty outburst of song would be far more natural. It is to be feared that the church of the present day, through a craving for excessive propriety, is growing too artificial; so that enquirers' cries and believers' shouts would be silenced if they were heard in our assemblies. This may be better than boisterous fanaticism, but there is as much danger in the one direction as the other. For our part, we are touched to the heart by a little sacred excess, and when godly men in their joy overleap the narrow bounds of decorum, we do not, like Michal, Saul's daughter, eye them with a sneering heart."[23]

---

[1] Jonathan Edwards, *Religious Affections*, edited by John Smith (New Haven: Yale University Press, 1969).

[2] Ibid., 98.

[3] Ibid., 108.

[4] Ibid., 109.

[5] Ibid., 113.

[6] Ibid., 120.

[7] Ibid., 93.

[8] Ibid., 95.

[9] Ibid., 99.

[10] Ibid., 100.

[11] Ibid., 102.

[12] Ibid., 119.

[13] Ibid., 117.

[14] Ibid.

[15] Ibid., 120-21.

[16] Ibid., 121.

[17] Ibid., 122-23.

[18] Ibid.

[19] Ibid., 115.

[20] Ibid.

[21] Ibid.

[22] Ibid., 121.

[23] Charles H. Spurgeon, *The Treasury of David* (Peabody, MA: Hendrickson Publishers, n.d.), Volume 1, exposition of the 32nd Psalm, 85

Epilogue

If you find yourself still hesitant about what I've described in this narration of my own spiritual journey, I want to challenge you to carefully consider why. It may well be that you have serious theological objections to what I've said. You may be thoroughly convinced that my experience is inconsistent with what you believe Scripture to teach. If that is the case, I can only encourage you to continue your study, to dig ever more deeply into God's Word and be willing, no matter the personal cost, to adjust your views to greater conformity to what God has infallibly revealed to us in Scripture. I pray that with God's help I will do the same.

But I suspect that a major factor in many of you is something other than biblical convictions. I know in my own case that my resistance to the sort of spiritual phenomena you've read about was largely the product of fear. Here is how I described it in my book on spiritual gifts:

> "My opposition to spiritual gifts was also energized by fear – the fear of emotionalism; the fear of fanaticism; the fear of the unfamiliar; the fear of rejection by those whose respect I cherished and whose friendship I did not want to forfeit; the fear of what might occur were I fully to relinquish control of my life and mind and emotions to the Holy Spirit; the fear of losing what little status in the evangelical community my hard work had attained.

> I'm talking about the kind of fear that energized a personal agenda to distance myself from anything that had the potential to link me with people who, I believed, were an embarrassment to the cause of Christ. I was faithful to the eleventh commandment of Bible-church evangelicalism: "Thou shalt not do at all what others do poorly." In my pride I had allowed certain extremists to exercise more of an influence on the shape of my ministry than I did the text of Scripture. Fear of being labeled or linked or in some way associated with the "unlearned" and "unattractive" elements in contemporary Christendom exercised an insidious power on

my ability and willingness to be objective in the reading of Holy Scripture. I am not so naïve to think that my understanding of Scripture is now free from subjective influences! But I am confident that at least fear, in this form, no longer plays a part.

By the way, if all this sounds like the arrogance and self-righteousness of someone who prized "being right" above everything else, that's precisely what it was."[1]

If any of this feels painfully familiar, consider the following story from John 9. I hope it speaks as loudly to you as it does to me.

John 9 and the Man Born Blind

Try to envision what it's like to be blind from birth. How would it feel never to have seen anything? Not the words on this page. Not the shoes on your feet. Not the smile on a friend's face. Nary a star in the sky above. Nothing. Just darkness. It's a terrifying thought, but try.

Unable to see, you're unable to work. So, you survive by begging. The problem is, you don't even know what food looks like. There's no way to tell if the object placed in your hand by a passerby is a rotten peach or a ripe kiwi. Who put it there, a man or woman? Were they repulsed by your condition or happy to see you? You'll never know, because rarely does anyone ask how you're doing or show an interest in your opinion on world affairs. Every day, day after day, you sit enveloped by darkness with nothing to do but listen to the voices around you and hope that a few people will have compassion.

Then one day, a day that started out like all the others . . . in darkness, you hear a group of men talking about you. Their words are familiar. You've heard them before, but they still cut deeply into your soul. Suddenly, another voice, one you've never heard before, rises above the others. This voice is devoid of blame and accusations, a voice filled not with questions but answers, a voice that resonates with love and understanding and . . . power.

Without warning, you feel something warm on your eyes. Is someone playing a practical joke? Over the years you've come to expect insensitive teenagers making fun of your condition. They'd hit you and run away, laughing. Sometimes they'd throw things. You tried to act as if it didn't matter, but it did. Are they at it again? Instinctively, you reach up to touch your eyes . . . it's gooey and wet.

"For heaven's sake! Someone's put mud on my eyes."

Before you can react or say anything else, there's that voice again.

"Go," he says, "and wash in the pool of Siloam."

Why the pool of Siloam? If he cares, why doesn't he just wipe them clean himself, especially if he's the one who put it there? But, then, it beats begging.

After enlisting the help of a friend, you make your way, stumbling, to the pool. Bending over, you wash the muddy mess from your eyes, still wondering whose voice it was and why he said . . .

"What! I can see! I can see!"

For the very first time, ever, you can see! Forty years of blindness, gone in an instant. Forty years of darkness and groping and despair and anger, washed away in the cool waters of Siloam.

No one can guess what thoughts must have rushed through the mind of this man. I can't imagine how he processed the light, the colors, the shapes, the sizes of all the things that he had, at most, only touched and heard about all those years. Perhaps his friend led him back to where he spent so many years begging for food. "There's where you sat," fumbling for words as he gasps in unbelief at what his own eyes tell him. He sees faces for the first time and begins to connect them to the voices he heard every day.

The people stare intently, pointing at his face.

"Is this the one who sat here begging for food?"

"Yes! Of course it is."

"No," say others. "The beggar was blind. It must be a twin brother we never knew about. Blind people don't just start seeing! That sort of thing just doesn't happen."

"No, it's me! I'm the one! I'm the beggar. I used to be blind but now I can see. This man put mud on my eyes and told me to wash in the pool of Siloam and I did and look, I can see!"

Finding the man who was responsible suddenly becomes the only thing of importance. He and his friends were debating whose sin had caused him to be blind in the first place. No doubt the beggar used to wonder about it himself. Who screwed up? Mom? Dad? Grandma? Or was it that uncle he never cared much about. Somehow, it really doesn't matter anymore. All he can remember is that man saying something about blindness and the glory of

God. He's not sure how they relate, but Wow! He can see! There will be plenty of time to theologize later on. Right now, there's too much to look at. So much lost time to make up.

"Boy, it sure is bright! Is that blue or brown? Oh well, soon enough I'll know which is what."

The people who knew this blind beggar and had seen him day in and day out are much at a loss as he is. We could speculate forever on what they were thinking, but of one thing we're sure: they immediately rush off to the religious authorities.

"If anyone can explain what happened, the Pharisees can. They'll know what to make of all this."

The response of the religious elite is nothing short of stunning. They launch a full-scale investigation. After all, they can't have some guy going around restoring sight to the blind! And on the Sabbath at that. The Pharisees are divided. For some, healing on the Sabbath is wrong. Therefore, whoever did it can't be from God. Others argue that if you can heal someone blind from birth you must be from God, the Sabbath notwithstanding!

One thing I've noticed over the years is that often the only people who seem to mind it when a miracle occurs are those to whom it doesn't happen. The person who is healed or delivered or touched by the manifest power of God cares little for the petty theological disputes that follow.

But maybe the whole thing's a hoax. Maybe this guy was never blind in the first place.

"I've been to those healing meetings before. I know how they plant perfectly healthy people in wheel-chairs and then pretend to heal them."

Yeah, sure. And this guy willingly sat begging for food for forty years as a "plant" for some religious charlatan.

Desperate for some answers, the Pharisees quiz the man's parents. They ask three short questions:

"Is he your son?"
"Was he really blind?"
"How is it that he now sees?"

To which they respond with three quick answers:

"Yes, he's our boy."

"Yes, he was born blind."

"We don't have a clue. He's an adult. Go ask him yourselves!"

The religious leaders and theologians of Jesus' day weren't much different from a lot of those today. They had their theological framework in place and nothing would be allowed to dismantle it. They revered tradition and custom and habit and interpreted anything that threatened them as most certainly not having come from God. After all, they had a doctrinal statement to maintain and personal comfort to protect and no amount of supernatural activity was enough to change their minds.

The frightening thing is how often we all use our religious commitments to justify keeping Jesus at arm's length. There is no sadder irony in the kingdom of God than the way we use our religious laws and traditions to quench the activity of the Holy Spirit.

In this case, some might think the Pharisees had a case. After all, no one had ever healed a blind man with spit and mud! Surely God would never employ a method so offensive and messy and ugly and lacking dignity and the religious sophistication we've come to expect (if not demand).

The fear of man may well be the most paralyzing power on earth. A fear so powerful that a mother and father who've just seen their own child miraculously healed of congenital blindness freeze when confronted by the religious authorities of their day. Too terrified to acknowledge a miracle. Too terrified to give God thanks for this magnificent and long-awaited display of mercy. Too terrified to celebrate with their son. Terrified of losing face with the religious establishment. Terrified of losing status in the temple.

This is no stranger who has regained his sight. This isn't the neighbor's kid. This is the child of their own bodies. Suddenly, in one incredible moment, all their years of anguish are over . . . and all they care about is their status and place in the community!

The long, dark days of doubt and weeping and anger are over. The years of arguing with God and prayers that often turned to protests are over. The countless hours of speculation ("Who had sinned that our son was born this way?" "Why does God hate us so?") are over. The sleepless nights and bitterness of heart and forced explanations from well-meaning friends . . . all are over. The anxiety of wondering who would care for him after we're dead, over. The whispers and finger-pointing of neighbors and family members, over. Forty years of living hell, over in one second.

Did two people ever have greater cause for celebration? Was ever there greater justification for throwing a party? Could joy and laughter and tears of sheer delight ever be more appropriate than now? Yet, all they could think about was what others will think of them should they acknowledge that this Jesus was really the Messiah after all. They can't even think of their son, of his joy and freedom and excitement.

"To heck with our son. We have a position in the community we've worked hard to gain."

Such is the power of fear.

I'd like to close with this prayer:

O gracious and all-glorious Heavenly Father! Forgive us our failure to hold high your inspired and infallible Word. Forgive us our failure to submit every thought, every dream, every purpose, every plan to the eternal authority of Holy Scripture. Ground us once again in your life-giving truth. Capture our hearts with the beauty of all you have revealed. Guard us lest we wander from the truth or yield to a rival claim. Stir our hearts to love it and cherish it and obey it to the glory of your name. O Spirit of the Father and the Son, fill us afresh and renew our hearts. Awaken passion for the Son that we may seek him with unbridled zeal and whole-souled hunger. Empower us with your gifts that we may minister and serve and speak in the fullness of your power. Energize our minds to know the Son in all his glory. Energize our wills to follow him without pause. Energize our affections to love him unashamedly and rejoice in him above all else. Amen."

---

[1] Sam Storms, *The Beginner's Guide to Spiritual Gifts*, 12-13

Addendum

*

When a Gifted Person Falls

My purpose here is not to address the question of whether those who have fallen should be restored to ministry, and, if so, what the conditions might be for that restoration. Rather, I want to speak to those who are suspicious of prophetic ministry because of the failure of one of its more gifted individuals.

When someone in ministry falls, we often respond in one of two ways. Some experience excessive bitterness, refuse to forgive, and vow never to trust religious leaders again. This may be an indication that they too highly elevated the individual, perhaps even thinking him or her to be beyond the reach of sin. Or perhaps they had placed a faith in this person that should be reserved for the Lord Jesus Christ alone.

Others are tempted to apply what I call "unsanctified mercy" and insist on the premature restoration of the one who has sinned. This has certainly been a dangerous tendency in some Pentecostal and charismatic circles. I've heard it said by a few who experienced moral failures: "God has forgiven me, so why can't the church?" To their way of thinking, restoration in one's personal relationship with God ought to lead to a corresponding *simultaneous* restoration to public ministry. Such thinking is, in my opinion, both unbiblical and often times disastrous to the person involved.

Both of these options are understandable but wrong. We should neither become cynical of the ministry nor give way to unholy sympathy. There is a better, more biblical approach. Perhaps it would be best if I simply set forth three key principles that I believe ought to govern how we think and respond when a trusted, beloved brother or sister in the faith falls.

First, it is only natural that we feel both appreciation and embarrassment. Those whose lives have been positively impacted by someone's ministry should continue to affirm it and resist any temptation to think it was spurious or that its benefits are now somehow tainted or soiled. On the other hand, there is good reason to feel a sense of shame for what occurred, for such events give cause to the world to mock the gospel we proclaim and hold dear.

Second, scandalous sin in a person's life does not necessarily invalidate what was believed to have been beneficial in their ministry. It may, but it need not. Certainly the case of someone like Judas Iscariot must be considered. The horrid nature of his betrayal of Jesus exposed the hypocritical and false commitment of his earlier life and "friendship" with our Lord. But others in the Bible have fallen without calling into question the spiritual authenticity of their faith or ministry. One thinks immediately of Samson, David, Peter, and Mark, just to mention a few more prominent cases. Samson's immoral tryst with Delilah, David's adultery with Bathsheba and complicity in the murder of Uriah, Peter's cowardly, public denial of Jesus, and Mark's abandonment of the apostle Paul, did not corrupt the fruit of their labors.

Neither should we think that someone's fall necessarily casts a shadow on the reality of his/her prophetic ministry in the years preceding the problem. We may still hold to our conviction that the individual was and is a Christian who deeply loves the Lord Jesus Christ and earnestly desires to honor his savior. We believe his/her prophetic gift was and is genuine. This is not to minimize the gravity of sin. It is simply to say that sin does not necessarily invalidate the reality of faith. If the person were *unrepentant* about his/her fall and *resistant* to discipline, a different conclusion might be warranted. But what if he/she has fully acknowledged the failure and has taken responsibility for it? What if he/she has submitted to spiritual authority and has complied with the requirements for restoration?

Third, moral failure does not mean that the prophetic promises given through this person are invalid. Such prophecies must be judged and weighed as the Scriptures instruct. Whether or not they are fulfilled is unrelated to the fact that the one who spoke them sinned subsequent to their delivery. The psalms that King David wrote prior to his adulterous relationship with Bathsheba did not suddenly lose their value or cease to be edifying to the people of God.

Clearly this is a difficult and controversial issue that is often complicated when the person involved is someone we personally know and love. Whatever decisions are ultimately made in such cases, we would do well to heed Paul's counsel to the Galatian church: "Brothers, if anyone is caught in any transgression, you who are spiritual should restore him in a spirit of gentleness. Keep watch on yourself, lest you too be tempted" (Galatians 6:1).

ENJOYING GOD MINISTRIES
(Psalm 16:11)

"Proclaiming the Power of Truth
and
The Truth about Power"

Biblical and Theological Resources
From the Ministry of
Dr. Sam Storms
www.SamStorms.com
P. O. Box 481814
Kansas City, Missouri 64148

Many Christians are either woefully deficient in their knowledge of Scripture or noticeably devoid of the experience of God's power. The Lord never intended this for his people. We have all seen firsthand the joyless intellectual arrogance the absence of spiritual power can produce, as well as the fanatical emotional excess that comes from the lack of theological integrity. Enjoying God Ministries was launched to help reverse this terribly destructive trend in the church.

But we must never forget that truth and power are not an end in themselves, but serve to evoke and energize enjoyment of God. *Enjoying God* is the end or goal or pinnacle we seek, for "God is most glorified in us when we are most satisfied [i.e., when we rejoice fully] in Him" (John Piper). Both the truth of Scripture and the power of the Spirit are necessary if we are to encounter Jesus in a place of intimacy and joy and experience the life-changing, sin-killing, God-exalting satisfaction of soul for which he created us.

Enjoying God Ministries exists to provide solid, substantive, Spirit-filled resources that will enable you to walk in the fullness of the knowledge and love of Jesus Christ. Access to these resources is available by visiting our website at www.SamStorms.com. If you would like for Dr. Storms to speak at your church or conference, or feel led to support this ministry, please contact him directly at sam@enjoyinggodministries.com, or visit the web site and click on "How Can I Support EGM?" Enjoying God Ministries is a tax-exempt, 501(c)(3) ministry, which means that all your financial support is fully tax-deductible.